STUDY GUIDE

Henry Borne

Holy Cross College

SOCIOLOGY

SIXTH EDITION

John J. Macionis

PRENTICE HALL, *Upper Saddle River, NJ 07458*

© 1997 by PRENTICE-HALL, INC.
Simon & Schuster / A Viacom Company
Upper Saddle River, New Jersey 07458

10 9 8 7 6 5 4 3 2 1

ISBN 0-13-465303-3
Printed in the United States of America

This Study Guide has been written to enhance the foundation of sociological ideas and issues which are presented in the text, _Sociology_, by John J. Macionis. To enable you to review and apply basic sociological concepts, methods, and theories, the Study Guide has been organized into several different sections to accompany each chapter in the text.

A *Chapter Outline* provides a basis for organizing segments of information from each chapter in the text. A section on *Learning Objectives* identifies the basic knowledge, explanations, comparisons, and understandings a student should have after reading and studying each chapter in the text. A section entitled *Chapter Review* consists of a brief review of the chapter in paragraph form, following the outline of each chapter. This is followed by a section entitled *Key Concepts* in which the key terms from the chapter are listed in alphabetical order. Some space is provided for the student to write out the definition for each of these terms. The fifth section for each chapter includes *Study Questions*, including true-false, multiple-choice, definition, and short-answer type questions. The next section provides the *Answers* for the Study Guide questions, including a listing of the page numbers where answers to these questions can be found. The final section, *Analysis and Comment* provides space for students to raise questions and make comments on the boxes in the text.

This Study Guide is intended to be a concise review and learning tool to accompany _Sociology_. It is complementary to this text and is not intended to stand alone as a brief text. It will provide the student with opportunities to more deeply benefit from the knowledge of sociology which John Macionis offers in his text.

On a personal note, I want to congratulate John Macionis for writing such an excellent text. His text is very clearly written and offers students a very meaningful sociological perspective on a broad range of important contemporary social issues. It has been my pleasure to have had the opportunity to write this Study Guide. I would also like to thank Nancy Roberts, Editor-in-Chief, Social Sciences and Sharon Chambliss, Associate Editor-- Sociology/Anthropology of Prentice Hall for their guidance and assistance during the writing of this Study Guide. It is indeed people like them who make Prentice Hall such a fine publisher. Finally, my love to my family-- Cincy, Ben, and Abby-- for their support and love.

HB

The Sociological Perspective

PART 1: CHAPTER OUTLINE

I.   The Sociological Perspective
        A. Seeing the General in the Particular
        B. Seeing the Strange in the Familiar
        C. Individuality in Social Context
II.   The Importance of Global Perspective
III.   The Sociological Perspective in Everyday Life
        A. Sociology and Social Diversity
        B. Sociology and Marginality
        C. Sociology and Social Crisis
        D. Benefits of the Sociological Perspective
        E. Applied Sociology
IV.   The Origins of Sociology
        A. Science and Sociology
        B. Social Change and Sociology
                1. A New Industrial Economy
                2. The Growth of Cities
                3. Political Change
V.   Sociological Theory
        A. The Structural-Functional Paradigm
        B. The Social-Conflict Paradigm
        C. The Symbolic-Interaction Paradigm
        D. Sports: Three Theoretical Paradigms in Action
                1. The Functions of Sports
                2. Sports and Conflict
                3. Sports as Interaction
VI.   Summary
VII.   Key Concepts
VIII.   Critical-Thinking Questions
IX.   Suggested Readings

PART II: LEARNING OBJECTIVES

1. To be able to define sociology and understand the basic components of the sociological perspective.
2. To be able to provide examples of how social forces in society affect our everyday lives.
3. To understand the significance of the research on suicide done by Emile Durkheim, showing the impact of social forces on individual behavior.
4. To recognize the importance of taking a global perspective in order to recognize how the U.S. society fits into the rest of the world.
5. To recognize factors in society that affect how people perceive the world sociologically.
6. To be able to identify important historical factors in the development of sociology.
7. To be able to describe an important sociological contribution made by each of the following sociologists: C. Wright Mills, Auguste Comte, Herbert Spencer, and W. E. DuBois.
8. To be able to identify and understand the differences between the three major theoretical paradigms used by sociologists.
9. To be able to provide illustrative questions raised about society using each of the three theoretical paradigms discussed in this chapter.
10. To be able to identify important theorists and researchers who have used the sociological perspective in their study of society, and discuss their respective contributions to the discipline.

PART III: CHAPTER REVIEW

The author begins the text with a review of some generalization about society that are based on sociological research. Sociology, suggests our author, studies how the social world guides our actions and life choices.

THE SOCIOLOGICAL PERSPECTIVE

Sociology is defined as *the systematic study of human society*. Sociology as a discipline is guided by a distinctive perspective. The qualities of this perspective are outlined, with illustrations for each being presented.

Seeing the General in the Particular

Sociologist Peter Berger made this statement referring to the fact that sociologists see *general* social patterns in the behavior of *particular* individuals. While not erasing our uniqueness as an individual, these social forces impinge on our lives in many unseen, yet very significant ways. Examples discussed include age, gender, and social class. A basic underlying question though is: What makes people do the things they do? A key feature of taking a sociological perspective is to look beyond *particular* events or people and understand how and why different *categories* of people behave differently. Each chapter of the text illustrates how the general structures of society affects our lives as individuals.

Seeing the Strange in the Familiar

This refers to the process of detaching oneself from the familiar ways of thinking in order to gain new insights that at first seem strange. The insight gained, according to sociologist Peter Berger, is that "things are not what they seem." Sociology pushes us to question the assumptions we are making about society, and reveals aspects of our social life which most people would not claim to be "obvious" facts.

For example, the question, Why did you come to this college? is typically responded to by students with personal answers. The sociological perspective focuses our attention on broader social factors such as family income, age, and government funding as conditions influencing our choice. Our autonomy as individuals is not lost using sociology, rather, it is strengthened as we gain understanding of how our lives are linked to others and to society. *Figure 1-1* (p. 4) shows data that indicate a connection between racial and ethnic categories and college attendance.

Individuality in Social Context

Sociologists point out that in our individualistic society, we tend to deny our lives are predictable and patterned. Suicide, a seemingly very personal act, is discussed to demonstrate the effect social forces have on human behavior. The research by Emile Durkheim on suicide clearly shows how impersonal social forces affect personal behavior. Records of suicide in central Europe during the last part of the 19th century were found by Durkheim to show certain social categories as having higher suicide rates than others. It was found that the degree of *social integration*, or how strongly a person is bound to others by social ties, had a significant influence on the patterns of suicide rates. *Figure 1-2* (p. 4) provides a contemporary view of suicide rates in the U.S. using the categories of race and sex. The **Social Diversity** box entitled "What's in a Name? How Social Forces Affect Personal Choice" (p. 5) further demonstrates social forces affecting personal choice.

THE IMPORTANCE OF GLOBAL PERSPECTIVE

Global perspective refers to *the study of the larger world and our society's place in it.* The point is addressed that not only must we study individual experiences in social context, but also study U.S. society as it is affected by the world around us. The **Global Sociology** box (p. 6) provides a brief demographic portrait of the world's human population.

Data on average per capita income suggests we are a very wealthy nation when compared to other nations. This fact provides us with certain choices and opportunities not found in other parts of the world. The **Windows on the World** box presenting *Global Map 1-1*: "Economic Development in Global Perspective" (p. 7). Three categories of societies are differentiated: (1) **High-income countries**, or *industrialized societies that are relatively rich,* (2) **Middle-income countries**, or *societies characterized by limited industrialization moderate-to-low* *personal income*, and (3) ***Low-income countries***, or *societies with little industrialization in which severe poverty is the rule.*

Three reasons for using the global perspective as an important component of the sociological perspective are discussed. These include: (1) *Societies the world over are increasingly interconnected,* (2) *A global perspective enables us to see that many human problems we face in the United States are more serious elsewhere,* and (3) *Thinking globally is an excellent way to learn more about ourselves.*

THE SOCIOLOGICAL PERSPECTIVE IN EVERYDAY LIFE

While Americans tend to understand social life along individualistic lines, there are three situations identified which tend to heighten a person's awareness of the presence of social forces.

Sociology and Social Diversity

Encountering social diversity is one such situation. Confronting unfamiliar social environments tends to broaden our perspective and makes us look for the patterns of behavior which in familiar places tend to be taken for granted. Examples might be visiting a foreign country or going to a strange neighborhood.

Sociology and Social Marginality

The term social marginality refers to the state of being excluded from social activity as an "outsider." African Americans, women, and the aged are used to illustrate how certain socially significant characteristics can place people on the "outside" of social life, and make them more aware of social patterns others take for granted.

Sociology and Social Crisis

Finally, social crisis can enhance sociological thinking. C. Wright Mills has suggested that certain historical periods have been represented by social disruption that has increased sociological awareness. The depression years of the 1930s and the decade of the 1960s are used as examples of such historical periods. Our author notes that sociological thinking can also foster social disruption, not merely being a result of it.

Benefits of the Sociological Perspective

Four general benefits of using the sociological perspective are reviewed. These include: (1) *The sociological perspective challenges familiar understandings about ourselves and others, so that we can critically assess the truth of commonly held assumptions.* (2) *The sociological perspective enables us to assess both opportunities and constraints that characterize our lives.* (3) *The sociological perspective empowers us to be active members in our society.* And (4) *The sociological perspective helps us to recognize human diversity and to confront the challenges of living in a diverse world.*

4

The **Profile** box on C. Wright Mills (p. 11) focuses on the concept of the *"sociological imagination."* This concept is defined as the quality of mind which enables a person to see the interplay of biography (personal, private life) and history (the broader social structure and social forces impinging upon us).

Applied Sociology

Sociology is more than just a discipline for enhancing intellectual growth. Sociology provides training for many jobs. Examples are discussed.

THE ORIGINS OF SOCIOLOGY

While "society" has been a topic of thought and discussion since the beginning of human history, sociological thinking is a recent historical phenomenon. The discipline of sociology is relatively young, and itself emerged as a product of particular social forces. Auguste Comte coined the term *sociology* in 1838. Auguste Comte's work is placed within historical context in the **Profile** box (p. 12). He divided sociology into two parts: how society is held together (*social statics*), and how society changes (*social dynamics*).

Science and Sociology

Emile Durkheim pointed out in the latter 19th century that the great philosophers from antiquity through the first half of the 19th century, using only philosophical and theological perspectives in their studies, concentrated on the qualities of imaginary "ideal" societies rather than on the analysis of what society was really like. Sociology was born when focus was given to understanding how society actually operates.

Auguste Comte argued that the key to achieving this was to use the scientific approach in studying society. He divided the history of the study of society into three distinct eras, which he labeled the *theological*, the *metaphysical*, and the *scientific*. The latter he called *positivism*, or *a means to understand the world based on science*.

Social Change and Sociology

Three key factors are identified as reshaping society during the 17th and 18th centuries. These include:

A New Industrial Economy

Rapid technological changes of the 18th century brought people in great numbers to work in factories, thus breaking down established patterns of social life.

The Growth of Cities

As factories spread across Europe, drawing people out of the countryside seeking employment due to the changing nature of the economy, this massive influx of people into cities created many social problems. The crises which emerged stimulated the development of the sociological perspective.

Political Change

The rapid economic and urban growth created a context for change in political thinking. Traditional notions of Divine Law were being replaced by ideas of individual liberty and individual freedom. Sociologists during this time reacted differently to the new social order. Auguste Comte and Karl Marx are briefly discussed to illustrate.

SOCIOLOGICAL THEORY

While the sociological perspective provides us with a unique vantage point from which to observe our social world, theory helps us to meaningfully organize and explain the linkages between specific observations we make. A *theory* is *a statement of how and why specific facts are related*. The basis upon which sociologists choose issues to study is called theory building. This is guided by a *theoretical paradigm*, or *a basic image of society that guides thinking and research*. Emile Durkheim's theory on suicide is discussed. The **Seeing Ourselves** box (p. 16) presents *National Map 1-1* which provides data on suicide rates. These can be used to do some "theorizing."

There are three principal theoretical paradigms used by sociologists. Each theory focuses the researcher's attention on particular types of questions about how society is organized, and each provides a different explanation about why certain patterns are found in society.

The Structural-Functional Paradigm

The *structural-functional paradigm* is a *framework for building theory that envisions society as a complex system whose parts work together to promote solidarity and stability*. The two basic components of this paradigm are *social structure*, or *relatively stable patterns of social behavior*, and *social functions*, which refer to *consequences for the operation of society*. Structural functionalists often liken society to the human body, with different parts of society being interdependent, much like the various organs of the body. The work of Herbert Spencer, one of the first to use structural-functionalism in the analysis of society, is highlighted in the **Profile** box (p. 17). His perspective has been labeled "*social Darwinism*."

Besides Herbert Spencer, other early structural-functionalists included Emile Durkheim and Auguste Comte. As sociology developed in the United States during the 20th century, researchers Talcott Parsons and Robert K. Merton further applied and developed the thinking of these early social scientists. Merton differentiated between what he called *manifest functions*, or *the recognized and intended consequences of any social pattern*, and *latent functions*, which are *consequences that are largely unrecognized and unintended*. Merton further points out that elements of social structure may be functional for one aspect of society and not for others. There may be *undesirable consequences for the operation of society*, or *social dysfunctions*. In critically evaluating this paradigm, it is pointed out that it is a conservative approach to the study of society which tends to ignore tension and conflict in social systems.

The Social-Conflict Paradigm

The *social-conflict paradigm* is *a framework for building theory that envisions society as an arena of inequality that generates conflict and change*. The unequal distribution of power and privilege is reviewed in the context of educational achievement to demonstrate the insights provided by this view of society. Karl Marx is perhaps the most famous social scientist using this paradigm for the analysis of society.

The work of W.E.B. DuBois is discussed in the **Profile** box (p. 20) illustrating how theorists using the social-conflict paradigm attempt not only to understand society, but also to reduce inequality.

Critical evaluation of this paradigm raises concern that social unity is ignored, and that in focusing on change, objectivity may be lost. Both of these first two paradigms concentrate on broad generalities in society, while failing to study particular people in specific contexts.

The Symbolic-Interaction Paradigm

The first two paradigms discussed focus on a *macro-level* orientation, meaning *a focus on broad social structures that characterize society as a whole*. An alternative approach is a *micro-level orientation*, meaning *a focus on social interaction in specific situations*. This third paradigm, *symbolic interactionism*, is *a framework that envisions society as a product of everyday interactions of individuals*. The symbolic-interactionist paradigm was greatly influenced by the work of Max Weber, a German sociologist of the late 18th and early 20th centuries. In the United states, during the 20th century, the work of George Herbert Mead, Erving Goffman, George Homans and Peter Blau was instrumental in the development of this paradigm. Mead's work on socialization, Goffman's work on "*dramaturgical analysis*," and Homan and Blau's work on "*social-exchange analysis*" are discussed in later chapters.

In critically analyzing this view it must be stressed that the focus is on how individuals personally experience society. This approach does not allow us to generalize findings to establish broad general patterns.

Each of the three paradigms provides a unique perspective for the development of greater understanding of society. *Table 1-1* (p. 22) reviews the orientations, their respective image of society, and illustrative questions representative of each theoretical paradigm.

Sports: Three Theoretical Paradigms in Action

Sports in America is discussed as an indispensable part of social life. The question becomes, What insights can the sociological perspective provide us concerning sports?

The Functions of Sports

The structural-functional paradigm reveals many functional consequences which sports has for society. For example, the values sports have in terms of positive application in other arenas of social life.

Sports and Social Conflict

The social-conflict paradigm provides an analysis of sports focusing upon the social inequalities within sports at all levels of competition. Gender, racial, and social class inequalities are addressed and illustrated.

Sports as Interaction

The symbolic-interactionists view sports as an ongoing process and not merely as some "system." The individual perceptions of specific participants concerning the reality as each experiences it becomes the focus.

No one paradigm is better than another in analyzing sports, or any other aspect of society. The sociological perspective is enriched by the controversy and debate brought about through the application in research of these different paradigms.

The **Controversy and Debate** box (p. 24), entitled "Is Sociology Nothing More than Stereotypes?" discusses how generalizations made by sociologists and stereotypes are different.

PART IV: KEY CONCEPTS

Define each of the following concepts in the space provided or on separate paper. Check the accuracy of your answers by referring to the key concepts section at the end of the chapter in the text as well as by referring to italicized definitions located throughout the chapter.

generalizations
global perspective
high-income countries
latent functions
low-income countries
macro-level orientation
manifest functions
metaphysical stage
micro-level orientation
middle-income countries
positivism
seeing the general in the particular
seeing the strange in the familiar

social-conflict paradigm
social dynamics
social dysfunctions
social function
social marginality
social statics
social structure
sociological imagination
sociology
stereotype
structural-functional paradigm
symbolic-interaction paradigm
theological stage
theoretical paradigm
theory

PART V: STUDY QUESTIONS

True-False

1. T   F   According to Peter Berger, the *sociological perspective* focuses our attention on *seeing the general in the particular*.

2. T   F   Approximately *sixty-six percent* of eighteen-to twenty-four-year-olds in the United States are enrolled in college.

3. T   F   Emile Durkheim's research on *suicide* illustrates the point that not all aspects of life can be meaningfully studied using the sociological perspective.

4. T   F   African Americans and females have higher *suicide rates* than whites and males.

5. T   F   Less than ten percent of the world's population lives in North America (Canada, United States, and Mexico).

6. T   F   The *discipline of sociology* first emerged in Europe during the 19th century.

7. T   F   *Positivism* is a means to understand the world based on science.

8. T   F   Sociology *emerged* and *developed* more quickly in the 19th century within those countries experiencing the most profound social transformations.

9. T   F   Herbert Spencer's view of society came to be known as *social Darwinism*.

10. T   F   *Latent functions* refer to social processes which appear on the surface to be functional for society, but which are actually dysfunctional for society.

11. T   F   The symbolic-interaction and social-conflict paradigms both operate from a *micro-level* orientation.

12.   T   F   A *generalization* is being defined by our author as an exaggerated description that one applies to all people in some category.

Multiple-Choice

1.   Which sociologist linked the incidence of suicide to the degree of social integration of different categories of people?

     (a)   Emile Durkheim   (d)   C. Wright Mills
     (b)   Max Weber   (e)   Karl Marx
     (c)   Herbert Spencer

2.   In the *global village* presented by our author, which of the following continents is represented by more than one-half of the village's residents?

     (a)   Europe   (d)   South America
     (b)   North America   (e)   Asia
     (c)   Africa

3.   Learning to understand our individual lives in terms of the social forces that have shaped them is a state of mind that C. Wright Mills called:

     (a)   positivism   (d)   hypothesis testing
     (b)   science   (e)   perspective
     (c)   sociological imagination

4.   Which one of the following theorists developed the concept of the "sociological imagination?"

     (a)   Auguste Comte   (d)   Karl Marx
     (b)   Max Weber   (e)   C. Wright Mills
     (c)   Emile Durkheim

5.   The term "sociology" was coined in 1838 by:

     (a)   Emile Durkheim   (d)   Auguste Comte
     (b)   Karl Marx   (e)   Max Weber
     (c)   Herbert Spencer

6.   *Positivism* is the idea that _____, rather than any other type of human understanding, is the path to knowledge.

     (a)   human nature   (d)   optimism
     (b)   religion   (e)   intuition
     (c)   science

10

7. Who founded *Hull House*, a Chicago settlement house, in a poor, inner-city neighborhood?

   (a) Emile Durkheim   (d) Max weber
   (b) Jane Addams   (e) Harriet Martineau
   (c) Jesse Bernard

8. A basic image of society that guides thinking and research, is the definition for:

   (a) a research design   (d) an hypothesis
   (b) a theoretical paradigm   (e) positivism
   (c) the sociological imagination

9. Herbert Spencer's ideas about society became known as:

   (a) social Darwinism   (d) dramaturgical analysis
   (b) conflict theory   (e) exchange theory
   (c) social learning theory

10. Which of the following sociological theorists used the *structural-functional paradigm* to understand society?

    (a) Peter Berger and C. Wright Mills
    (b) Karl Marx and Robert Merton
    (c) Emile Durkheim and Max Weber
    (d) Herbert Spencer and Robert Merton
    (e) none of the above

11. Consequences of social structure which are largely *unrecognized* and *unintended* are called:

    (a) paradigms   (d) latent functions
    (b) manifest functions   (e) social dysfunctions
    (c) social marginality

12. Which of the following theoretical perspectives is best suited for analysis using the *macro-level* orientation?

    (a) dramaturgical analysis   (d) labeling theory
    (b) social exchange theory   (e) social-conflict theory
    (c) symbolic-interactionism

13. The questions, How is society experienced? And, how do individuals attempt to shape the reality perceived by others? are most likely to be asked by a researcher using which of the following theoretical paradigms?

    (a)   structural-functionalism   (d)   social-conflict
    (b)   symbolic-interactionism   (e)   none of the above
    (c)   social Darwinism

14. Which of the following aspects of social life is used in the text to illustrate the insights provided by the theoretical paradigms used by sociologists?

    (a)   war   (d)   bureaucracy
    (b)   sports   (e)   family
    (c)   education

Fill-In

1. The systematic study of human society is the general definition for _____.
2. The three major components of the *sociological perspective* are: Seeing the _____, seeing the _____, and _____.
3. *Global Map 1-1* illustrates the relative economic development of the world. There are three categories of countries identified, including _____ countries, _____ countries, and _____ countries.
4. Being excluded from social activity as an "outsider" is termed _____.
5. Auguste Comte termed the study of how society held itself together as _____ _____, and how social changes as _____ _____.
6. Auguste Comte asserted that scientific sociology was a result of a progression throughout history of thought and understanding in *three stages*, the _____, _____, and _____.
7. The development of sociology as an academic discipline was shaped within the context of three *revolutionary changes in Europe* during the 17th and 18th centuries. These included a new _____ _____, the growth of _____, and _____ change.
8. An explanation of the relationship between two or more social facts is called a _____.
9. A basic image of society that guides thinking is called a _____ _____.
10. Emile Durkheim's work as a *structural-functionalist* primarily was concerned with social _____.
11. The *recognized* and *intended consequences* of any social pattern are referred to as _____ functions.
12. W.E.B. Du Bois, one of sociology's pioneers, believed sociologists should direct their

efforts to contemporary _____, and for him the vexing issues of _____ was the paramount social concern.

13. The *symbolic-interaction paradigm* takes a _____ approach, meaning a focus on social interactions in specific situations.

14. A _____ is an exaggerated description hat one applies to all people in some category.

Definition and Short-Answer

1. Describe the characteristics of the *global village* presented by the author. What are your reactions to these characteristics?

2. Differentiate between the concepts *manifest* and *latent functions* and provide an example for each.

3. Discuss Emile Durkheim's explanation of how *suicide rates* vary between different categories of people. Explain how this research demonstrates the application of the sociological perspective.

4. What three key *societal changes* during the 17th and 18th centuries were significant for the emergence of sociology as a scientific discipline?

5. What are the three key aspects of the *sociological perspective*? Define each.

6. What are the four basic *benefits* of using the sociological perspective?

7. What are the three major *theoretical paradigms* used by sociologists? Identify the key questions raised by each.

8. Discuss the contributions to sociology made by the following theorists: Robert K. Merton, Karl Marx, and W. E. B. Du Bois.

PART VI: ANSWERS TO STUDY QUESTIONS

True-False

1.	T	(p. 2)	6.	T	(p. 11)	11.	F	(p. 21)
2.	F	(p. 3)	7.	T	(p. 13)	12.	F	(p. 24)
3.	F	(p. 4)	8.	T	(p. 15)			
4.	F	(pp. 4-5)	9.	T	(p. 17)			
5.	T	(p. 6)	10.	F	(p. 18)			

Multiple-Choice

1.	a	(p. 4)	6.	c	(p. 13)	11.	d	(p. 18)
2.	e	(p. 6)	7.	b	(p. 15)	12.	e	(p. 21)
3.	c	(p. 11)	8.	b	(p. 16)	13.	b	(p. 22)
4.	e	(pp. 10-11)	9.	a	(p. 17)	14.	b	(p. 23)
5.	d	(pp. 11-12)	10.	d	(pp. 17-18)			

1.   sociology (p. 2)
2.   general in the particular, strange in the familiar, individuality in social context (pp. 2-4)
3.   high-income, middle-income, low-income (p. 7)
4.   social marginality (p. 9)
5.   social statics, social dynamics (p. 12)
6.   theological, metaphysical, scientific (pp. 12-13)
7.   industrial economy, cities, political (p. 14)
8.   theory (p. 15)
9.   theoretical paradigm (p. 16)
10.   solidarity (p. 17)
11.   manifest (p. 18)
12.   problems, race (p. 20)
13.   micro-level (p. 21)
14.   stereotype (p. 24)

PART VII: ANALYSIS AND COMMENT

Go back through the chapter and write down in the spaces below key points from each of the following boxes. Then, for each of the boxes identified, write out three questions concerning the issues raised which you feel would be valuable to discuss in class.

Profiles

C. Wright Mills (1916-1962)

   Key Points:

   Questions:

Herbert Spencer (1820-1903)

   Key Points:

   Questions:

Auguste Comte (1798-1857)

   Key Points:

   Questions:

W.E.B. DuBois (1868-1963)

   Key Points:

   Questions:

Social Diversity

"What's in a Name? How Social Forces Affect Personal Choice"

Key Points: Questions:

Global Sociology

"The Global Village: A Sociological Snapshot of Our World"

Key Points: Questions:

Controversy and Debate

"Is Sociology Nothing More Than Stereotypes?"

Key Points: Questions:

Seeing Ourselves

"National Map 1-1: Suicide Rates Across the U.S."

Key Points: Questions:

Window on the World

"Global Map 1-1: Economic Development in Global Perspective"

Key Points: Questions:

Sociological 2 Investigation

PART 1: CHAPTER OUTLINE

I.   The Basics of Sociological Investigation
      A. Science as One Form of "Truth"
      B. Common Sense versus Scientific Evidence
II.   The Elements of Science
      A. Concepts, Variables, and Measurement
          1. Reliability and Validity of Measurement
          2. Relationships Among Variables
      B. The Ideal of Objectivity
      C. Some Limitations of Scientific Sociology
      D. The Importance of Subjective Interpretation
      E. Politics and Research
      F. Gender and Research
      G. Feminist Research
      H. Research Ethics
III.   The Methods of Sociological Research
      A. Testing a Hypothesis: The Experiment
          1. An Illustration: The Stanford County Prison
      B. Asking Questions: Survey Research
          1. Population and Sample
          2. Questionnaires and Interviews
          3. An Illustration: Studying the African-American Elite
      C. In the Field: Participant Observation
          1. An Illustration: Street Corner Society
      D. Using Available Data: Secondary and Historical Analysis
          1. An Illustration: A Tale of Two Cities
      E. Technology and Research
      F. The Interplay of Theory and Method
IV.   Putting It All Together: Ten Steps in Sociological Investigation
V.   Summary
VI.   Key Concepts

PART II: LEARNING OBJECTIVES

1.   To understand the requirements fundamental to using sociological investigation.
2.   To understand how the four ways of knowing facts affect what is considered "true."
3.   To become familiar with the basic elements of science and how they are used in sociological investigation.
4.   To understand the limitations of the scientific study of our social world.
5.   To recognize the importance of subjective interpretation as part of the process of scientific investigation.
6.   To see how research is affected by gender and politics.
7.   To begin to view ethical considerations involved when studying people.
8.   To become familiar with the major research methods used by sociologists, and to be able to compare and contrast the various procedures involved in each.
9.   To be able to discuss the relative advantages and disadvantages of the different research methods.
10.   To be able to discuss each of the four examples of sociological research provided in the text, including research design used, variables identified and studied, findings, and interpretations.
11.   To be able to identify and describe each of the ten steps in carrying out a research project using sociological investigation.

PART III: CHAPTER REVIEW

Research by Lois Benjamin, an African-American sociologist, concerning well-educated African-Americans is discussed as an example of *doing sociology*, the process of *sociological investigation*. Her research illustrates the components of the sociological perspective, especially that of *seeing the general in the particular*. Racism and its affects on the African-American "elite" is the focus of her work.

THE BASICS OF SOCIOLOGICAL INVESTIGATION

There are two basic requirements identified as underlying sociological investigation: (1) Look at the world using the sociological perspective, and (2) Be curious and ask questions.

A fundamental issue being raised in this chapter concerns how we recognize information as being true. The requirements identified above are only the beginning of learning about the process of studying society using sociology. The focus now is on how sociologists find answers to questions about society.

Science as a Form of "Truth"

How do we come to know something to be true? Four ways of knowing are being identified. These include: faith, recognition of expertise, agreement through consensus, and science. *Science* is the basis of sociological investigation, and is defined as *a logical system that bases knowledge on direct, systematic observation*. Science is based on **empirical evidence**, meaning *evidence that we can verify using our senses*.

Common Sense versus Scientific Evidence

Six common sense statements considered to be true by many North Americans are identified in the text. However, using scientific evidence these statements are contradicted by empirical facts. For example, the accuracy of the statement that most poor people ignore opportunities to work is seriously brought into question when discovering the empirical evidence that one-half of all poor people in the U.S. are either children or the aged.

As a scientific discipline, sociology can provide us with a framework through which to critically evaluate the many kinds of information we are being exposed to, and enable us to more systematically consider the assumptions we are making about social life.

THE ELEMENTS OF SCIENCE

Sociologists see society in a similar fashion to how natural scientists see the physical world. Sociological investigation uses empirical evidence to provide specific answers to questions concerning social life. There are a number of important components of scientific investigation. These include:

Concepts, Variables, and Measurement

Sociologists use concepts to identify elements of society. A **concept** is *a mental construct that represents some part of the world, inevitably in a simplified form*. For example, terms like family, society, and social class are concepts sociologists use to help orient us to our social world. A **variable** is *a concept whose value changes from case to case*. For example, social class varies with some people being identified as middle-class and others as working-class, etc. **Measurement** is *the process of determining the value of a variable in a specific case*. For example, the factors of family income and occupation can be used to determine what social class a particular person or family is in. The process of creating measurements for variables can be very complicated. Variables can be measured in many different ways, so any measurement used will be arbitrary. Further, we cannot provide a measurement, for example, of every Untied States citizen.

Sociologists must make use of *statistical measures* often called descriptive statistics. The first **Sociology of Everyday Life** box identifies three useful, and often used, descriptive measures *(mean, median, and mode)* using earnings as an illustration (p. 33).

The last example indicates how variables can be operationalized. **Operationalizing a variable** means *to specific exactly what is to be measured in assigning a value to a variable*. For instance, as mentioned earlier, social class can be measured using income and occupation.

18

Reliability and Validity of Measurement

Careful and specific operationalization is critical, but there are two other important issues concerning the measurement of variables to be considered. First, there is the issue of *reliability*, or *the quality of consistency in measurement*. For example, does a person taking several different math achievement tests score equivalently on each? If not, one or more of the tests are not reliable. The second issue is that of *validity*, or *the quality of measuring precisely what one intends to measure*. The question here is, is the measurement device really measuring what it purports to measure? For example, are math tests truly measuring math skills and knowledge, or are they possibly measuring some other quality in a person like obedience to rules?

Relationships Among Variables

Sociological investigation enables researchers to identify *cause and effect* relationships among variables. In cause and effect relationships we are saying one variable *(independent)* causes a change or effect in another variable *(dependent)*. Determining real cause and effect is a difficult and complex process. While variables may be *correlated*, meaning *that two or more variables are related or change together in some way*, it does not necessarily mean that one causes the change in the other(s). The concept *spurious correlation* refers to *an apparent, although false, association between two (or more) variables caused by some other variable*. **Figure 2-1** (p. 35) outlines an example using the variables population density, income level, and juvenile delinquency.

Using scientific *control*, meaning *the ability to neutralize the effect of one variable in order to assess the relationships among other variables*, researchers can check for spuriousness.

In summary, to conclude that a cause and effect relationship exists, at least three conditions must be established:

(1) a correlation exists between the variables
(2) the independent variable precedes the dependent variable in time
(3) no evidence exists that a third variable is responsible for a spurious correlation between the two variables

The Ideal of Objectivity

Researchers must make every effort to neutralize their personal biases and values. Complete neutrality *(objectivity)* is seen as an ideal rather than as a reality in science, and is defined as a state of personal neutrality in conducting research.

Max Weber argued that research may be *value-relevant*, or of personal interest to the researcher, but the actual process of doing the research must be *value-free*. One way biases are controlled is through *replication*, or *repetition of research by other investigators*.

Some Limitations of Scientific Sociology

To apply the logic of science to our social world several important limitations must be recognized:

    (1)   Human behavior is too complex to allow sociologists to predict precisely any individual's actions.

    (2)   Because humans respond to their surroundings, the mere presence of a researcher may affect the behaviors being studied.

    (3)   Social patterns change constantly; what is true in one time or place may not hold true in another.

    (4)   Because sociologists are part of the social world they study, being value-free when conducting social research can be difficult.

The Importance of Subjective Interpretation

Some sociologists argue removing all subjectivity from research is undesirable. First, they say, science is more than mere procedures. The elements of imagination and curiosity are critical. Second, science alone cannot grasp the complexity of human motivation and feelings. Third, data gathered through scientific research doesn't speak for itself. *Interpretation* of findings is a quality hard to quantify. Sociology is an art as well as a science.

Politics and Research

Researchers like Alvin Gouldner argue that politics is part of every aspect of our lives. Political neutrality is a myth. Everything social involves power relationships, and science is no exception. He suggests sociologists support certain values.

Gender and Research

Gender, or *the significance members of a society attach to being female or male*, is being identified as an important political dimension of research. Values influence research in terms of gender. Dangers to sound research that involve gender include: *androcentricity, overgeneralizing, gender sensitivity, double-standard, and interference*. Each of these is briefly discussed.

Feminist Research

While still evolving, the feminist approach primarily focuses on the condition of women in society, and sees women as generally experiencing a subordinate position relative to men. Therefore, feminist researchers reject Weber's value-free approach. The issue is raised by most other researchers that science and politics cannot be mixed.

Research Ethics

Yet another issue concerns how research affects the people being studied. The American Sociological Association has a set of formal guidelines for the conduct of social research, including technical competence, awareness of bias, safety and privacy, discussion with subjects concerning risks involved, accurate presentation of purpose of research, full reporting of findings and identification of any organizational affiliations of the research effort.

There are also global dimensions to research ethics. The cultural backgrounds of people in different societies can be very different from our own. The **Social Diversity** box (pp. 40-41) which is entitled "Conducting Research with Hispanics" identifies five useful tips for sociological investigators who study people of Spanish descent. These include: (1) *being careful with terms*, (2) *realizing that cultural values may differ*, (3) *realizing that family dynamics may differ*, (4) *realizing that attitudes toward time and efficiency may differ*, and (5) *realizing that attitudes toward space may differ*.

THE METHODS OF SOCIOLOGICAL RESEARCH

A *research method* is defined as *a systematic plan for conducting research*. Four of the most commonly used methods are presently introduced, each with particular strengths and limitations for the study of social life.

Testing a Hypothesis: The Experiment

The *experiment is a research method for investigating cause and effect under controlled conditions*. This type of research tends to be explanatory. Experiments are typically designed to test a specific *hypothesis*, or *unverified statement of a relationship between variables*. The ideal experiment involves three steps leading to the acceptance or rejection of the hypothesis. The three steps are: measurement of the dependent variable, exposure of the dependent variable to the independent variable, remeasurement of the dependent variable. The separation of subjects into *control* and *experimental* groups is also discussed.

The issue of the awareness of subjects being studied and how this affects their behavior is reviewed. Distortion in research caused by such awareness is called the *Hawthorne effect*, so labeled after a company in which an experiment was done on work productivity and this effect was first identified.

An Illustration: The Stanford County Prison

Philip Zimbardo's classic study focuses on the structural conditions in prisons. The hypothesis being tested was that the character of prison itself, and not the personalities of the prisoners or guards, is the cause of prison violence. Twenty-four volunteers, deemed to be physically and emotionally healthy, participated in this mock prison experiment which was scheduled to run for two weeks. Because of the stress created, the experiment had to be canceled within a week.

Asking Questions: Survey Research

A *survey* is *a research method in which subjects respond to a series of items in a questionnaire or interview*. It is the most widely used of the research methods. Surveys can be used to do explanatory research, but are also useful for descriptive research, or research focusing on having subjects describe themselves or some social setting.

Population and Sample

A *population* is defined as *the people who are the focus of research*. Generally, contacting all members of a population is impossible, so samples are taken from the population to be studied. *Samples* are *a part of a population selected to represent the whole*. The **Sociology of Everyday Life** box entitled "National Political Surveys" provides an illustration of a particular type of survey, called a poll (p. 44).

The most critical issue concerns how a researcher knows the sample truly is representative of the population, meaning, Does the sample reflect the sample qualities present in the population? *Random selection* techniques are used to help ensure the probability that inferences made from the results of the sample actually do reflect the nature of the population as a whole.

Questionnaires and Interviews

Selection of the subjects is only one step in a survey. Another step requires the researcher to develop a specific plan for asking and recording questions. Two general techniques are used:
questionnaires and interviews.

A *questionnaire* is *a series of written questions a researcher supplies to subjects requesting their responses*. Two basic types of questions asked have *open-ended* and *closed-ended* formats. Generally, surveys are mailed to subjects who are asked to complete a form and return it. This technique is called a *self-administered survey*. A problem exists however in that many forms do not get returned.

An *interview* is *a series of questions a researcher personally administers to respondents*. This strategy has advantages, including more depth, but also involves the disadvantages of extra time and money, and the influence of the researcher's presence on the subjects' responses.

For both questionnaires and interviews, how the questions are asked is extremely important. Poor questions will lead to poor research results and conclusions.

An Illustration: Studying the African-American Elite

Lois Benjamin's survey research on the effects of racism on talented African-American men and women is discussed. Her use of *snowball sampling* and interviews as part of her research design is reviewed. The eagerness of respondents to participate, their high degree of emotion in responding to questions, and the effects of the research on them is also discussed. **Table 2-1** (p. 46) summarizes some of her data. Also, some findings presented in tabular form is focused on in the **Critical Thinking** box (p. 47) which

22

also addresses on how to properly read a table. In the **Seeing Ourselves** box (p. 51) *National Map 2-1* shows the residential patterns of affluent minorities.

In the Field: Participant Observation

Participant observation is *a method by which researchers systematically observe people while joining in their routine activities*. The approach is very common among cultural anthropologists who use *fieldwork* as the principal method to gather data in the form of *ethnographies*. Sociologists typically use the *case study* approach, a type of participant observation, when doing exploratory research. This is very valuable when there is not a well defined understanding of the social patterns being investigated.

Participant observation has two sides, the participant and observer, sometimes referred to as the insider-outsider roles. These can come into conflict with one another. Field notes, or the daily record kept by researchers, will reveal not only the conclusions of the research, but also the experience of the research itself. Such participant observation is classified as a form of **qualitative research**, or *investigation by which a researcher gathers impressionistic, not numerical data*. Surveys, on the other hand, are examples of **quantitative research**, or *investigation by which a researcher collects numerical data*.

An Illustration: Street Corner Society

In the 1930s, William F. Whyte conducted what was to become one of the classic participant observation studies. He sought to study a poor, Italian, urban neighborhood of Boston (which he called Cornerville) to determine the true social fabric of the community. His work reveals the conflict between the roles of participant and observer, involvement and detachment. The role of a *key informant* is highlighted as part of this research process.

Using Available Data: Secondary and Historical Analysis

Secondary analysis is a research method in which researchers utilize data collected by others. Advantages of this approach are the considerable saving of time and money, and the typically high quality of Census Bureau research often used for such purposes. However, problems are also involved, including the possibility that data was not systematically gathered, or not directly focused on the interests of the researcher. Durkheim's research on suicide is an example of using secondary analysis.

An Illustration: A Tale of Two Cities

A study by E. Digby Baltzell using secondary research focuses on the question of the apparent influence of religious doctrine in two different parts of colonial America on achievement orientation. Issues of the application of the sociological imagination, operationalization of variables, and theory building are addressed in this presentation of his research.

23

We are reminded that sociological investigation is a complex process, involving scientific skills, personal values, and a lively imagination. *Table 2-2* (p. 53) summarizes the four research methods discussed in this chapter, including applications, advantages and limitations of each method.

Technology and Research

The effects of recent developments in information technology, including the internet, are briefly discussed.

The Interplay of Theory and Method

The obtaining of facts is not the final goal of science. Beyond facts is the issue of the development of theory, or combining facts into meaning. Two processes of logical thought are used by scientists. **Deductive logical thought** is *reasoning that transforms general ideas into specific hypotheses suitable for scientific testing.* Zimbardo's prison research is a good example of this type of thinking. **Inductive logical thought** involves *reasoning that builds specific observations into general theory.* Baltzell's research illustrates this type of thinking. *Figure 2-2* (p. 56) diagrams this interplay of theory and method.

As discussed in the **Controversy and Debate** box (pp. 54-55) statistics must be interpreted very carefully. Examples of how people "lie" with statistics are illustrated.

PUTTING IT ALL TOGETHER: TEN STEPS IN SOCIOLOGICAL INVESTIGATION

The general guidelines for conducting sociological research follow these steps:

(1) Define the topic of investigation.
(2) Find out what others have learned about the topic.
(3) Assess the requirements for carrying out the research.
(4) Specify the research questions.
(5) Consider ethical issues.
(6) Devise a research strategy.
(7) Gather the data.
(8) Interpret the data.
(9) State your conclusions.
(10) Share your results.

PART IV: KEY CONCEPTS

Define each of the following concepts in the space provided or on separate paper. Check the accuracy of your answers by referring to the key concepts section at the end of the chapter in the text as well as referring to italicized definitions located throughout the chapter.

androcentricity
cause and effect
concept
control
correlation
deductive logical thought
dependent variable
empirical evidence
experiment
gender
Hawthorne effect
hypothesis
independent variable
interview
mean
measurement
median
mode
objectivity
operationalizing a variable
participant observation
population
qualitative research
quantitative research
questionnaire
reliability
replication
research method
sample
science
secondary analysis
spurious correlation
survey
validity
value-free
value-relevant
variable

PART V: STUDY QUESTIONS

True-False

1. T F Research by Lois Benjamin focused on *lower-class* African Americans and how they deal with racism.
2. T F Our author suggests that a major strength of sociology is that it is much like using *common sense*.
3. T F A *concept* is defined as the process of determining the value of a variable in a specific case.
4. T F The *mode* is the statistical term referring to the value which occurs most often in a series of numbers.
5. T F When two variables are related in some way, they are said to demonstrate *correlation*.
6. T F If two variables are *correlated*, by definition one is an independent variable and one is a dependent variable.
7. T F Max Weber argued that people involved in scientific research must strive to be *value-free*.
8. T F *Androcentricity* refers to approaching an issue from a male perspective.
9. T F A *hypothesis* is being defined as an unverified statement of a relationship between variables.
10. T F The *interview* is the most common form of data gathering for researchers using the participant-observation method.
11. T F Lois Benjamin used a technique known as *snowball sampling* as a data gathering method in her research on African-Americans.
12. T F Most *field research* is *exploratory* and *descriptive*.
13. T F E. Digby Baltzell's historical study on Boston and Philadelphia supports research linking attitudes toward achievement with religious doctrine.
14. T F The *first step* in the scientific research process should be to determine what research design will be used to obtain the data.

Multiple-Choice

1. _____ evidence is information we can verify with our senses.

   (a) common sense
   (b) empirical
   (c) intrapsychic
   (d) holistic
   (e) qualitative

2. Specifying exactly what is to be measured in assigning a value to a variable is called:

   (a) validity   (d) reliability
   (b) objectivity   (e) empirical evidence
   (c) operationalizing a variable

3. The descriptive statistic which represents the value that occurs *midway* in a series of numbers is called the:

   (a) mode   (d) median
   (b) correlation   (e) average
   (c) mean

4. The quality of *consistency* in measurement is known as:

   (a) spuriousness   (d) objectivity
   (b) reliability   (e) validity
   (c) empirical evidence

5. Measuring what one intends to measure is the quality of measurement known as:

   (a) reliability   (d) control
   (b) operationalization   (e) objectivity
   (c) validity

6. Several limitations of scientific sociology are reviewed in chapter 2. Which of the following is <u>not</u> identified as a limitation involved in sociological research?

   (a) Human behavior is too complex to allow sociologists to predict precisely any individual's actions.
   (b) Because humans respond to their surroundings, the mere presence of a researcher may affect the behavior being studied.
   (c) Social patterns change constantly; what is true one time or place may not hold true in another.
   (d) Because sociologists are part of the social world they study, being value-free when conducting social research can be difficult.
   (e) Few quantitative techniques are appropriate for sociologists to utilize in their analysis of data.

7. What is Alvin Gouldner's argument about sociological research?

(a) Sociologists have a choice about which values are worth supporting.
(b) Sociologists must remain completely objective, supporting no particular values.
(c) Values actually play an insignificant role in scientific research.
(d) The only values appropriate within the context of the sociological research process are those which represent the scientific method.
(e) Scientific research has the capacity to test absolute truths about social reality.

8. An unverified statement of a relationship between variables is a(n):

(a) correlation
(b) logical deduction
(c) hypothesis
(d) logical induction
(e) theory

9. The prison research conducted by Philip Zimbardo is an example of the use of which research method?

(a) survey
(b) case study
(c) participant-observation
(d) experiment
(e) secondary analysis

10. Which approach was used by Lois Benjamin in her study of talented African-Americans?

(a) participant observation
(b) secondary analysis
(c) a laboratory experiment
(d) a survey using interviews
(d) a field experiment

11. E. Digby Baltzell's study of important and successful Americans is an example of which research method?

(a) experiment
(b) participant observation
(c) secondary analysis
(d) survey
(e) case study

12. If a researcher begins a sociological investigation with general ideas about the world which then are used to produce specific hypotheses suited for scientific testing, the process is known as:

(a) inductive logical thought
(b) a qualitative methodology
(c) empirical analysis
(d) deductive logical thought
(e) speculative reasoning

Fill-In

1. Four *ways of knowing* include:_____, _____,
   _____, and _____.
2. _____ evidence is information we can verify with our senses.
3. A _____ is a mental construct that represents some part of the world, inevitably in a simplified way.
4. _____ refers to a relationship by which two (or more) variables change together, such as the extent of crowding and juvenile delinquency.
5. In a cause and effect relationship, the variable which causes the change in the _____ variable is called the _____ variable.
6. The ability to *neutralize the effect* of one variable so that the relationship among other variables can be more precisely measured is called _____ _____.
7. *Cause and effect* rest on three conditions: _____,
   _____, and _____.
8. The state of complete *personal neutrality* in conducting research is referred to as
   _____.
9. _____ distinguished between *value-relevant* choice of research topics and *value-free* conduct of sociological investigation.
10. _____ refers to the significance members of a society attach to being female or male.
11. A _____ _____ is a systematic plan for conducting research.
12. One strategy for neutralizing outside influences when using the experimental method is dividing subjects into an _____ group and a _____ group.
13. The _____ _____ refers to a change in a subject's behavior caused simply by the awareness of being studied.
14. In survey research, a _____ is defined as the people who are the focus of research.
15. _____ is a method in which researchers systematically observe people while joining in their routine activities.
16. The Zimbardo prison research is an illustration of _____ logical thought.

Definition and Short-Answer

1. What are the two *requirements* which underlie the process of sociological investigation?
2. What are the four *ways of knowing* discussed in the text? Please describe and provide an illustration for each.
3. What are the three factors which must be determined to conclude that a *cause and effect* relationship between two variables may exist?
4. Margaret Eichler points out five dangers to sound research that involves *gender*. Please identify and define each.
5. Define the concept *hypothesis*. Further, write your own hypothesis and operationalize the variables which you identify.

6. Describe Lois Benjamin's research methods and conclusions? What are the relative strengths and weaknesses of her research?

7. What are the five areas of concern identified in the Social Diversity box (pp. 40-42) regarding research with Hispanics?

8. What are the four major *research designs* used by sociologists? Describe each, comparing their relative advantages and disadvantages.

9. What are the twin roles of the research involved in participant observation?

10. What are the basic *steps* of the sociological research process? Please briefly describe each step in the process.

11. What are Alvin Gouldner's points concerning politics and research?

12. Review Max Weber's points concerning *objectivity* in science.

13. Compare and contrast W.F. Whyte's participant observation study "Street Corner Society" with E.D. Baltzel's historical study on Puritans and Quakers.

PART VI: ANSWERS TO STUDY QUESTIONS

True-False

1.	F	(p. 29)	6.	F	(p. 34)	11.	T	(p. 46)
2.	F	(p. 31)	7.	T	(p. 36)	12.	T	(p. 48)
3.	F	(p. 32)	8.	T	(p. 38)	13.	T	(p. 51)
4.	T	(p. 33)	9.	T	(p. 41)	14.	F	(pp. 55-56)
5.	T	(p. 34)	10.	F	(p. 43)			

Multiple Choice

1.	b	(p. 31)	7.	a	(p. 38)
2.	c	(p. 33)	8.	c	(p. 41)
3.	d	(p. 33)	9.	d	(p. 42)
4.	b	(p. 33)	10	d	(p. 45)
5.	c	(p. 33)	11.	c	(p. 50)
6.	e	(p. pp. 36-37)	12.	d	(p. 53)

Fill-In

1. faith, expertise, social agreement, science (p. 30)
2. empirical (p. 31)
3. concept (p. 32)
4. correlation (p. 34)
5. independent, variable (p. 34)
6. control (p. 35)
7. a demonstrated correlation, independent variable precedes the dependent variable in time, controlling for spurious relationships (p. 35)
8. objectivity (p. 36)

9. Max Weber (p. 36)
10. gender (p. 38)
11. research method (p. 40)

PART VII: ANALYSIS AND COMMENT

Sociology of Everyday Life

"Three Useful (and Simple) Statistical Measures"

    Key Points: Questions:

"National Political Surveys"

    Key Points: Questions:

Critical Thinking

"Table Reading: An Important Skill"

    Key Points: Questions:

Social Diversity

"Conducting Research With Hispanics"

    Key Points: Questions:

Controversy and Debate

"Can People Lie With Statistics?"

    Key Points: Questions:

Seeing Ourselves

"National Map 2-1 Affluent Minorities across the United States"

    Key Points: Questions:

Culture

PART I: CHAPTER OUTLINE

I. What is Culture?
   A. Culture and Human Intelligence
   B. Culture, Nation, and Society
II. The Components of Culture
   A. Symbols
   B. Language
      1. Is language uniquely human?
      2. Does language shape reality?
   C. Values and Beliefs
      1. Key Values of U.S. Culture
      2. Values: Inconsistency and Conflict
      3. Values in Action: The Games People Play
   D. Norms
      1. Mores and Folkways
      2. Social Control
   E. "Ideal" and "Real" Culture
   F. Material Culture and Technology
III. Cultural Diversity: Many Ways of Life in One World
   A. High Culture and Popular Culture
   B. Subculture
   C. Multiculturalism
   D. Counterculture
   E. Cultural Change
   F. Ethnocentrism and Cultural Relativity
   G. A Global Culture?
IV. Theoretical Analysis of Culture
   A. Structural-Functional Analysis
   B. Social-Conflict Analysis
   C. Sociobiology

PART II: LEARNING OBJECTIVES

1. To understand the sociological meaning of the concept culture.
2. To understand the relationship between human intelligence and culture.
3. To know the components of culture and to be able to provide examples of each.
4. To understand the debate concerning multiculturalism in U.S. culture.
5. To be able to discuss the issue of whether language is uniquely human.
6. To understand the Sapir-Whorf hypothesis.
7. To be able to identify the major U.S. values and to recognize their interrelationships with one another and with other aspects of our culture.
8. To be able to provide examples of the different types of norms operative in a culture.
9. To explain how subcultures and countercultures contribute to cultural diversity.
10. To have a basic appreciation for the significance of multiculturalism as an issue.
11. To be able to differentiate between ethnocentrism and cultural relativism.
12. To be able to discuss factors which suggest a "global" culture is being created in our world.
13. To be able to compare and contrast analyses of culture using structural-functional, social-conflict, and sociobiological paradigms.
14. To be able to identify the consequences of culture for human freedom and constraint.

PART III: CHAPTER REVIEW

The variety of cultures found around the world is truly amazing. To illustrate, a story concerning the use of a *feng shui* master by Taiwanese business people working in the United States is presented. Another example is told in the **Global Sociology** box (p. 64) concerning anthropologist Napoleon Chagnon's first visit to the territory of the Yanomamo culture in the tropic rain forest of southern Venezuela. In this instance, the degree of difference was great enough for the researcher that he experienced *culture shock*, or *the personal disorientation that comes from encountering an unfamiliar way of life*.

WHAT IS CULTURE?

Culture is defined as *the beliefs, values, behavior, and material objects that constitute a people's ways of life*. Sociologists differentiate between *non-material culture*, *the intangible world of ideas created by members of a society*, and *material culture*, *the tangible things created by members of a society*.

Sociologically, culture is viewed in the broadest possible sense, referring to everything that is part of a people's way of life. Our lives become meaningful to us through culture. Our lifestyles are not determined by *instincts*, or biological forces, as is true in large degree for other species. We are the only species whose survival depends on what we learn through culture, rather than by what we are naturally given through biology.

Culture and Human Intelligence

The primate order among mammals, of which our species is a part, emerged some 65 million years ago. Humans diverged from our closest primate relatives some 12 million years ago. However, our common lineage remains apparent. This includes, grasping hands, ability to walk upright, great sociability, affective and long-lasting bonds for childrearing and protection.

Fossil records indicate the first creatures with clearly human characteristics lived about 2 million years ago, which is relatively recent in terms of evolutionary time. Our species, *homo sapiens* (meaning thinking person) evolved a mere 40,000 years ago. Civilization based on permanent settlements has existed only for the last 12,000 years.

A major point being made is that human culture and biological evolution are linked. Over evolutionary time, instincts have gradually been replaced by "mental power," enabling us to actively fashion the natural environment. This process of having human nature changed from instinct to culture has allowed great human diversity to be created.

Culture, Nation, and Society

Three important concepts are differentiated in this section. *Culture* refers to a shared way of life. A *nation* is a political entity (a place within designated borders). Finally, a *society* refers to the organized interaction of people in a nation or within some other boundary.

THE COMPONENTS OF CULTURE

Even though considerable cultural variation exists, all cultures share five components: *symbols, language, values, norms,* and *material objects*.

Symbols

This component underlies the other four. A **symbol** *is anything that carries a particular meaning recognized by people who share culture.* Symbols serve as the basis for everyday reality. Often taken for granted, they are the means through which we make sense of our lives. Symbols vary cross-culturally and change over time. To some degree symbols even vary within a single culture. Examples for each type of variation are presented. The **Global Sociology** box (pp. 66-67) presents the differences in meaning of gestures in other cultures.

Language

The significance of language for human communication is vividly illustrated by the story of Helen Keller recounting the moment she acquired language and a symbolic understanding of the world, through the help of her teacher Ann Sullivan. *Language* is *a system of symbols that allows members of a society to communicate with one another*. All cultures have a spoken language, though not all have a written language. The Yanomamo, for example, have no written language. *The process by which one generation passes culture to the next*, is *cultural transmission*. Like our genes, our language is rooted in our ancestry. Transmitting culture through speech is known as *oral cultural transmission*. Language is the key to human imagination. Given the infinite combinations of symbols possible, and hence ideas, human creativity appears to be boundless. **Global Map 3-1** (p. 69) shows regional use of the world's three most widely spoken languages.

Is language uniquely human?

While virtually all nonhuman animal communication seems largely rooted in instinct, there is some scientific evidence to suggest certain other animals have at least rudimentary ability to use symbols. Research with chimps has found them capable of attaching words to objects and create simple sentences. While not having the physical ability to form sounds of human speech, nor, at least as yet, being able to demonstrate the capability of transmitting what they learn to other members of their species, it appears they do "experience" culture to some degree. Specific research with a chimp named *Kanzi* is discussed.

Does language shape reality?

Two anthropologists specializing in linguistic studies during the first half of this century, Edward Sapir and Benjamin Whorf, have argued that language is more than simply attaching labels to the "real world." They reject the view that language merely describes a single reality. The ***Sapir-Whorf hypothesis*** holds that *people perceive the world through the cultural lens of language*. Language then determines, to a large degree, our reality. Culture is thereby shaped by language.

Values and Beliefs

Values are defined as *culturally defined standards by which people assess desirability, goodness, and beauty, and which serve as broad guidelines for social living*. They are broad principles, evaluations, and judgments from the standpoint of a given culture. They are learned through socialization and help shape the development of our personality. Although in our diverse society few cultural values are shared by everyone, there are several central values which are widely accepted in U.S. society. Values underlie *beliefs*, or *specific statements that people hold to be true*.

Key Values of U.S. Culture

Sociologist Robin Williams has identified ten such values, including *equal opportunity, achievement and success, material comfort, activity and work, practicality and efficiency, progress, science, democracy and free enterprise, freedom, and racism and group superiority.*

Values: Inconsistency and Conflict

The values people hold vary to some degree by age, sex, race, ethnicity, religion, and social class. Individuals are likely to experience some inconsistency and conflict with their personal values. Further, the dominant values identified above contain certain basic contradictions. Examples of such situations are discussed in the text, making reference to the concept of *status inconsistency*. Further, values change over time. The traditional value of individual responsibility is apparently in the process of eroding in our society. The **Sociology of Everyday Life** box entitled "A New Culture of Victimization" (pp 72-73) discusses this trend.

Values in Action: The Games People Play

Sociologist James Spates has studied how children's games, like king of the mountain and tag, provide experiences for children which stress basic American values. Lessons are learned about what our culture defines as important, like competition.

Norms

Norms are defined as *rules and expectations by which a society guides the behavior of its members*. They can be *proscriptive*, mandating what we must not do, or *prescriptive*, stating what we must do. They can change over time, as illustrated by norms regarding sexual behavior. Some are meant to apply to all situations and all people, while others apply to only certain people and vary situation to situation.

Mores and Folkways

Norms vary in terms of their degree of importance. *Mores* refer to *societies standards of proper moral conduct*. *Folkways* are *a society's customs for routine, casual interaction*. These concepts were first developed by sociologist William Graham Sumner.

Social Control

Norms provide for conformity. *Sanctions* are positive and negative responses to the behavior of people that reward conformity and punish deviance. They are an important part of our cultural system of *social control*, or the *various means by which members of society encourage conformity to norms*. Through socialization we internalize cultural norms and impose constraints on our own behavior, hopefully avoiding *guilt* and *shame*.

"Ideal" and "Real" Culture

Values and norms are not descriptions of actual behavior, but rather reflect how we believe members of a culture should behave. Therefore, it becomes necessary to distinguish between *ideal culture* or *social patterns mandated by cultural values and norms*, and *real culture* or *actual social patterns that only approximate cultural expectations*.

Material Culture and Technology

Material and nonmaterial culture are very closely related. *Artifacts*, or tangible human creations, express the values of a culture. For instance, the Yanomamo value militaristic skill, and devote great care to making weapons. In the U.S. we value independence and individuality, and we have 150 million privately owned automobiles to express these qualities. *Figure 3-1* (p. 75) shows data that indicates the love of cars in the United States.

Material culture also reflects a culture's *technology*, or *knowledge that a society applies to the task of living in the physical environment*. Technology is the link between culture and nature. The point is made that while we attempt to manipulate our natural environment, most technologically "simple" cultures attempt to adapt to their natural worlds. Also, advances in technology act as double-edged swords, creating both positive and negative effects for the quality of life. Technology also varies within a culture. The Amish in the United States illustrate this latter point.

CULTURAL DIVERSITY: MANY WAYS OF LIFE IN ONE WORLD

The United States is the most *multicultural* of all the industrial nations, while Japan is the most *monocultural*. The U.S. is described as a "patchwork quilt" of many peoples. *Figure 3-2* (p. 76) presents data concerning recorded immigration to the United States, by region of birth, for two different historical periods. While during the latter part of the 19th century most immigrants came from European nations, more recently the vast majority are coming from Asia and Latin America.

High Culture and Popular Culture

The concept of "cultured" is being sociologically critiqued in this section. Not all cultural patterns are equally accessible to all members of a society. *High culture* refers to *cultural patterns that distinguish a society's elite*, while *popular culture* designates *cultural patterns that are widespread among a society's population*. The issue of culture as a process of mass production in the U.S. is also discussed. In the **Seeing Ourselves** box (p. 78), *National Map 3-1* uses the popularity of two different forms of bread to show where in the United States the "cultural upper crust" resides.

Subcultures

Sociologists define *subculture* as *cultural patterns that set apart some segment of a society's population*. Subcultures can be based on age, ethnicity, residence, sexual preference, and many other factors.

Ethnicity is perhaps the most recognized dimension with which to identify cultural diversity. While the U.S. is considered by many to be a "melting pot" where people from many different racial and ethnic backgrounds blend together, but great diversity still exists, and is perhaps increasing. A problem exists however in that cultural differences involve not only *variety*, but *hierarchy*.

Multiculturalism

This discussion focuses on the debate in our society over whether we as a nation should stress cultural diversity or the common elements of our people. How do we strike a balance within the Latin phrase *E Pluribus Unum* (out of many, one)? For example, an important proposal being addressed in Congress and in state legislatures is whether English should be designated as the official language of the United States. In the **Seeing ourselves** box (p. 80), *National Map 3-2* shows where in the U.S. there are large numbers of children whose first language is not English.

Multiculturalism is *an educational program recognizing past and present cultural diversity in U.S. society and promoting the equality of all cultural traditions*. The "singular pattern" focus in our culture is called *Eurocentrism*, *the dominance of European (particularly English) cultural patterns* . An alternative pattern currently being developed by some multiculturalists to counter these biases is called *Afrocentrism*, or a view that focuses on *the dominance of African cultural patterns*.

Multiculturalists are suggesting that their perspective will help us develop a more meaningful understanding of our own *past*, *present*, *ethnic diversity*, and *world interdependence*. However, there are critics of multiculturalism who say that it encourages divisiveness rather than unity, it erodes any claim to a common truth, and that it may not actually help minorities.

Counterculture

A *counterculture* is defined as *cultural patterns that strongly oppose those widely accepted within a society*. Members of countercultures are likely to question the morality of the majority group and engage in some form of protest activities. Typically the majority group will respond with the imposition of varying degrees of social control. The Ku Klux Klan, Black Panthers, and Hippies are examples of countercultures in our society.

Cultural Change

Cultural change is continuous, though its rate may vary greatly. *Table 3-1* (p. 81) presents data on the changing attitudes of college students, comparing cohorts from 1968 and 1995. Patterns of both change and consistency are found.

The interconnections between elements of culture must be kept in mind. *Cultural integration* refers to *the close relationship among various elements of a cultural system*. On the other hand, ***cultural lag*** refers to *the fact that cultural elements change at different rates, which may disrupt a cultural system*.

Cultural change is set into motion by three different causes *invention, discovery*, and *diffusion*. Illustrations for each are presented in the text.

Ethnocentrism and Cultural Relativity

Ethnocentrism is *the practice of judging another culture by the standards of one's own culture*. It creates a biased evaluation of unfamiliar practices. A comparison between the U.S. and the Yanomamo illustrates this concept. Further, *Figure 3-2* (p. 84) entitled "The View From Down Under," suggests that North Americans view themselves "above" other countries in the Western Hemisphere.

Cultural relativism refers to *the practice of judging a culture by its own standards*. The issue of cultural sensitivity related to U.S. business ventures overseas is discussed. Tension between these two views of cultural diversity continues to pose difficult problems for U.S. citizens abroad. General guidelines to use when encountering other cultures are presented.

A Global Culture?

Many differences and conflicts exist between cultures, societies, kinship groups, etc., and, more than ever before, there is also more contact between them. The author asks if we are witnessing the birth of a global culture. It is pointed out that global connections involve:

1. *The global economy: the flow of goods*
2. *Global communication: the flow of information*
3. *Global migration: the flow of people*

Further, three important limitations to the global culture thesis are addressed. These include that the flow of goods, information, and people is "uneven," that it is being assumed that people everywhere want and can afford various goods and services, and while certain cultural traits are found more and more throughout the world it should not be assumed that the meanings attached to them are the same.

THEORETICAL ANALYSIS OF CULTURE

Culture is an extremely complex phenomenon. To understand culture and its components requires a macro-level analysis.

Structural-Functional Analysis

Research using this approach draws on the philosophical doctrine of *idealism*, which holds that ideas are the basis of human reality. Stability of a culture, a positive quality, is based on its core values. Cultures are understood as organized systems devised to meet human needs. Therefore, ***cultural universals***, or *traits that are part of every known culture*, are sought and studied. Limitations of this perspective include an underestimation of culture conflict, and downplaying the extent of change in society.

Social-Conflict Analysis

The focus among researchers using this paradigm is the social conflict generated by inequality among different categories of people in a culture. The question of why certain values are dominant in a culture rather than some others is central to this view. Karl Marx, using the philosophical doctrine of *materialism*, argued that the way we deal with the material world (i.e., through capitalism) powerfully affects all other dimensions of our culture. In the **Controversy and Debate** box (p. 90), the concept of *cultural conflict*, or *political opposition, often accompanied by social hostility, rooted in different cultural values*, is discussed. The question is asked: "What are the culture wars?"

A limitation of the social-conflict perspective is an underestimation of the extent of integration in society. Both structural-functional and social-conflict views need to be used to provide insights to gain a fuller understanding of culture.

Sociobiology

Sociobiology is *a theoretical paradigm that explores ways in which our biology affects how humans create culture*. This view poses an interesting challenge to the sociologist's focus on culture as the dominant force in human life. Sociobiologists argue that Charles Darwin's theory of *natural selection*, which is based on four basic principles (discussed on p. 89), applies to human evolution as it does to all other species.

Controversy exists concerning the application of Darwin's insights to humans. Sociobiologists focus on the existence of certain cultural universals as evidence that culture is determined to a significant degree by biology. For example, they point out, our fondness for sweet things is no accident, but is rooted in our primate ancestry. Our distant ancestors who lived in trees primarily ate ripe fruit. This strategy for survival, based on genetic coding, has been passed through the generations to us humans living today. Also discussed is the "double-standard" which exists regarding the sexual activity of males and females. Sociobiologists say that males and females are genetically driven toward different reproductive strategies, "quantity" and "promiscuity" for males, "quality" and "selectivity" for females.

This approach has been criticized, based on historical patterns, of supporting racism and sexism. Also, to date, there is lack of scientific proof of their assertions.

CULTURE AND HUMAN FREEDOM

Culture as Constraint

Through evolution, culture has become our means of survival. However, it can have negative consequences. For example, by having the ability to symbolically experience the world by attaching meanings to it we are susceptible to alienation and the stress created by inconsistent or conflicting values.

41

Culture as Freedom

While being dependent on culture and constrained by our particular way of life, the capacity for creating change, or shaping and reshaping our existence, appears limitless. Culture is a liberating force to the extent we develop an understanding of its complexity and the opportunities available within it for change and autonomy.

PART IV: KEY CONCEPTS

Define each of the following concepts in the space provided or on separate paper. Check the accuracy of your answers by referring to the key concepts section at the end of the chapter in the text as well as referring to italicized definitions located throughout the chapter.

Afrocentrism
counter culture
cultural conflict
cultural integration
cultural lag
cultural relativity
cultural transmission
cultural universals
culture
culture shock
discovery
diffusion
ethnocentrism
Eurocentrism
folkways
high culture
ideal culture
invention
language
material culture
materialism
mores
multiculturalism
natural selection
nonmaterial culture
norms
popular culture
prescriptive norms
proscriptive norms
real culture

Sociology of Everyday Life

"Don't Blame Me! The New Culture of Victimization"

Key Points: Questions:

Window on the World

"Global Map 3-1 Language in Global Perspective"

Key Points: Questions:

Seeing Ourselves

"National Map 3-1 Who's the Upper-Crust? High Culture and Popular Culture"

Key Points: Questions:

"National Map 3-2 Language Diversity Across the United States"

Key Points: Questions:

Society

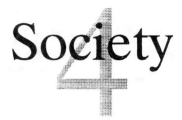

PART I: CHAPTER OUTLINE

I.   Gerhard Lenski and Jean Lenski: Society and Technology
     A. Hunting and Gathering Societies
     B. Horticultural and Pastoral Societies
     C. Agrarian Societies
     D. Industrial Societies
     E. Postindustrial Societies
     F. The Limits of Technology

II.   Karl Marx: Society and Conflict
     A. Society and Production
     B. Conflict in History
     C. Capitalism and Class Conflict
     D. Capitalism and Alienation
     E. Revolution

III.   Max Weber: The Rationalization of Society
     A. Tradition and Rationality
     B. Rationality, Calvinism, and Industrial Capitalism
     C. Rational Social Organization
          1. Rationality and Bureaucracy
          2. Rationality and Alienation

IV.   Emile Durkheim: Society and Function
     A. Structure: Society Beyond Ourselves
     B. Function: Society in Action
     C. Personality: Society in Ourselves
     D. Modernity and Anomie
     E. Evolving Societies: The Division of Labor

V.   Critical Evaluation: Four Visions of Society
          1. How Have Societies Changed?
          2. Why Do Societies Change?
          3. What Holds Societies Together?
          4. Are Societies Improving?

VI.   Summary
VII. Key Concepts
VIII. Critical-Thinking Questions
IX. Suggested Readings

PART II: LEARNING OBJECTIVES

1. To give answers to the questions "How do societies differ?", "What do societies have in common?" and "How and why do societies change?"
2. To be able to differentiate between the four "visions" of society discussed in this chapter.
3. To explain the sociocultural evolution from hunting and gathering societies to industrial societies as developed by Gerhard and Jean Lenski.
4. To contrast the different types of societies described by the Lenskis on the basis of their historical period, productive technology, population size, settlement pattern and social organization.
5. To explain the model of society based on conflict and change developed by Karl Marx.
6. To be able to discuss the perspective of Marx on the concepts of capitalism, communism, revolution, alienation, and materialism.
7. To explain the role of rationality in modern society developed by Max Weber.
8. To be able to identify Weber's qualities of rationality in modern society.
9. To describe Emile Durkheim's functional view of society, including his analyses of the influence of social facts and the role of the division of labor in society.

PART III: CHAPTER REVIEW

We are introduced at the start of this chapter to the significant scientific discovery in 1991 of the "*Iceman,*" whose 5,300 year old frozen remains were found in a glacier near the border of Austria and Italy. A most interesting finding was the material artifacts found with the body, suggesting a fairly advanced society existed many generations ago.

The concept *society* refers to *people who interact in defined territory and share culture.* In this chapter four separate visions of society are discussed; each addresses questions which concern forces that shape human life. The visions include: (1) Gerhard Lenski and Jean Lenskis' focus on the importance of *technology,* (2) Karl Marx's understanding of the key role *social conflict* plays in society, (3) Max Weber's illustration of the significance of *human ideas,* and (4) Emile Durkheim's analysis of the patterns of *social solidarity.*

GERHARD LENSKI AND JEAN LENSKI: SOCIETY AND TECHNOLOGY

Until about 10,000 years ago the hunting and gathering type of society was the only one in existence. Comparing present day hunting and gathering type societies with modern technologically "advanced" societies raises many interesting questions. The Lenskis focus their research on **sociocultural evolution**, or *the process of change that results from a society's gaining new information, particularly technology.* The relationship of society to the physical environment is studied, with society being understood as being like a living organism. A key variable determining the rate of change in a society is the amount of technological information available. The Lenskis and their approach are highlighted in the **Profile** box (p. 96). Based on their view, four general types of societies are distinguished.

Hunting and Gathering Societies

Hunting and gathering refers to simple technology for hunting animals and gathering vegetation. Only a very small number of such societies are still in existence today. Examples include the Aborigines of Australia and the Pygmies of Central Africa. Typical characteristics of people using this subsistence strategy include small bands of people, a nomadic lifestyle over large territories, stratification based only on age and sex, and characterized by few positions of leadership. Most recognize a *shaman*, or spiritual leader. Social organization tends to be simple and equal, being organized around the family. Life expectancy at birth is relatively low, however in environments with ample food supplies the quality of life is good, with much leisure time.

Horticultural and Pastoral Societies

Approximately 10-12,000 years ago plants began to be cultivated. **Horticulture** is *technology based on using hand tools to cultivate plants*. This strategy first appeared in the Middle East and Southeast Asia, and through diffusion spread through Europe and Asia. Some societies, like the Yanomamo, combine horticulture with hunting and gathering strategies.

In regions where horticulture was impractical societies based on **pastoralism** or *technology based on the domestication of animals* emerged. Settlements using horticultural subsistence become linked through trade roots, with many having populations in the thousands. Both horticultural and pastoral societies tend to have a more complex social organization and have increased specialization. *Material surpluses*, or more resources than necessary to sustain day-to-day living, become possible with these lifestyles, and this is often linked to greater social inequality. These societies given their increased technological development are more productive than hunting and gathering societies. However, the Lenskis suggest this was often accompanied by ethical regression.

Agrarian Societies

Agrarian societies emerged about 5,000 years ago and are based on **agriculture**, or *the technology of large-scale farming using plows harnessed to animals or more powerful sources of energy*. Technological change during this period was so dramatic that the Lenksis have argued it was the era of the "dawn of civilization." The use of the plow increased soil fertility as well as made agriculture more efficient. This also greatly increased the surplus of food available. Irrigation was developed at this time. The power of the elite greatly increased, supported by religious beliefs and the expanding political power structure. The **Social Diversity** box (p. 100) discusses factors in sociocultural evolution, such as the development of metal, which helped propel men into an even stronger position of social dominance.

Industrial Societies

Industrialism is *the technology that powers sophisticated machinery with advanced sources* *of energy*. The muscle power of humans and animals are no longer the basis of production and tools and machinery become more complex and efficient owing to the incorporation of metal alloys, such as steel. *Figure 4-1* (p. 101) shows the increasing rate of technological innovation during the 19th century, bringing about vast social changes. A major shift was occurring from production within families to production within factories. Great population increases occurred as health conditions began to improve. Occupational specialization became even more pronounced and cultural values became more heterogeneous.

Postindustrial Societies

Postindustrialism refers to *technology that supports an information-based economy*. The primary form of production centers on the creation, processing, storage, and application of information. The technological breakthrough which sparked the emergence of the postindustrial society was the computer.

As sociocultural evolution continues, economic, social, and political inequality is decreasing. *Table 4-1* (pp. 102-103) summarizes basic points concerning the social stages in societal evolution, including the historical period for each, their productive technologies, population size, settlement patterns, and social organization.

The Limits of Technology

The point is made that while the technological abilities of industrial societies are unparalleled in history they offer no "quick fix" for social problems. Further, advances in our technological level cause some problems, for example, loss of personal freedom, loss of community, and pollution.

KARL MARX: SOCIETY AND CONFLICT

Marx's thinking focused on a fundamental contradiction of industrial society, How could vast social inequality exist given the new industrial technology with its phenomenal productive capability? The central focus of Marx's work was on the idea of *social conflict*, which means *struggle between segments of society valued resources*. For Marx, the most significant type of social conflict results from the manner in which society produced material goods. The **Profile** box (p. 105) discusses some of the controversy surrounding Marx's research and theory.

Society and Production

Marx designated a very small part of the population as *capitalists*, or *people who own factories and other productive enterprises*. Their goal was profit. The vast majority of people however were termed the *proletariat*, meaning *people who provide labor necessary to operate factories and other productive enterprises*. Labor is exchanged by these people for wages. Fundamental conflict exists between the competing needs of these two groups.

Marx's analysis of society followed the philosophical doctrine of *materialism* in asserting that the system of producing material goods can shape all of society. All societies are composed of *social institutions*, or *the major spheres of social life, or society's subsystems, organized to meet basic human needs*. He labeled the economic system the *infrastructure* and all other social institutions as the *superstructures*. *Figure 4-2* (p. 106) illustrates this philosophical viewpoint.

Marx seriously questioned the supposed "truths" of capitalist society which he saw as being based on the operation of the market-place. He believed capitalism promoted *false consciousness*, or *explanations of social problems grounded in the shortcomings of individuals rather than the flaws of society.*

Conflict in History

Marx understood historical change in society as operating in both gradual evolutionary and rapid revolutionary processes. He believed early hunting and gathering societies to be represented by *communism*, or the equal production of food and other material as a common effort shared more or less equally by everyone. He saw horticultural, pastoral, agrarian, and industrial societies as based on systems of inequality and exploitation. The concepts *bourgeoisie* (French, meaning "of the town") and proletariat are discussed further within the framework of social history during the period of industrialization.

Capitalism and Class Conflict

Marx viewed all social history as one of *class conflict*, or *the antagonism between entire classes over the distribution of wealth and power in society*. Social change involved workers first becoming aware of their shared oppression and then organizing and acting to address their problems. The process involved replacing false consciousness with *class consciousness*, or *the recognition by workers of their unity as a class in opposition to capitalists and, ultimately, to capitalism itself.*

Capitalism and Alienation

For Marx, *alienation* meant *the experience of isolation resulting from powerlessness*. Workers perceive themselves as a mere commodity. Four ways industrial capitalism alienates workers are identified: (1) alienation from the *act of working*, (2) alienation from the *products of work*, (3) alienation from *other workers*, and (4) alienation from *human potential*.

The **Sociology of Everyday Life** box (p. 109) discusses the relationship between alienation and industrial capitalism. Excerpts from the book *Working* by Studs Terkel, illustrate how repetitive tasks on the job creates alienation.

Revolution

Marx viewed revolution as the only way to change the nature of society. The type of system he saw as replacing industrial capitalism was socialism, which he believed was a more humane and egalitarian type of productive system.

MAX WEBER: THE RATIONALIZATION OF SOCIETY

Weber made many contributions to sociology, perhaps more than any other sociologist. One of the most significant was his understanding about how our social world differs from societies of early times. His work reflects the philosophical approach of *idealism* which emphasizes the importance of human ideas in shaping society. New ways of thinking, not merely technology, and materialistic relationships was the major force in social change.

Weber's life and times are briefly reviewed in the **Profile** box (p. 111). A conceptual tool used by Weber in his research was the concept *ideal-type*, defined as *an abstract statement of the essential characteristics of any social phenomenon*.

Tradition and Rationality

Weber differentiated between two types of societies in terms of how people viewed the world. The first is characterized by *tradition*, or *sentiments and beliefs passed from generation to generation*. The other is characterized by *rationality*, or *deliberate, matter-of-fact calculation of the most efficient means to accomplish a particular goal*. This process of change from tradition to rationality he termed the *rationalization of society*, denoting *the historical change from tradition to rationality as the dominant mode of human thought*. Industrialization was an expression of this process. The *Window on the World* box includes *Global Map 4-1* (p. 112) which presents information on the global distribution of high technology. Great differences are revealed.

Rationality, Calvinism, and Industrial Capitalism

Weber points out that industrial capitalism developed where Calvinism was widespread. This is discussed as an example of how the power of ideas shapes human social development. A central doctrine of this religion was *predestination*, creating visions of either damnation or salvation, but in the hands of God not the people. Anxious to know their fate people looked for signs of God's favor. Some reassurance was to be found in personal success and achievement.

Rational Social Organization

Weber believed rationality shaped modern society in various ways. Rational organization involves the following seven traits: (1) creating distinctive social institutions, (2) large-scale organizations, (3) specialized tasks, (4) personal discipline, (5) awareness of time, (6) technical competence, (7) impersonality. Each of the seven are described.

Rationality and Bureaucracy

While traditional societies had such systems, they were not based on rationality. Modern day society becomes characterized by a type of social organization called *bureaucracy*. Weber viewed this as the clearest expression of a rational world.

Rationality and Alienation

Weber, like Marx, was critical of modern society, but for different reasons. For Weber, economic inequality was not the major problem, rather dehumanization and alienation were what troubled society most. Weber saw individuality being constricted by modern rationality.

EMILE DURKHEIM: SOCIETY AND FUNCTION

Emile Durkheim's work is briefly introduced to us in the **Profile** box (p. 115). He was a major architect of the structural-functional paradigm.

Structure: Society Beyond Ourselves

Central to the work of Durkheim is the concept of *social fact*, or any pattern that is rooted in society rather than the experience of individuals. Examples are values and norms of a society. Further, Durkheim observed society as being characterized by three elements. The first is that society is *structured*. Second, society has *power* as these structural patterns shape our thoughts and actions. Third, these patterns can be viewed as "facts" because they have an *objective existence* apart from any individual's subjective experience of them. Society is something which is more than the sum of its parts. The power of society is experienced as morality for the individual.

Function: Society in Action

Function is another concept important in the understanding of Durkheim's view of society. The significance of social facts is to be discovered in the functional contribution to the general life of society, not in the experience of individuals. His perspective leads us to view the functional consequences of any social phenomenon, even crime for example.

Personality: Society in Ourselves

According to Durkheim, society exists not only beyond us, having a life of its own, but also within us. Personalities are built through the internalization of social facts. Suicide, discussed in chapter 1, illustrates this point.

Modernity and Anomie

The diminishing regulation of people by society creates individualism and creates *anomie, a condition in which society provides little moral guidance to individuals*. In the modern word, striking a balance between individual desires and social guidance is difficult.

Evolving Societies: The Division of Labor

Durkheim differentiated between two types of solidarity which gave characterized societies over history. For most of history human societies were dominated by a collective conscience, or moral consensus. Durkheim termed this *mechanical solidarity*, meaning *social bonds, based on shared morality, that unite members of preindustrial societies*. Likeness was the rule in society. As this type declined it was replaced by *organic solidarity*, or *social bonds, based on specialization, that unite members of industrial societies*. So Durkheim saw history in terms of a growing *division of labor*, or *specialized economic activity*. Therefore, modernity rests less on *moral consensus* and more on *functional interdependence*.

Durkheim, like Weber and Marx had concern about modern society and its effect on the individual. The dilemma for Durkheim was the fact that the positive benefits of modern society, such as technological advances and personal freedoms, were accompanied by diminishing morality and the danger of anomie.

CRITICAL EVALUATION: FOUR VISIONS OF SOCIETY

The concluding section focuses on the four questions raised at the beginning of this chapter using each of the four visions provided by the Lenskis, Marx, Weber, and Durkheim. These are:

How Have Societies Changed?

The sociocultural evolution model used by the Lenskis focuses on technology in answering this question. Marx's conflict approach focuses on historical differences in the productive system. And, while Weber focused on characteristics of human thought, Durkheim concentrated on how societies differ in terms of how they are bound together.

Why Do Societies Change?

The Lenskis see change occurring through technological innovation. Marx saw class struggles as the "engine of history." Weber's idealist approach focused on how ideas contribute to social change. Finally, Durkheim believed the expanding division of labor was the main force behind the increasing complexity of society.

What Holds Societies Together?

The Lenskis would answer by focusing on cultural patterns. Marx argued that only through cooperative enterprise could a united society develop. Weber saw unity created through a society's distinctive world view. Durkheim focused on the factor of social integration.

Are Societies Improving?

The views of the Lenskis and Marx are mixed on this point. Weber had a rather pessimistic view, while Durkheim had the most optimistic view of this group of theorists. The **Controversy and Debate** box (p. 119) presents summaries of national surveys concerning feelings of optimism in the United States today.

PART IV: KEY CONCEPTS

Define each of the following concepts in the space provided or on a separate paper. Check the accuracy of your answers by referring to the key concepts section at the end of the chapter in the text as well as referring to italicized definitions located throughout the chapter.

agriculture
alienation
anomie
bourgeoisie
bureaucracy
capitalists
class consciousness
class conflict
collective consciousness
division of labor
false consciousness
horticultural society
hunting and gathering society
idealism
ideal-type
infrastructure
materialism
material surplus
mechanical solidarity
organic solidarity
pastoralism
proletariat
rationalization of society
rationality
social fact
social institutions
society
sociocultural evolution
superstructure
tradition

PART V: STUDY QUESTIONS

True-False

1.   T   F   As used sociologically, the concept of *society* refers to people who interact in a defined territory and share a culture.

PART VI: ANSWERS TO STUDY QUESTIONS

True-False

1.	T	(p. 95)	6.	T	(p. 99)	11.	T	(p. 110)
2.	T	(p. 95)	7.	F	(p. 100)	12.	T	(p. 113)
3.	T	(p. 97)	8.	F	(p. 102)	13.	F	(p. 116)
4.	F	(p. 99)	9.	T	(p. 104)	14.	F	(p. 117)
5.	F	(p. 98)	10.	F	(p. 105)	15.	T	(p. 117)

Multiple-Choice

1.	e	(p. 95)	8.	c	(p. 107)
2.	b	(p. 96)	9.	d	(p. 107)
3.	b	(p. 98)	10.	b	(p. 110)
4.	d	(pp. 98-99)	11.	e	(p. 111)
5.	a	(p. 99)	12.	e	(p. 116)
6.	d	(p. 100)	13.	a	(p. 116)
7.	d	(p. 105)	14.	c	(p. 117)

Fill-In

1. technology, social solidarity (p. 95)
2. sociocultural (p. 96)
3. horticultural (p. 98)
4. material surplus (p. 98)
5. capitalists, proletariat (p. 104)
6. infrastructure, superstructure (p. 105)
7. false consciousness (p. 107)
8. alienation (p. 108)
9. ideas (p. 110)
10. ideal type (p. 110)
11. tradition (p. 111)
12. social facts (p. 116)
13. organic solidarity (p. 117)

PART VII: ANALYSIS AND COMMENT

Profiles

"Gerhard Lenski and Jean Lenski"

Key Points: Questions:

"Karl Marx" (1818-1883)

    Key Points: Questions:

"Max Weber" (1864-1920)

    Key Points: Questions:

"Emile Durkheim" (1858-1917)

    Key Points: Questions:

Social Diversity

"Technology and the Changing Status of Women"

    Key Points: Questions:

Sociology of Everyday Life

"Alienation and Industrial Capitalism"

Key Points: Questions:

Controversy and Debate

"Is Society Getting Better or Worse?"

Key Points: Questions:

Window on the World

"Global Map 4-1 High Technology in Global Perspective"

Key Points: Questions:

Socialization

5

PART I: CHAPTER OUTLINE

I. The Importance of Social Experience
   A. Human Development: Nature and Nurture
   B. Social Isolation
      1. Effects of Social Isolation in Nonhuman Primates
      2. Effects of Social Isolation on Children
II. Understanding the Socialization Process
   A. Sigmund Freud: The Elements of Personality
      1. Basic Human Needs
      2. Freud's Model of Personality
      3. Personality Development
   B. Jean Piaget: Cognitive Development
      1. The Sensorimotor Stage
      2. The Preoperational Stage
      3. The Concrete Operations Stage
      4. The Formal Operations Stage
   C. Lawrence Kohlberg: Moral Development
   D. Carol Gilligan: Bringing in Gender
   E. George Herbert Mead: The Social Self
      1. The Self
      2. The Looking-Glass Self
      3. The I and the Me
      4. Development of the Self
III. Agents of Socialization
   A. The Family
   B. Schooling
   C. The Peer Group
   D. The Mass Media

PART II: LEARNING OBJECTIVES

1.   To understand the "nature" versus "nurture" debate regarding socialization.
2.   To explain the effects of social isolation on humans and other primates.
3.   To identify the key components in Sigmund Freud's model of personality.
4.   To identify and describe Jean Piaget's stages of cognitive development.
5.   To be able to describe and critique the stage model of moral development as outlined by Lawrence Kohlberg.
6.   To be able to discuss the gender differences in moral reasoning as suggested by the research of Carol Gilligan.
7.   To explain the contributions of George Herbert Mead to the process of socialization.
8.   To be able to compare and contrast the theories of Freud, Piaget and Mead concerning socialization and human development.
9.   To compare and contrast the spheres of socialization (family, schooling, etc.) in terms of their effects on an individual's socialization experiences.
10.   To compare and contrast the modes of socialization in childhood, adolescence, adulthood, and old age.
11.   To describe death as a stage in the life course as viewed by Elizabeth Kubler-Ross.
12.   To describe the social experience of life within a total institution.
13.   To discuss the issue of the extent to which socialization constrains human freedom.

PART III: CHAPTER REVIEW--KEY POINTS

THE IMPORTANCE OF SOCIAL EXPERIENCE

We are told the story of Anna, a young girl who was raised in a context devoid of meaningful social contact. Kingsley Davis, a sociologist, studied the six year old girl, and described her as being more an object than a person. What Anna had been deprived of was *socialization*, or *the lifelong social experience by which individuals develop their human potential and learn patterns of their culture*. Socialization is the foundation of **personality**, referring to *a person's fairly consistent patterns of thinking, feeling, and acting*. In Anna's case, personality just did not develop.

Human Development: Nature and Nurture

Naturalists during the later 19th century, applying Charles Darwin's theory of evolution, claimed that all human behavior was instinctive. By the end of the 19th century this was clearly the dominant mode through which human behavior was understood. Sociologists, however, see human nature itself as being shaped by cultural context.

Psychologist John Watson challenged the naturalistic perspective and developed an approach called *behaviorism,* claiming that all human behavior was learned within particular social environments. He was convinced learning--or *nurture*--was more important than biology--or *nature*. The work of anthropologists illustrating the great cultural variation existing around the world supports Watson's view.

Contemporary sociologists do not argue that biology plays no role in shaping human behavior. At the very least, human physical traits are linked to heredity. Also, certain characteristics such as intelligence, potential to excel in music and art, and personality characteristics seem to be influenced by heredity. The current position on this issue among sociologists is that nature and nurture are not so much in opposition as they are inseparable.

Social Isolation

For obvious ethical reasons research on the effects of social isolation has been limited to the study of animals. A few rare cases, like Anna's, of human isolation have been investigated.

Effects of Social Isolation on Nonhuman Primates

Classic research by Harry and Margaret Harlow using rhesus monkeys has illustrated the importance of social interaction for other primates besides humans. Using various experimental situations with artificial "mothers" for infant monkeys they determined that while physical development occurred within normal limits, emotional and social growth failed to occur. One important discovery was that monkeys deprived of mother-infant contact, if surrounded by other infant monkeys, did not suffer adversely. This suggested the importance of social interaction in general rather than specifically a maternal bond. A second conclusion was that monkeys who experienced short-term isolation (3 months or less) recovered to normal emotional levels after rejoining other monkeys. Long-term separation appears to have irreversible negative consequences.

Effects of Isolation in Children

The cases of Anna, Isabelle, and Genie, all of whom suffered through years of isolation and neglect as young children are reviewed. Each case suggests that while humans are resilient creatures, extreme social isolation results in irreversible damage to emotional, cognitive and behavior domains of personality development.

UNDERSTANDING THE SOCIALIZATION PROCESS

Sigmund Freud: The Elements of Personality

While trained as a physician, Freud's most important contribution became the development of psychoanalysis and the study of personality development.

Basic Human Needs

Freud saw biological factors having a significant influence on personality, though rejected the argument that human behavior reflected biological instinct. He conceived instincts as general urges and drives. He claimed humans had two basic needs. One he labeled *eros*, or a need for bonding. Another be called the death instinct, or *thanatos*, which related to an aggressive drive.

Freud's Model Of Personality

Freud's perspective combined both these basic needs and the influence of society into a unique model of personality. He argued the personality is comprised of three parts. One is the **id**, representing *the human being's basic drives*, which are unconscious and demand immediate satisfaction. Another, representing *a person's conscious efforts to balance innate, pleasure-seeking drives with the demands of society*, he labeled the **ego**. Finally, the human personality develops a **superego** which is *the operation of culture within the individual*. There is basic conflict between the id and the super-ego which the ego must continually try to manage. If the conflict is not adequately resolved personality disorders result.

Personality Development

The controlling influence on drives by society is referred to as *repression*. Often a compromise between society and the individual is struck, where fundamentally selfish drives are redirected into socially acceptable objectives. This process is called *sublimation*.

While being controversial, Freud's work highlights the internalization of social norms and the importance of childhood experiences in the socialization process and the development of personality.

Jean Piaget: Cognitive Development

A prominent psychologist of the 20th century, Piaget's work centered on human *cognition*, or how people think and understand. He was concerned with not just what a person knew, but how the person knows something. He identified four major stages of cognitive development. Biological maturation and social experience are seen as important.

The Sensorimotor Stage

The *sensorimotor stage* is described as *the level of human development at which individuals experience the world only through sensory contact*. This stage lasts for about the first two years of life. The understanding of symbols does not exist during this period. The child experiences the world only in terms of direct physical contact.

The Preoperational Stage

The *preoperational stage* is described as *the level of human development at which individuals first use language and other symbols*. This stage extends from the age of two to the age of seven. Children continue to be very egocentric during this time, having little ability to generalize concepts. An experiment is discussed illustrating this point.

The Concrete Operations Stage

The third stage in Piaget's model is called the *concrete operational stage* and is described as *the level of human development at which individuals first perceive causal connections in their surroundings*. This period typically covers the ages of seven to eleven. Cause and effect relationships begin to be understood during this period. The ability to take the perspective of other people also emerges.

The Formal Operations Stage

The fourth stage is the *formal operational stage* and is described as *the level of human development at which individuals think abstractly and critically*. This stage begins about age twelve. The ability to think in hypothetical terms is also developed.

Piaget viewed the human mind as active and creative. Research now is focusing on the cross- cultural relevance of this model and to what extent males and females develop differently through these stages. Further, some evidence suggests that almost one-third of the adults in the U.S. do not reach stage four.

Lawrence Kohlberg: Moral Development

Kohlberg extended Piaget's work to the issue of moral reasoning. He identifies three stages of moral development, including the *preconventional, conventional, and postconventional*. In the first stage moral reasoning is tied to feelings of pleasure and avoidance of pain. In the second, specific cultural norms dominant moral reasoning for the person. In the third stage more abstract ethical principles are involved. Many of the same criticisms raised about Piaget's model apply to Kohlberg's work. Also, he only used males in his research which limits generalizability.

Carol Gilligan: Bringing in Gender

Gilligan's research, which is highlighted in the **Profile** box (p. 130) focuses on a systematic comparison of moral development for females and males. Her work indicates that the moral reasoning of girls and boys is different. Girls tend to use a *care and responsibility perspective,* while boys tend to use a *justice perspective.* Each are discussed. One question about her work is whether the differences are the result of nature or nurture.

George Herbert Mead: The Social Self

Questions such as, What exactly is social experience? And, How does social experience enhance our humanity? were central to Mead's research on the socialization process. Mead's analysis is often referred to as *social behaviorism.* This view is similar to Watson's behaviorism, however Mead's work was not limited to the study of behavior only. Mead's work also concerned mental processes. Mead's life and career are reviewed in the **Profile** box (p. 132).

The Self

Mead understood the basis of humanity to be the *self, a dimension of personality composed of an individual's self-awareness and self-image.* For Mead, the self was a totally social phenomenon, inseparable from society. The connection between the two was explained in a series of steps, the emergence of the self through *social experience,* based on the *exchange of symbols,* and occurring within a context in which people take the role of the other, or *taking the other's point of view* into account during social interaction.

The Looking-Glass Self

The process of taking the role of the other can be more meaningfully understood using Charles Horton Cooley's concept of the **looking-glass self.** This term designates *the image people have of themselves based on how they believe others perceive them.*

The I and The Me

An important dualism is suggested by Mead's idea that the self thinks about itself. The two components include: (1) the self as subject by which we initiate social action. This subjective part of the self Mead labeled the *I.* And, (2) the self as object, concerned how we perceive ourselves from the perspective of others. This objective aspect Mead called the *Me.* All social interaction is seen as the continuous interplay of these two aspects of the self.

Development of the Self

Mead minimized the importance of biology in personality development. Further, while seeing early childhood experiences as significant, he did not see developmental stages closely linked to age. The key was social experience, not maturation. Mead also saw infants as responding to others only in terms of imitation. As the use of symbols emerges the child enters a *play* stage, in which role-taking occurs. Initially, the roles are modeled after significant others, especially parents. Through further social experience children enter the *game* stage where the simultaneous playing of many roles is possible. The final stage involves the development of a **generalized other**, or *widespread cultural norms and values we use as references in evaluating ourselves. Figure 5-1* (p. 133) illustrates the development of the self as a process of gaining social experience.

AGENTS OF SOCIALIZATION

The Family

The family is identified as the most important agent of socialization. The process of socialization within this institution is discussed as being both intentional and unconscious. While parenting styles vary, the most important aspect in parent-child relations seems to be *attention* paid by parents to their children. The family is the initial source for transmission of culture to the child.

The social class of the family has been shown to have a considerable bearing upon the values and orientations children learn. This point is elaborated using the research of Melvin Kohn who found that middle-class and working-class parents stress different values for their children.

Schooling

It is within the context of school that children begin to establish contact with people from a diversity of social backgrounds. The expressed objective purpose of the school experience is the imparting of knowledge, math, reading, etc. However, there exists a *"hidden curriculum"* which also teaches children important cultural values.

It is within the educational environment that evaluations are made of children based on universal standards on *how they perform* instead of *who they are*. Schooling is critical for obtaining the knowledge and skills necessary for adult roles.

The Peer Group

Peer group socialization typically occurs outside the context of adult supervision. A **peer group** is defined as *a social group whose members have interests, social position, and age in common*. Some research provides evidence suggesting that the conflict between parents and their adolescent children is more apparent than real. A major feature operative during adolescence is referred to as **anticipatory socialization**, or *social learning directed toward gaining a desired position*.

72

The Mass Media

The *mass media* are *impersonal communications directed to a vast audience*. This includes television, newspapers, radio, etc. While it attempts to be factual, many sociologists have argued that the mass media offers a biased perspective on society, presenting the established elites in a favorable light. *Figure 5-3* (p. 138) show data concerning the political views of the influential Hollywood elite. The influence of television on thought and behavior is discussed. Also, *National Map 5-1* presented in the **Seeing Ourselves** box (p. 136) provides a look at television viewing and newspaper reading patterns across the U.S. Also, *Figure 5-2* (p. 135) shows data concerning the distribution of television sets in different countries around the globe. The **Social Diversity** box (p. 137) illustrates an example of advertising involving racial and ethnic biases.

SOCIALIZATION AND THE LIFE COURSE

While focus is given to childhood in terms of the significance of socialization this process is lifelong. Social experience is viewed in this section as being structured during different stages of the life course.

Childhood

The novel by Charles Dickens about Oliver Twist is briefly discussed to provide a portrait of Oliver's life, one very different from contemporary American childrens' experience.

Childhood in our culture lasts roughly the first twelve years of life. It is a period characterized by freedom from responsibilities. It is an expanding period in technologically advanced societies. However, some research, especially on affluent families, suggests it actually may be getting shorter as a period. The "hurried child" pattern reflects this idea. In primitive societies less differentiation is made between childhood and adulthood. It is stressed however that child labor is very common in poorer countries around the world, as is illustrated in *Global Map 5-1* in the **Window on the World** box (p. 140).

An interesting example of how differences between childhood and adulthood is understood in primitive cultures is provided by comparing sex among children through research by anthropologist Margaret Mead. Such research is used to suggest that childhood is far from just being an inevitable consequence of biological maturation.

Adolescence

This period emerged as a distinct life cycle stage during industrialization. This period corresponds roughly to the teen years. The social turmoil often associated with this stage appears to be the result of inconsistences in the socialization process as opposed to being based on physical changes. Examples concerning the status of teens in relation to voting and drinking are discussed.

Adulthood

Eleanor Roosevelt's life is briefly reviewed to illustrate two major characteristics of this stage of life. First, it is a period when most of our life's accomplishments occur. Second, especially toward the end of this stage, people reflect upon what they have accomplished.

Early Adulthood

This period lasts approximately from the early 20's to age 40. While personality is largely set by this time, certain transitions, life unemployment, divorce, or a serious illness can result in significant personality changes. This period is dominated by meeting day-to-day responsibilities and achieving goals set earlier in life. The juggling of conflicting priorities also characterizes this period.

Middle Adulthood

This period lasts roughly between the ages of 40 to 60. A distinctive quality of this period is reflection on personal achievements in light of earlier expectations. Differences between men and women are discussed, including family roles and attractiveness.

Old Age

This period begins during the mid-60s. The status of the aged varies greatly cross-culturally. In rapidly changing modern societies the aged tend to be defined as marginal or even obsolete. This period is quite different from previous ones as it is characterized by the leaving of roles instead of entering new ones.

Dying

Elizabeth Kubler-Ross has written extensively on the process of death as an orderly transition involving five distinct stages, *denial, anger, negotiation, resignation,* and *acceptance.* As society changes, particularly with more people living into old age, our conception of both old age and death are changing.

The Life Course: An Overview

In summarizing the vast amount of research on socialization discussed in this chapter, our author makes four general conclusions: (1) although linked to the biological process of aging, the essential characteristics of each stage of socialization are constructions of society, (2) each period provides different problems and transitions, (3) the process varies by social background, and (4) experiences during the life course must be understood within the context of past historical periods. A *cohort* is *a category of people with a common characteristics, usually age.* Age-cohorts are influenced by the same economic and cultural factors, so members typically display similar attitudes and values.

RESOCIALIZATION: TOTAL INSTITUTIONS

A *total institution* is defined as *a setting in which people are isolated from the rest of society and manipulated by an administrative staff*. Erving Goffman has identified three distinct qualities of such institutions: (1) they control all aspects of the daily lives of the residents, (2) they subject residents to standardized activities, and (3) they apply formal rules and rigid scheduling to all activities. This structure is designed to achieve the policy of **resocialization**, or *radically altering an inmate's personality through deliberate manipulation of the environment* is understood as a two part process--the destruction of the individual's self-conception, and the systematic building of another one. A process known as *institutionalization* often occurs whereby residents become dependent on the structure of the institution and are unable to function outside the institution.

While society affects both our outward behavior and inner-most feelings, we are not merely puppets. Even though we are further influenced by biological forces, our existence as humans provides tremendous opportunity for freedom, spontaneity, and creativity. The question "Are we free within society?" is addressed in the **Controversy and Debate** box (p. 145).

PART IV: KEY CONCEPTS

Define each of the following concepts in the space provided or on separate paper. Check the accuracy of your answers by referring to the key concepts section at the end of the chapter in the text as well as by referring to italicized definitions located throughout the chapter.

adolescence
adulthood
anticipatory socialization
behaviorism
childhood
cognition
cohort
concrete operations stage
ego
eros
formal operations stage
game stage
generalized other
hidden curriculum
I
id
institutionalized
looking-glass self
mass media

me
object permanence
old age
peer group
personality
preoperational stage
resocialization
repression
self
sensorimotor stage
significant other
social behaviorism
socialization
sublimation
superego
taking the role of the other
thanatos
total institution

PART V: STUDY QUESTIONS

True-False

1. T F As defined by our author, the concept of *personality* does not concern behavior.

2. T F John Watson was a 19th century psychologist who argued that human behavior was largely determined by *heredity*.

3. T F The Harlows' research on *rhesus monkeys* concerning social isolation illustrates that while short-term isolation can be overcome, long-term isolation appears to cause irreversible emotional and behavioral damage to the monkeys.

4. T F The cases of Isabelle, Anna, and Genie support the arguments made by naturalists that certain personality characteristics are determined by *heredity*.

5. T F Sigmund Freud envisioned biological factors as having *little or no* influence on personality development.

6. T F Carol Gilligan's research focuses on how *gender* affects moral reasoning.

7. T F George Herbert Mead argued that biological factors played *little or no* role in the development of the self.

8. T F George Herbert Mead's concept of the *generalized other* refers to widespread cultural norms and values we use as a reference in evaluating ourselves.

9.   T   F   The concept *hidden curriculum* relates to the important cultural values being transmitted to children in school.

10.   T   F   *Childhood* in technologically advanced societies is much more similar to adulthood than it is in preindustrialized societies.

Multiple-Choice

1. The story of *Anna* illustrates the significance of _____ in personality development.

    (a)   heredity   (d)   ecological forces
    (b)   social interaction   (e)   historical processes
    (c)   physical conditions

2. Which of the following is representative of Sigmund Freud's analysis of personality:

    (a)   biological forces play only a small role in personality development
    (b)   the term instinct is understood as very general human needs in the form of urges and drives
    (c)   the most significant period for personality development is adolescence
    (d)   personality is best studied as a process of externalizing social forces

3. Sigmund Freud's model of personality *does not* include which of the following elements:

    (a)   superego   (c)   self
    (b)   id   (d)   ego

4. Culture existing within the individual Sigmund Freud called:

    (a)   thanatos   (d)   the id
    (b)   eros   (e)   the superego
    (c)   the ego

5. According to Jean Piaget, which of the following best describes the preoperational stage of cognitive development:

    (a)   the level of human development in which the world is experienced only through sensory contact
    (b)   the level of human development characterized by the use of logic to understand objects and events
    (c)   the level of human development in which language and other symbols are first used
    (d)   the level of human development characterized by highly abstract thought
    (e)   none of the above

6. The stages of preconventional, conventional, and postconventional are found in which developmental stage model?

   (a) Piaget's cognitive development model
   (b) Freud's psychoanalytic model
   (c) Watson's behaviorist model
   (d) Mead's self model
   (e) Kohlberg's moral development model

7. According to research by Carol Gilligan, *males* tend to use a _____ perspective concerning moral reasoning.

   (a) justice
   (b) visual
   (c) independent
   (d) mechanical

8. G. H. Mead's perspective has often been described as:

   (a) psychological pragmatism
   (b) psychoanalysis
   (c) social behaviorism
   (d) behaviorism
   (e) naturalism

9. The concept of the *looking-glass self* refers to:

   (a) Freud's argument that through psychoanalysis we can uncover our unconscious
   (b) Piaget's view that through biological maturation and social experience individuals become able to logically hypothesize about thoughts without relying on concrete reality
   (c) Watson's behaviorist notion that one can see through to a person's mind only by observing their behavior
   (d) Cooley's idea that a person's self-conception is based on the responses of others

10. Melvin Kohn's research on social class and socialization of children within the family found that compared to middle-class parents, working-class parents were more likely to stress the value of _____ for their children.

   (a) conformity
   (b) affection
   (c) independence
   (d) achievement
   (e) success

11. The process of social learning directed toward gaining a desired position is called:

   (a) resocialization
   (b) looking-glass self
   (c) socialization
   (d) anticipatory socialization

12. Latest statistics show that the average U.S. family has a television on in the house how many hours per day:

(a) 7 (c) 13
(b) 3 (d) 10

Fill-In

1. A _____ is defined as a person's fairly constant pattern of thinking, feeling, and acting.
2. The approach called _____ developed by John Watson in the early 20th century provided a perspective which stressed learning rather than instincts as the key to personality development.
3. According to Sigmund Freud, the _____ represents the conscious attempt to balance the innate pleasure-seeking drives of the human organism and the demands of society.
4. Sigmund Freud termed society's controlling influence on the drives of each individual as _____, whereas he called the process of transforming fundamentally selfish drives into more socially acceptable objectives as _____.
5. Jean Piaget's work centered on human _____.
6. Jean Piaget's model of *cognitive development* focused not on what children knew about the world but _____ they comprehended the world.
7. According to Carol Gilligan, in terms of *moral reasoning*, boys tend to take a _____ perspective, while girls tend to take a _____ perspective.
8. George Herbert Mead defined the _____ as a dimension of personality composed of the individual's self-awareness and self-image.
9. George Herbert Mead identified two components of the *self*, the _____, or self as subject, and the _____, or self as object.
10. In George Herbert Mead's theory of personality development, three *stages* are identified, including the _____, _____, and _____.
11. The process of social learning directed toward gaining a desired position is called _____.
12. Elisabeth Kubler-Ross described *death* as an orderly transition involving five distinct *responses*, including _____, _____, _____, _____, and _____.
13. A category of people with a common characteristic, usually their age is called a -_____.
14. Because they are settings in which people are isolated from the rest of society and manipulated by an administrative staff, prisons and mental hospitals are examples of _____.

Definition and Short-Answer

1. Briefly review the history of the *nature-nurture* debate concerning human development.
2. Review the cases of *social isolation* described in the text. What are the effects of social isolation on nonhuman primates? What are the effects of social isolation on children?
3. According to Sigmund Freud, what are the basic *components* of personality? What stages of human development does Freud's identify?
4. According to Jean Piaget, what are the *stages* of cognitive development? What are the characteristics of each stage?
5. Differentiate between the three *stages* of moral development according to Lawrence Kohlberg. How does Carol Gilligan's research enhance Kohlberg's model? What are the two moral reasoning perspectives she identifies? Describe these and provide illustrations from your own experience.
6. What is G. H. Mead's theory of personality development? What are the stages identified in his model? What is the "self" and how does it develop?
7. What are the major *agents* of socialization? Briefly describe how each influences human development.
8. What are the two major characteristics of *adulthood*? Briefly describe each.
9. According to Kubler-Ross, what are the *stages of death*? Define each.
10. What is a *total institution*? What are their three primary characteristics? Provide an example of a total institution.
11. Discuss the similarities and differences between the developmental theories of Freud, Piaget, Kohlberg, and Mead.

PART VI: ANSWERS TO STUDY QUESTIONS

True-False

1.	F	(p. 123)	6.	T	(p. 130)
2.	F	(p. 124)	7.	T	(p. 131)
3.	T	(p. 125)	8.	T	(p. 133)
4.	F	(p. 126)	9.	T	(p. 134)
5.	F	(p. 127)	10.	F	(p. 139)

Multiple-Choice

1.	b	(p. 123)	7.	a	(p. 130)
2.	b	(p. 127)	8.	c	(p. 130)
3.	c	(p. 127)	9.	d	(p. 131)
4.	e	(p. 127)	10.	a	(p. 134)
5.	c	(p. 128)	11.	d	(p. 135)
6.	e	(p. 129)	12.	a	(p. 137)

1.   personality (p. 123)
2.   behaviorism (p. 124)
3.   ego (p. 127)
4.   repression/sublimation (p. 127)
5.   cognition (p. 128)
6.   how (p. 128)
7.   justice, care and responsibility (p. 130)
8.   self (p. 131)
9.   I, Me (p. 131)
10. imitation, play, game (p. 132)
11. anticipatory socialization (p. 135)
12. denial, anger, negotiation, resignation, acceptance (p. 142)
13. cohort (p. 143)
14. total institutions (p. 143)

PART VII: ANALYSIS AND COMMENT

Profile

"George Herbert Mead" (1863-1931)

    Key Points: Questions:

"Carol Gilligan: Socialization and Girl's Self-esteem"

    Key Points: Questions:

81

Social Diversity

"How Do the Media Portray Minorities?"

    Key Points: Questions:

Controversy and Debate

"Are We Free Within Society?"

    Key Points: Questions:

Seeing Ourselves

"National Map 5-1 T.V. Viewing and Newspaper Reading Across the U.S."

    Key Points: Questions:

Window on the World

"Global Map 5-1 Child Labor in Global Perspective"

    Key Points: Questions:

Social Interaction In Everyday Life

PART I: CHAPTER OUTLINE

I.   Social Structure: A Guide To Everyday Living

II.   Status
   A. Status Set
   B. Ascribed Status and Achieved Status
   C. Master Status

III.   Role
   A. Role Set
   B. Role Conflict and Role Strain
   C. Role Exit

IV.   The Social Construction of Reality
   A. The Thomas Theorem
   B. Ethnomethodology
   C. Reality-Building in Global Perspective

V.   Dramaturgical Analysis: "The Presentation of Self"
   A. Performances
   B. Nonverbal Communication
   C. Gender and Personal Performances
      1. Demeanor
      2. Use of Space
      3. Staring, Smiling, and Touching
   D. Idealization
   E. Embarrassment and Tact

VI.   Interaction in Everyday Life: Two Illustrations
   A. Language: The Gender Issue
      1. Language and Control
      2. Language and Function
      3. Language and Attention

PART II: LEARNING OBJECTIVES

1.   To identify the characteristics of social interaction and social structure.
2.   To explain the relationship between social structure and individuality.
3.   To distinguish between the different types of statuses and roles and the interconnection between them.
4.   To describe the importance of role in social interaction.
5.   To explain the social construction of reality.
6.   To understand the theoretical approach within the symbolic-interaction paradigm known as ethnomethodology.
7.   To know the importance of performance, nonverbal communication, idealization, and embarrassment to the "presentation of self."
8.   To describe dramaturgical analysis.
9.   To be able to discuss the significance of gender for social interaction, including the differing perspectives of females and males in different social contexts.
10.   To be able to use gender and humor as illustrations of how people construct meaning in everyday life.

PART III: CHAPTER REVIEW

In the beginning of this chapter we are introduced to two people who are lost in an unfamiliar part of a city while they are driving to another couples home. One person is a female and the other is a male. Each has a different perspective on the situation they are in. The male does not want to ask for directions, the female does. Why is this so typically the pattern in our society? This chapter focuses on *social interaction*, or *the process by which people act and react in relation to others*. Social meaning is created through such activity.

SOCIAL STRUCTURE: A GUIDE TO EVERYDAY LIVING

People act in patterned ways based on social influences with their respective societies. An illustration from Vietnam provides an example of this fact.

STATUS

A *status* refers to *a recognized social position that an individual occupies*. Each involves certain rights, privileges, obligations and expectations that are widely recognized. Statuses guide the behavior of people in different social situations, and are an important part of how people define themselves.

Status Set

Status set refers to *all the statuses a person holds at a given time*. An example would include being a father, accountant, male, and husband. Status sets are both complex and changeable.

Ascribed Status and Achieved Status

An *ascribed status* is *a social position that someone receives at birth or assumes involuntarily later in life*. In contrast, an *achieved status* refers to *a social position that someone assumes voluntarily and that reflects personal ability and effort*. Most often there is a combination of ascribed and achieved factors in each of our statuses.

Master Status

A *master status* is *a status that has exceptional importance for social identity, often shaping a person's entire life*. In our society, one's occupation often comprises this position. The **Social Diversity** box (p. 152) points out that physical disability becomes the master status for many people. Ascribed statuses such as race and sex are discussed as other examples of positions which act as a person's master status.

ROLE

The concept *role* refers to *behavior expected of someone who holds a particular status*. Ralph Linton describes it as the dynamic expression of a status. However, sociologists differentiate between actual role performance and role expectations society attaches to a role. Like statuses, roles are *relational*, meaning they organize our behavior toward other people.

Role Set

Generally, a person has many more roles than statuses, as each status typically has multiple roles attached. Robert Merton defines a *role set* as *a number of roles attached to a single status*. *Figure 6-1* (p. 153) provides an illustration of a status set and role set.

Role Conflict and Role Strain

The concept *role conflict* refers to *incompatibility among roles corresponding to two or more statuses*. Even the roles attached to a single status can create problems for an individual. *Role strain*, referring to *incompatibility among roles corresponding to a single status*, describes this situation. Prioritizing roles is one strategy used to resolve this condition. Another way to deal with role strain is by insulating roles from one another, limiting involvement in particular roles to only certain specific times of the day or week.

Role Exit

Role exit is the process by which people disengage from social roles that have been central to their lives. Helen Ebaugh, herself an ex-nun, discusses the process of becoming an "ex." This includes critical reflection, imagining alternative roles, adopting new roles, developing a new sense of self, grappling with changing responses, forming new relationships, and learning new skills. In our modern society role exits are becoming more common over the life course.

THE SOCIAL CONSTRUCTION OF REALITY

While statuses and roles structure our lives, we as individuals have considerable ability to shape patterns of interaction with others. The phrase *social construction of reality* refers to *the process by which people creatively shape reality through social interaction*. Social interaction is understood as a process of negotiation which generates a changing reality. Examples from literature are discussed to illustrate this process.

The Thomas Theorem

One observation made by sociologists is that *situations that we define as real are real in their consequences*. This has become known as the *Thomas theorem*.

Ethnomethodology

One approach to understanding the ways humans shape reality is called *ethnomethodology* which is based on the symbolic-interaction paradigm. Harold Garfinkel coined the term, defined as *the study of the way people make sense of their everyday lives*. Garfinkel did research in which he had students deliberately refuse to "play the game." This approach highlights awareness of many unnoticed patterns of everyday life.

Reality-Building in Global Perspective

Human creativity draws on what is available in the surrounding culture. Variation exists between subcultures in any given society, and cross-culturally in terms of how reality is fashioned. A question raised in the **Seeing Ourselves** box, *National Map 6-1* (p. 156) asks where baseball fans are found across the United States. This varies by region of the country.

DRAMATURGICAL ANALYSIS: "THE PRESENTATION OF SELF"

Another approach to understanding the social interaction of everyday life is *dramaturgical analysis* developed by Erving Goffman. This approach is defined as *the investigation of social interaction in terms of theatrical performance.* Goffman theorized that statuses and roles are used to create impressions. Central to this analysis is the process called the *presentation of self,* meaning *an individual's effort to create specific impressions in the minds of others.* This process is also referred to as *impression management.*

Performances

Goffman referred to the conscious and unconscious efforts of people in conveying information about themselves as *performances.* These would include dress, tone of voice, objects being carried, etc. An interesting analysis of physicians and their offices is discussed to illustrate this idea.

Nonverbal Communication

Novelist William Sansom's description of a fictional character named Mr. Preedy walking across a beach in Spain is used to illustrate the process of *nonverbal communication.* This concept refers to *communication using body movements, gestures, and facial expressions rather than speech.* Types of smiles, eye contact and hand movements are reviewed to further highlight *body language.*

The question of the universality of the expression of different emotions is discussed in the **Global Sociology** box (p. 158). Paul Ekman studied emotions around the world and found that while the reality of our emotions is rooted in biology, there are three ways in which emotional life differs cross-culturally. These include: what triggers an emotion varies from one society to another, people display emotions according to the norms of their culture, and societies differ in terms of how people cope with emotions.

Ekman's research also suggests examples of nonverbal clues which can be identified to tell if a person is telling a lie. He suggests four types of information provided by a performer should be carefully observed, including--*words, voice, body language, and facial expression.* In *Figure 6-3* (p. 161) readers are asked "Which is the honest face?"

Gender and Personal Performances

How societies link human traits to being female or male is very important to take into account when studying personal performances.

Demeanor

Demeanor refers to general conduct or deportment. It tends to vary by an individual's power. Given that men are more likely than women to be in positions of dominance it is suggested that women must craft their performances to maintain subordinance.

Use of Space

Power is a key here as well. Masculinity has been traditionally associated with greater amounts of **personal space**, or *the surrounding area to which an individual makes some claim to privacy*. Also, men tend to intrude on a woman's space more often than women intruding on a man's space.

Staring, Smiling, and Touching

While women tend to maintain interactions through sustaining eye contact longer than men do, men tend to stare more. Meanings associated with smiling also seem to vary with gender. Touching patterns also vary, with men tending to touch women more than women touch men. Various rituals are created in which men tend to express their dominance over women.

Idealization

Goffman suggests that we attempt to idealize our intentions when it comes to our performances. The context of a hospital involving physicians making their rounds with patients is used to illustrate how people, in this case doctors, try to convince people they are abiding by ideal cultural standards.

Embarrassment and Tact

As hard as we may try to craft perfect performances, slip-ups do occur and may cause *embarrassment*, or the recognition that we have failed through our performance to convince our audience. Oftentimes audiences will ignore flaws in performances, using *tact* to enable the performance to continue. This is because embarrassment causes discomfort for all present.

While life is not a scripted play, Shakespeare's "All the world's a stage" idea does portray our relationships within social structure to some extent.

INTERACTION IN EVERYDAY LIFE: TWO ILLUSTRATIONS

Language: The Gender Issue

The content of communication is both manifest, or what is explicitly stated, and latent, which conveys much more information. One such latent message concerns the relative social definitions of men and women. Language functions to define the sexes in at least three ways.

Language and Control

One example of this is that males tend to attach female pronouns to valued objects, consistent with the concept of possession. Another illustration is women changing their name when they marry.

Language and Value

Language conveys different levels of status in many subtle ways. Typically, the masculine terms carry higher status.

Language and Attention

The English language seems to almost ignore what is feminine. This is reflected in our pronoun usage. Some very interesting research by Deborah Tannen concerning gender and language are discussed in the **Sociology of Everyday Life** box (p. 171). She suggests that linguistic differences separate the sexes.

Humor: Playing With Reality

Another example of the sociological importance of everyday interaction is in the analysis of humor. The issue of why something is funny is virtually never analyzed critically by people.

The Foundation of Humor

Humor emerges out of ambiguity and double meanings involving two differing definitions of the situation, a contrasting of the *conventional* and the *unconventional*. Examples of this are given to illustrate this idea. The key to a good joke seems to lie in the opposition of realities.

The Dynamics of Humor: "Getting It"

To get the joke the listener must understand the two realities, the conventional and the unconventional. Examples of different levels of complexity of jokes on this dimension are provided. People derive satisfaction and even "insider status" by being able to "piece together" the realities to "get the joke."

Topics of Humor

While humor is universal, what is viewed as funny is not. Yet, humor is everywhere closely tied to what is controversial. There is also a fine line between what is funny and what is "sick."

Functions of Humor

The universality of humor reflects its function as a safety-valve. Sentiments can be expressed that might be dangerous to relationships if taken seriously. Humor also allows us to explore alternatives to the status quo.

Humor and Conflict

Humor is often used by different groups in society to question the interests of those they oppose. Finally, humor allows some freedom as with it we are never prisoners of the present.

PART IV. KEY CONCEPTS

Define each of the following concepts in the space provided or on separate paper. Check the accuracy of your answers by referring to the key concepts section at the end of the chapter in the text as well as by referring to italicized definitions located throughout the chapter.

achieved status
ascribed status
demeanor
dramaturgical analysis
ethnomethodology
humor
idealization
master status
nonverbal communication
performance
personal space
presentation of self
role
role conflict
role exit
role expectations
role performance
role set
role strain
social interaction
status
status set
social construction of reality
Thomas theorem

<u>Fill-In</u>

1. social interaction (p. 149)
2. status (p. 150)
3. ascribed (p. 151)
4. role strain (p. 153)
5. social construction of reality (p. 154)
6. Thomas (p. 155)
7. ethnomethodology (p. 155)
8. dramaturgical (p. 157)
9. words, voice, body language, facial expressions (p. 160)
10. personal space (p. 161)
11. control, value, attention (p. 164)
12. conventional/unconventional (p. 166)

PART VII: ANALYSIS AND COMMENT

Social Diversity

"Physical Disability as Master Status"

    Key Points: Questions:

Seeing Ourselves

"National Map 6-1 Baseball Fans Across the United States"

    Key Points: Questions:

Global Sociology

"Human Emotions in Global Perspective"

Key Points: Questions:

Sociology of Everyday Life

"Gender and Language: You Just Don't Understand"

Key Points: Questions:

Groups and Organizations

PART II: LEARNING OBJECTIVES

1. To explain the differences among primary groups, secondary groups, aggregates, and categories.
2. To identify the various types of leaders associated with social groups.
3. To compare and contrast the research of Asch, Milgram and Janis on group conformity.
4. To explain the importance of reference groups to group dynamics by understanding Stouffer's research on soldiers.
5. To distinguish between ingroups and outgroups.
6. To see the relevance of group size and social diversity to the dynamics of social groups.
7. To be able to identify the types of formal organizations.
8. To be able to identify the primary characteristics of bureaucracy.
9. To compare and contrast the small group and the formal organization on the basis of their respective activities, hierarchies, norms, criteria for membership, relationships, communications, and focuses.
10. To be able to identify the outcomes of the informal side of bureaucracy.
11. To be able to identify and discuss the problems of bureaucracy.
12. To be able to discuss the issue of the "McDonaldization" of society.

13. To understand the effects of power and opportunity on employees and the effects of humanizing bureaucracy.
14. To compare and contrast formal organizations in the U.S. and Japan and to understand formal organizations in a more global perspective.

PART III: CHAPTER REVIEW- KEY POINTS

The introduction to this chapter relates the amazing success story of McDonald's. In 1954 Ray Kroc bought the interests of the McDonald brother's restaurants in California. This chapter gives insight into the extent to which *social groups*, from families to *formal organizations*, have meaning in our lives.

SOCIAL GROUPS

A *social group* is defined as *two or more people who identify and interact with one another*. While we each have our own individuality, the "we" feeling that can only be achieved in social groups is central to our existence as human beings.

Groups, Categories, and Crowds

Category

Not all collections of individuals are social groups. People who share a status in common are defined as a *category*. Potentially, members of categories and aggregates could become social groups given certain circumstances.

Aggregate

An *aggregate* is defined as a number of people who are in the same place at the same time.

Crowd

A *crowd* refers to a large number of people in proximity to one another who do interact to a greater or lesser extent.
Under certain circumstances members of these different collectivities could be transformed into a group. Examples are presented.

Primary and Secondary Groups

Charles Horton Cooley, who is highlighted in the **Profile** box (p. 175) studies the extent to which people have personal concern for each other in social interaction settings. He distinguished between primary and secondary groups. *Primary groups* are defined as a *small social group whose members share personal and enduring relationships*.

These *primary relationships* are characterized as ends in and of themselves. They are critical in the socialization process. Members are considered unique and not interchangeable. *Secondary groups* are defined as *a large and impersonal social group whose members pursue a specific interest or activity*. They are typically short-term with narrowly-defined relationships and are seen as a means to an end. The term *secondary relationships* applies to this type of group. The distinction in real life is not always as clear as these definitions might suggest. *Table 7-1* (p. 176) provides a summary of the key differences between primary and secondary groups.

While primary groups have *personal orientation*, secondary groups have *goal orientation*. In the **Seeing Ourselves** box (p. 177) *National Map 7-1* takes a look at people's tendency to sue each other as an indicator of the quality of our social relationships.

Group Leadership

Leadership plays a critical role in group dynamics. Research shows that leadership has less to do with individual traits and more to do with the needs of the group itself.

Two Leadership Roles

Research also reveals that there are usually two types of leaders in social groups held by separate individuals. *Instrumental leadership* refers to *group direction that emphasizes the completion of tasks*. *Expressive leadership* *focuses on collective well-being*. This differentiate is also linked to gender, with men typically taking the instrumental role and women taking the expressive role in leadership positions.

Three Leadership Styles

Leaders also vary in the ways in which they include others in the decision-making process. Three decision-making styles are identified. One is *authoritarian* leadership which focuses on instrumental concerns. This type of leader makes decisions on their own, demanding strict compliance from subordinates. Another type is the *democratic* leader who takes a more expressive approach, seeking to include all members in the decision-making process. A third type is labeled *laissez-faire*. Leaders using this approach tend to downplay their power, allowing the group to function on its own.

Group Conformity

Group conformity is another dimension of group dynamics in which members seek the satisfaction of being like other members. Three research projects illustrate the importance of group conformity to the sociological understanding of group processes.

Asch's Research

Solomon Asch conducted an experiment in which naive subjects were asked to answer questions concerning the length of lines. Five to seven secret accomplices of the experimenter comprised the rest of the group. They purposely gave incorrect answers. Often the naive subject would give a "wrong" answer in order to conform. *Figure 7-1* (p. 178) illustrates an example of the lines used in this experiment.

Milgram's Research

Stanley Milgram conducted an experiment which naive subjects believed was about learning and memory. The naive subject played the role of a "teacher" and the accomplice played the role of a "learner." If learners failed to correctly remember word pairs given by the teacher, the teacher was instructed by Milgram (a legitimate authority figure) to electrically shock the learner. His research suggests that people comply with almost blind obedience to authority figures. Further, if encouraged by others in a group situation, subjects were likely to administer even higher voltage shocks. The learners were not actually being shocked at all, but were play-acting as if they were. Naive subjects involved in this research found it to be a very stressful experience and this type of research remains very controversial.

Janis's Research

Irving Janis researched the actions of high government officials by examining historical documents. He theorized that people in groups can be led to engage in behavior that violates common sense. Janis discusses three factors which affect decision-making processes and create **groupthink**, or *the tendency of group members to conform by adopting a narrow view of some issue.* The Kennedy administration's decision to invade Cuba is used as an example of this phenomenon.

Reference Groups

The term **reference group** signifies *a social group that serves as a point of reference in making evaluations or decisions.* These groups can be primary or secondary. They are a major factor involved in anticipatory socialization processes.

Stouffer's Research

Stouffer conducted research on the morale and attitudes of soldiers in World War II in order to investigate the dynamics of reference groups. Stouffer found what appeared to be a paradox: Soldiers in branches with higher promotion rates were more pessimistic about their own chances of being promoted than soldiers in branches with lower rates of promotion. This is explained however by the identification of the groups against which the soldiers measured their progress. In relative terms, those soldiers in branches with higher rates felt deprived.

101

Ingroups and Outgroups

Two other kinds of groups provide us with standards against which we evaluate ourselves. People tend to perceive certain groups as more attractive to belong to than others. An *ingroup* is *a social group commanding a member's esteem and loyalty*. This group exists in relation to *outgroups*, or *social groups toward which one feels competition or opposition*. This dichotomy allows us to sharpen boundaries between groups and to highlight their distinctive qualities. The operation of the group dynamics created by these distinctions affect broader social patterns in society, such as social inequality between blacks and whites.

Group Size

Group size significantly influences how members socially interact. As a group's membership is added to arithmetically, the number of possible relationships increases in a geometric progression. *Figure 7-2* (p. 181) provides an illustration.

The Dyad

Georg Simmel studied social dynamics in small social groups. He differentiated between the *dyad*, *a social group with two members*. This type of group is less stable than larger groups. Both members must actively participate in the relationship. Also, dyads tend to be more intense than other groups, thus making them less stable. But, dyads have the potential to be the most meaningful social bond we ever experience.

The Triad

The *triad*, *a social group with three members*. The triad is more stable than the dyad. The third person, should the relationship between the other two members become strained, can act as a mediator. As groups get larger they become more stable as the loss of even several members does not threaten the group's existence.

There is no ideal size for a group. As a rule people find more *pleasure* in smaller groups and find more *satisfaction* through accomplishing tasks in larger groups.

Social Diversity

This section focuses on the research by Peter Blau who identifies four ways in which the structure of social groups regulates intergroup association. The four factors include *group size*, *heterogeneity* of group members, *social parity* within the group, and *physical boundaries*.

Networks

The term *network* refers to *a web of social ties that links people who identify and interact little with one another*. Little sense of membership is felt by individuals in the network and only occasionally do they come into contact. Some can be operating at a primary level, but most are secondary in nature. Demographic characteristics, such as age, education, and residence patterns influence the likelihood of a person's involvement in networks. Such ties may be weak, but can serve as an important resource--*who you know is more important than what you know.* New information technology has generated a global network--the *internet*, which is discussed in the **Sociology of Everyday Life** box (p. 183). The **Window on the World** box (p. 184) presents *Global Map 7-1* which puts cyberspace in global perspective.

FORMAL ORGANIZATIONS

Today our lives seem focused around *formal organizations*, or *large, secondary groups that are organized to achieve their goals efficiently.* The U.S. government is the nation's largest formal organization, employing more than 5 million people.

Types of Formal Organizations

Amitai Etzioni uses the variable of how members relate to the organization as a criteria for distinguishing three types of formal organizations.

Normative Organizations

People join *normative organizations* to pursue some goal they consider morally worthwhile. Voluntary associations like the PTA, the Red Cross, and the Lions Club would be examples. Traditionally, because women had been excluded from the labor force they have had higher participation rates in such organizations than men. *Figure 7-3* (p. 186) provides a global snapshot of membership in cultural or educational organizations for selected countries.

Coercive Organizations

Coercive organizations serve as a form of punishment (prisons) and treatment (mental hospitals). People are separated from the rest of society within distinct physical boundaries and are labeled as inmates or patients.

Utilitarian Organizations

Utilitarian organizations provide material benefits for members in exchange for labor. Most people must join at least one such organization in order to "make a living."

Origins of Bureaucracy

Formal organizations date back thousands of years. The type of formal organization called *bureaucracy* emerged as a result of changes occurring in societies in Europe and North

103

America during the Industrial Revolution. A bureaucracy is an organizational model rationally designed to perform complex tasks efficiently.

Characteristics of Bureaucracies

Bureaucracy is *an organizational model rationally designed to perform complex tasks efficiently.* Our nation's telephone system is illustrated to show examples of the scope and capacity of bureaucracies.

Max Weber identified six basic characteristics or elements of the ideal bureaucracy. These include: *specialization, hierarchy of offices, rules and regulations, technical competence, impersonality,* and *formal, written communications.*

In contrast to small groups, like a family, which have intrinsic value for its members, the organizational model of bureaucracy has at its heart a goal-oriented approach. It works to promote efficiency. *Table 7-2* (p. 188) differentiates between the qualities of each.

The Informal Side of Bureaucracy

While in principle bureaucracy has a highly formal structure, in reality not all behavior in bureaucracies fits precisely the organizational rules. While it is the position or office which is supposed to carry the power, the personalities of the occupants are important factors. Also, "grapevines" become an important source of information and interaction within such systems.

Problems of Bureaucracy

Bureaucracy is not without its problems, and can be very unresponsive to individual needs. Being fair to the system of bureaucracy, some problems are the result of the fact organizations are not truly bureaucratic. Bureaucracies due tend to dehumanize those it serves through its impersonal operation. It also often alienates those who work within them.

Bureaucratic Alienation

Max Weber was concerned about the *dehumanizing* potential of bureaucracy. *Impersonal* treatment is a source of *alienation.* Weber was very pessimistic in this regard about the future of humanity.

Bureaucratic Inefficiency and Ritualism

The image of *red tape* is closely tied to bureaucracies. *Bureaucratic ritualism* signifies a *preoccupation with rules and regulations to the point of thwarting an organization's goals.* This process tends to reduce performance and stifle creativity of members.

<h1 align="center">Bureaucratic Inertia</h1>

Bureaucracies seem to have lives of their own. *Bureaucratic inertia* refers to *the tendency of bureaucratic organizations to perpetuate themselves*.

<h2 align="center">Oligarchy</h2>

Robert Michels observed the fact that *oligarchy*, or *the rule of the many by the few*, was a typical outgrowth of bureaucracy. He suggested that individuals in high levels within a bureaucratic hierarchy tend to accumulate power and use it to promote their own objectives.

<h2 align="center">Parkinson's Law and the Peter Principle</h2>

Waste and incompetence are also features of bureaucracies. Parkinson's law, for example, states that "work expands to fill the time available for its completion." Also, the Peter principle states that bureaucrats are promoted to their level of incompetence. Both seem evident in bureaucratic systems to some degree.

Gender and Race in Organizations

Rosabeth Moss Kanter, who is introduced in the **Profile** box (p. 192), points out that ascribed statuses such as gender and race often determine who holds power in bureaucratic hierarchies. Such stratification in term dramatically affects a person's on-the-job performance. Widely shared responsibility and opportunities for advancement in the company seem to be highly correlated with worker performance and creativity. *Figure 7-4* (p. 191) illustrates evidence to such inequality.

Humanizing Bureaucracy

Humanizing bureaucracy means *fostering a more democratic organizational atmosphere that recognizes and encourages the contributions of everyone*. This seems to produce happier employees and better profits. Humanized organizational environments have certain basic characteristics which fall into three broad categories. These include: *social inclusiveness, sharing of responsibilities,* and, *expanding opportunities for advancement*.

Self-Managed Work Teams

More organizations today are moving away from the top-down chain of command structure. Members of self-managed work teams have the skills necessary to carry out tasks with minimal supervision. Productivity seems to be positively affected by this approach to organizational structure.

Organizational Environment

Organizational environment refers to *a range of factors external to an organization that affects its operation*. This would include *technology*, *politics*, the *economy*, *population patterns*, and *other organizations*. Each of these factors is briefly discussed.

The McDonaldization of Society

The effects of McDonald's goes beyond the sale of food. It's organizational principles are steadily coming to dominate our society.

McDonaldization: Four Principles

The four principles identified and described include: *efficiency, calculability, predictability*, and *control through automation*.

Can Rationality be Irrational?

Max Weber warned in the early part of this century of the price paid for efficiency--*dehumanization*. Could the McDonald system take control of us? George Ritzer briefly provide critique of McDonaldization.

Formal Organizations in Japan

Japan's economic success during the past few decades has raised great interest among U.S. citizens. Their formal organizations reflect their culture's collective identity and social solidarity. We here in the U.S. on the other hand, have stressed individuality. Japan's approach to constructing organizations makes bureaucracies remarkably personal. Five distinctions between Japanese and Western formal organizations are highlighted by William Ouchi. These include: *hiring and advancement, lifetime security, holistic involvement, nonspecialized training*, and *collective decision making*. The **Controversy and Debate** box (p. 197) addresses the issue of whether large organizations are threatening to personal privacy. In the **Seeing Ourselves** box (p. 199) *National Map 7-2* shows data focusing on concerns about privacy in different parts of the country.

GROUPS AND ORGANIZATIONS IN GLOBAL PERSPECTIVE

In recent years there has been a shift in focus from organizations themselves to organizational environments in which they operate. The Japanese success with more humanized and personal organizational environments has illustrated that organizations need not be impersonal. Collective identity and responsibility seems to be compatible with high organizational productivity.

PART IV: KEY CONCEPTS

Define each of the following concepts in the space provided or on a separate paper. Check the accuracy of your answers by referring to the key concepts section at the end of the chapter in the text as well as by referring to italicized definitions located throughout the chapter.

aggregates
authoritarian leader
bureaucracy
bureaucratic inertia
bureaucratic ritualism
category
coercive organization
democratic leader
dyad
expressive leadership
formal organizations
groupism
groupthink
humanizing bureaucracy
ingroup
instrumental leader
laissez-faire leader
McDonaldization
network
normative organization
oligarchy
organizational environment
outgroup
Parkinson's law
Peter principle
primary group
secondary group
social group
triad
utilitarian organization

PART V: STUDY QUESTIONS

True-False

1. T   F   While members of *aggregates* could become transformed into a social group, by definition members of *categories* cannot be transformed into groups.

2.   T   F   *Expressive leadership* emphasizes the completion of tasks.

3.   T   F   Stanley Milgram's research on *group conformity* patterns illustrated that most individuals are skeptical about the legitimacy of authority for people in positions of power.

4.   T   F   Samuel Stouffer's research on soldier's attitudes toward their own promotions during World War II demonstrates the significance of *reference groups* in making judgments about ourselves.

5.   T   F   According to research by Georg Simmel, larger groups tend to be more stable than small groups, such as dyads.

6.   T   F   *Networks* tend to be more enduring and provide a greater sense of identity than most other types of social groups.

7.   T   F   *Normative organizations* are defined as those which impose restrictions on people who have been labeled as deviant.

8.   T   F   *Bureaucracy* is being defined in the text as an organizational model rationally designed to perform complex tasks efficiently.

9.   T   F   *Parkinson's Law* and the *Peter Principle* relate to processes of bureaucratic waste and incompetency.

10.   T   F   Rosabeth Kanter's research on hierarchies in organizations demonstrates that those members of a bureaucracy who have restricted opportunities often are the people who demonstrate the most creativity and have the highest aspirations for achievement.

11.   T   F   Worker participation programs, like those traditionally found in Japan, are becoming more popular in the U.S.

12.   T   F   *Nepotism* was a larger factor in the development of formal organizations in Japan than in the U.S.

Multiple-Choice

1.   A social group characterized by long-term personal relationships usually involving many activities is a _____.

    (a)   primary group   (d)   aggregate
    (b)   secondary group   (e)   normative organization
    (c)   category

2.   Which of the following is *not* true of primary groups:

    (a)   they provide security for their members
    (b)   they are focused around specific activities
    (c)   they are valued in and of themselves
    (d)   they are viewed as ends in themselves

3. Which of the following theorists differentiated between *primary* and *secondary* groups:

(a) Max Weber
(b) Amitai Etzioni
(c) Emile Durkheim
(d) Charles Horton Cooley
(e) George Herbert Mead

4. Which of the following is *not* identified in the text as a type of leadership decision-making style:

(a) laissez-faire
(b) democratic
(c) authoritarian
(d) utilitarian

5. Promoting group goals in social groups is least adequately accomplished when the leader is _____ in terms of decision-making style.

(a) instrumental
(b) democratic
(c) authoritarian
(d) laissez-faire

6. Which researcher concluded that people are not likely to question group opinion even when common sense dictates that they should:

(a) Irving Janis
(b) Hans Windler
(c) Stanley Jacobson
(d) Charles Kanter

7. The Kennedy administration's decision to invade Cuba is used as an example of:

(a) ingroups and outgroups
(b) reference groups
(c) bureaucracy
(d) oligarchy
(e) groupthink

8. Amitai Etzioni constructed a typology of formal organizations. Organizations such as the PTA, Red Cross and United Way illustrate the type of organization he called:

(a) utilitarian
(b) coercive
(c) normative
(d) oligarchical

9. Which of the following is *not* a type of formal organization as identified by Amitai Etzioni:

(a) coercive
(b) normative
(c) hierarchial
(d) utilitarian

10. *Bureaucratic ritualism* is:

   (a)   the process of promoting people to their level of incompetence
   (b)   the tendency of bureaucratic organizations to persist over time
   (c)   the rule of the many by the few
   (d)   a preoccupation with rules and regulations as ends in themselves rather than as means toward organizational goals

11. Robert Michels identified one of the limitations of bureaucracy which involves the tendency of bureaucracy to become an *oligarchy* because:

   (a)   technical competence cannot be maintained
   (b)   bureaucrats abuse organizational power
   (c)   bureaucrats get caught up in rule-making
   (d)   specialization gives way to generalist orientations

12. According to Rosabeth Kanter's research:

   (a)   proper application of technology is the most significant factor in the success of bureaucracies
   (b)   oligarchy actually is the most effective bureaucratic structure during times of rapid technological change
   (c)   people are the company's most important resource
   (d)   humanizing bureaucracies would diminish productivity
   (e)   none of the above

Fill-In

1. A _____ _____ is defined as two or more people who identify with one another and have a distinctive pattern of interaction.
2. Political organizations are examples of _____ *groups*.
3. _____ *leadership* refers to group leadership that emphasizes the completion of tasks.
4. _____ *leaders* focus on instrumental concerns, make decisions on their own, and demand strict compliance from subordinates.
5. Irving Janis studied the group process he called _____ that reduces a group's capacity for critical reflection.
6. A social group that consists of *two* members is a _____.
7. Peter Blau points out four ways in which the composition of social groups affects intergroup associations. These include: _____ _____ turn inward, _____ _____ turn outward, _____ _____ promotes contact, and _____ _____ foster social boundaries.

8. Amitai Etzioni identifies three *types of formal organizations*, distinguished by why people participate, including _____, _____, and

    _____.

9. A _____ is an organizational model rationally designed to perform complex tasks efficiently.

10. According to Max Weber, the *six characteristics of a bureaucracy* include: _____, _____ ___ _____, _____ ___ _____, _____ _____, _____, _____, _____ _____.

11. Preoccupation with rules and regulations to the point of thwarting and organization's goals _____ _____.

12. _____ _____ is the term used to describe the tendency for bureaucratic organizations to persist over time.

13. Three paths to a more *humane organizational structure* include: _____ _____, _____, and _____ _____ ___ _____.

14. Factors found in the *organizational environment* include: _____, _____, ___ _____, _____ _____, and _____ _____.

15. The four basic organizational principles of the *McDonaldization* of society include: _____, _____, _____ and _____ _____ _____.

16. The cultural emphasis on individual achievement in our society finds its parallel in Japanese _____.

Definition and Short-Answer

1. Differentiate between the *qualities* of bureaucracies and small groups. In what ways are they similar?

2. What are the three factors in *decision-making* processes in groups that lead to "groupthink?"

3. What are the major *problems* of bureaucracy? Provide an example for each.

4. In what ways do bureaucratic organizations in Japan differ from those in the U.S.? What are the consequences of these differences? Will their way work in the U.S. Why?

5. Provide two examples of a *coercive* organization.

6. Differentiate between the concepts "aggregate" and "category."

7. Identify the basic *types of leadership* in groups (in terms of both "styles" and "decision-making" approach) and provide examples of the advantages and disadvantages for each type.

8. What are the three "paths" to a more *humane* organizational structure? How does Rosabeth Kanter's research relate to the humanizing of bureaucracy?

9. Review Peter Blau's research concerning how the structure of social groups regulates intergroup association.

10. Review the research by Janis, Milgram, and Asch concerning group conformity.
11. What are factors relating to the *organizational environment*? Provide an example for each.
12. What is meant by the phrase "the *McDonaldization* of society?" What are the four principles of McDonaldization? What are the arguments concerning its *irrationality*?
13. Discuss evidence presented in this chapter concerning the significance of gender and race in organizations.
14. What are the basic *characteristics* of bureaucracy? Define and provide an illustration for each from personal experience.
15. Review the evidence presented by Rosabeth Kanter concerning inequalities based on gender and race in formal organizations. Make specific reference to *Figure 7-4*.

PART VI: ANSWERS TO STUDY QUESTIONS

True-False

1.	F	(p. 174)	6.	F	(p. 183)	11.	T	(p. 197)
2.	F	(p. 176)	7.	F	(p. 185)	12.	F	(p. 198)
3.	F	(p. 178)	8.	T	(p. 186)			
4.	T	(pp. 179-80)	9.	T	(p. 191)			
5.	T	(p. 181)	10.	F	(p. 192)			

Multiple-Choice

1.	a	(pp. 174-75)	7.	e	(p. 179)
2.	b	(pp. 174-75)	8.	c	(p. 185)
3.	d	(pp. 174-75)	9.	c	(p. 185)
4.	d	(p. 177)	10.	d	(p. 189)
5.	d	(p. 177)	11.	b	(p. 190)
6.	a	(p. 179)	12.	c	(p. 192)

Fill-In

1. social group (p. 174)
2. secondary (p. 176)
3. instrumental (p. 176)
4. authoritarian (p. 177)
5. groupthink (p. 179)
6. dyad (p. 181)
7. large groups, heterogeneous groups, social parity, physical boundaries (pp. 182-83)
8. utilitarian, normative, coercive (p. 186)
9. bureaucracy (p. 186)
10. specialization, hierarchy of offices, rules and regulations, technical competence, impersonality, and formal, written communications (pp. 186-87)

11. bureaucratic ritualism (p. 193)
12. bureaucratic inertia (p. 193)
13. social inclusiveness, sharing of responsibility, expanding opportunities for advancement (p. 193)
14. technology, politics, the economy, population patterns, other organizations (p. 194)
15. efficiency, calculability, predictability, control through automation (pp. 195-96)
16. groupism (p. 198)

PART VII: ANALYSIS AND COMMENT

Profiles

"Charles Horton Cooley" (1864-1929)

    Key Points: Questions:

"Rosabeth Moss Kanter"

    Key Points: Questions:

Global Sociology

"The Japanese Model: Will It Work In the United States?"

    Key Points: Questions:

Sociology of Everyday Life

"The Internet: Welcome to Cyberspace!"

Key Points: Questions:

Seeing Ourselves

"National Map 7-1 The Quality of Relationships: Lawsuits Across the U.S."

Key Points: Questions:

Window on the World

"Global Map 7-1 Cyberspace: A Global Network"

Key Points: Questions:

Deviance

8

VI.   Crime
       A. The Components of Crime
       B. Types of Crime
       C. Criminal Statistics
       D. The "Street" Criminal: A Profile
              1. Age
              2. Gender
              3. Social Class
              4. Race and Ethnicity
       E. Crime In Global Perspective
VII.   The Criminal Justice System
       A. Police
       B. Courts
       C. Punishment
              1. Retribution
              2. Deterrence
              3. Rehabilitation
              4. Societal Protection
VIII. Summary
IX.   Key Concepts
X.   Critical-Thinking Questions
XI.   Suggested Readings

PART II: LEARNING OBJECTIVES

1.   To explain how deviance is interpreted as a product of society from the sociological perspective.
2.   To explain the historical and recent biological explanations for deviance.
3.   To evaluate the explanatory views of biological theories of deviance.
4.   To explain the psychological explanation of deviance.
5.   To evaluate the explanatory views of psychological theories of deviance.
6.   To explain the sociological explanations of deviance focusing upon the main sociological paradigms.
7.   To compare and contrast different theories representative of these main paradigms.
8.   To evaluate empirical evidence used to support these different sociological theories of deviance.
9.   To be able to identify the components of crime and distinguish between the types of crime.
10.   To know the limitations of criminal statistics.
11.   To identify, describe, and evaluate the elements of our criminal justice system.

116

PART III: CHAPTER REVIEW

This chapter addresses a number of questions concerning deviance. For instance, How do societies confront what is "offensive and disagreeable"? How and why does deviance occur? And, do all people who violate norms become labeled as deviants?

WHAT IS DEVIANCE?

Deviance is *the recognized violation of cultural norms.* It is a very broad concept. Many characteristics are used by members of society in identifying deviance. One familiar type of deviance is *crime*, or *the violation of norms a society formally enacts into criminal law*. A special category of crime is *juvenile delinquency*, or *the violation of legal standards by the young*. It is pointed out that deviance can be negative or positive, but that it stems from *difference* that causes us to react to another person as an "outsider."

Social Control

Social control is a part of any society and involves the regulation of the behavior of individuals. Like deviance, it takes many forms, both positive and negative, and involves a complex process. Serious deviance may provoke a response from the *criminal justice system*, or *a societal reaction to alleged violations of law utilizing police, courts, and prison officials*. *How* society defines deviance, *whom* individuals target as deviant, and *what* people decide to do about nonconformity are all key issues.

The Biological Context

During the latter part of the 19th century Caesare Lombroso, an Italian physician who worked in prisons, suggested that criminals have distinctive physical traits. Lombroso's research was scientifically flawed.

During the middle of this century William Sheldon suggested that body structure was a critical link to criminal behavior. He reported a positive correlation between muscular, athletic body type and criminality. Subsequent research by Sheldon and Eleanor Glueck has supported this argument; however, they argue that the body structure is not the cause of the delinquency. They stress the importance of social processes in provoking certain types of people to become delinquent.

Recent genetic research has rejuvenated interest in the study of biological causes of criminality. To date no conclusive evidence connects criminality to any specific genetic flaws. How it is that specific behavior comes to be defined as deviant cannot be answered using this biological perspective. Overall, research findings lead us to the understanding that the interaction of genetic and social influences is significant in affecting the patterns of deviant behavior in society.

Personality Factors

Psychological explanations of deviance concentrate on personality abnormalities, and so like biological theories are focused on "individualistic" characteristics. *Containment theory* posits the view that juvenile delinquency (among boys) is a result of social pressure to commit deviant acts in the absence of moral values and a positive self-image. Longitudinal research conducted by Walter Reckless and Simon Dinitz during the 1960s supported this conclusion.

There are several weaknesses in the psychological approach to deviance. First, most serious crime is committed by people who are not psychologically abnormal. Second, cross-cultural differences in what is deemed normal and abnormal tends to be ignored. And three, the fact that people with similar psychological qualities are not equally as likely to be labeled deviant is not considered.

The Social Foundations of Deviance

Deviance is not simply a matter of free choice or personal failings. Both conformity and deviance are shaped by society. Our author points out this is evident in three ways. *Deviance varies according to cultural norms; People become deviant as others define them that way; And, both rule making and rule breaking involve social power.*

STRUCTURAL-FUNCTIONAL ANALYSIS

Emile Durkheim: The Functions of Deviance

While on the surface deviance may appear to be harmful only for society, Emile Durkheim asserted that deviance is an integral part of all societies and serves four major functions. These include *affirming cultural values and norms, clarifying moral boundaries, promoting social unity, and encouraging social change*. Examples for each are presented.

An Illustration: The Puritans of Massachusetts Bay

Kai Erikson's historical research on this highly religious society supports Durkheim's theory concerning the functions of deviance. For these people deviance helped clarify various moral boundaries. Over time, he noted, what was defined as deviant changed as social and environmental conditions changed. However, what remained constant was the proportion of people viewed as deviant.

Robert Merton: Strain Theory

According to Merton, deviance is encouraged by the day-to-day operation of society. Analysis using strain theory points out imbalances between institutionalized *means* available to different groups of people and the cultural *goals* in society. As a result of this structured inequality of opportunity, some people are prone to deviance. Four adaptive strategies, or deviant responses, are identified by Merton: *innovation, ritualism, retreatism, and rebellion. Figure 8-1* (p. 208) outlines the components of this theory. *Conformity,* or the acceptance of both cultural goals and means is seen as the result of successful socialization and the opportunity to pursue these goals through socially approved means.

As insightful as Merton is in recognizing the importance of social structural elements in causing deviance, there are some inadequacies of this approach. First, it is difficult to measure precisely how much deviance is actually caused by strain. Second, some kinds of deviance, like mental illness and homosexuality, are not adequately explained using this perspective. Third, Merton is not precise about why one response to strain is chosen over another by an individual. And fourth, the extent to which the variability of cultural values creates different concepts of personal success is not incorporated into this model very well.

Deviant Subcultures

Researchers Richard Cloward and Lloyd Ohlin have attempted to extend the work of Merton utilizing the concept of *relative opportunity structure*. They argue criminal deviance occurs when there is limited opportunity to achieve success and also limited availability of illegitimate opportunities. They further suggest that criminal subcultures emerge to organize and expand systems of deviance. Al Capone's life is an example. In poor and highly transient neighborhoods "conflict subcultures" (i.e., violent gangs) are more often the form this process takes. Those who fail to achieve success using legitimate means are likely to fall into "retreatist subcultures" (i.e., alcoholics).

Albert Cohen found that deviant subcultures occur more often in the lower classes and are based on values that oppose the dominant culture. Walter Miller, while agreeing that deviant subcultures are more likely to develop in the lower classes, suggests that the values which emerge are not a reaction against the middle-class way of life. Rather, he suggests that their values emerge out of daily experiences within contexts of limited opportunities. He described six focal concerns of these delinquent subcultures, *trouble, toughness, smartness, excitement, fate,* and *autonomy*.

Structural-functional analysis focuses our attention on the linkage between deviance and social norms and structures. However, three limitations to this approach are pointed out. First, functionalists assume a single, dominant culture even though research reveals U.S. society to be comprised of a variety of cultural patterns with competing ideas about what constitutes deviance. Second, the assumption that deviance occurs primarily among the poor is a weakness of the subcultural theories of deviance. Third, the view that the definition of being deviant will be applied to all who violate norms is inadequate.

SYMBOLIC-INTERACTION ANALYSIS

The symbolic-interaction paradigm focuses attention on the creation of different social realities in society and the extent to which these create distinguishable understandings of what deviance is.

Labeling Theory

Labeling theory, *the assertion that deviance and conformity result, not so much from what people do, but from how others respond to those actions*. This view stresses the relativity of deviance. Of critical significance to proponents of this perspective is the process by which people label others as deviant. The idea that reality is relative to time and space is illustrated in the **Global Sociology** box (p. 212) which describes cockfighting and asks whether it is a cultural ritual or a vicious abuse of animals.

Primary and Secondary Deviance

Edwin Lember has distinguished between the concepts of *primary deviance*, relating to activity that is initially defined as deviant, and *secondary deviance*, corresponding to a person who accepts the label of deviant.

Stigma

Erving Goffman suggested secondary deviance is the beginning of a *deviant career*. This typically results as a consequence of acquiring a **stigma**, or *a powerfully negative social label that radically changes a person's self-concept and social identity*. Some people may go through a "*degradation ceremony*," like a criminal prosecution, where a community formally condemns the person for deviance allegedly committed.

Retrospective Labeling

Retrospective labeling is *the interpretation of someone's past consistent with present deviance*. In this case, other people selectively rethink the "deviant's" past, arguing all the evidence was there that would inevitably become a problem.

Labeling and Mental Illness

Theorist Thomas Szaz has argued the concept "mental illness" should stop being applied to people. He says that only the "body" can become ill, and mental illness is therefore a myth. Szaz suggests the label mental illness is attached to people who are different and who worry the status quo of society. It acts as a justification for forcing people to comply with cultural norms.

Erving Goffman concurs with this perspective to the extent that he feels oftentimes a person is sent to a mental institution for the benefit of the status quo. The label of mental illness becomes an extremely powerful stigma and can act as a self-fulfilling prophecy.

The Medicalization of Deviance

Over the last fifty years the field of medicine has had a tremendous influence on how deviance has been understood and explained. The *medicalization of deviance* relates to *the transformation of moral and legal issues into medical matters.* Instead of seeing conformity and deviance as matters of "bad" and "good," we conceive the dichotomy as one of "well" versus "sick." The general view of alcoholism in our society is a good illustration of this process in recent years.

The Significance of Labels

Whichever approach is used, moral or medical, will have considerable consequences for those labeled as deviant. Questions concerning the effects of *who responds* to deviance, *how people respond* to deviance, and the *personal competence* of the person labeled as deviant are also addressed.

Sutherland's Differential Association Theory

Edwin Sutherland suggests that deviance is learned through association with others. Accordingly, a person's likelihood of violating norms is dependent upon the frequency of association with those who encourage norm violation. This perspective is known as *differential association* theory.

Hirschi's Control Theory

Travis Hirschi's point in *control theory* is that what really requires explanation is conformity. He suggests conformity results from four types of social controls: *attachment, commitment, involvement,* and *belief.* Once again, a person's position in the social structural system is important in determining one's likelihood of being involved in subcultural deviance.

SOCIAL-CONFLICT ANALYSIS

Deviance and Power

Social inequality serves as the basis of social-conflict theory as it relates to deviance. Certain less powerful people in society tend to be defined as deviant. This pattern is explained in three ways. First, the norms of society generally reflect the interests of the status quo. Second, even if the behavior of the powerful is questioned they have the resources to resist deviant labels. And third, laws and norms are usually never questioned, being viewed as "natural."

Deviance and Capitalism

Steven Spitzer has suggested that deviant labels are attached to people who interfere with capitalism. These people he refers to as "problem populations." Four qualities of capitalism are critical to recognize in order to understand who is labeled as deviant. These are: private ownership, production labor, respect for authority, and acceptance of the status quo.

White-Collar Crime

The concept **white-collar crime**, or *crimes committed by persons of high social position in the course of their occupations*, was defined by Edwin Sutherland in the 1940s. This type of crime involves powerful people taking illegal advantage of their occupational position. While it is estimated that the harm done to society by white-collar crime is greater than street crime, most people are not particularly concerned about this form of deviance. Research has found that *crime in the suites*, as white-collar crime is often called, is typically dealt with in terms of *civil law* instead of *criminal law*--the former referring to general regulations involving business dealings between private parties, and the latter dealing with an individual's moral responsibilities to society. The case of Michael Milken and his breaching of securities and exchange laws is discussed.

Social-conflict theory focuses our attention on the significance of power and inequality in understanding how deviance is defined and controlled. However, several weaknesses of this approach have been identified. The assumption that the rich and powerful directly create and control cultural norms is questionable given the nature of our political process. Further, the approach seems to overgeneralize the cost of white-collar crime relative to street crime. Finally, the approach suggests that only when inequality exists is there deviance, yet all societies exhibit types of deviance, and as Durkheim has pointed out deviance can be functional.

Table 8-1 (p. 216) summarizes the major contributions of each of the sociological explanations of deviance.

DEVIANCE AND SOCIAL DIVERSITY

Deviance and Gender

The significance of gender in the study of deviant behavior has historically been ignored in sociological research. The behavior of males and females has tended to be evaluated using different standards and the process of labeling has been sex-biased. The **Critical Thinking** box (pp. 218-219) discusses the myths surrounding date rape which helps to perpetuate a double standard.

Hate Crimes

A **hate crime** involves *a criminal act against a person or person's property by an offender motivated by racial or other bias*. While having a long history in our society, the government has only been tracking them since 1990. Recent research suggests gays and lesbians are often the target of such crimes. The **Critical Thinking** box (p. 220) takes a look at the issue of the *motivation* of the offender as a factor in determining the amount of punishment for the offender if found guilty. In the **Seeing Ourselves** box (p. 217) *National Map 8-1* shows us how different states have mandated legislation with harsher penalties for hate crimes.

CRIME

What is viewed as criminal varies over both time and place. What all crime has in common is that perceived violations bring about response from a formal criminal justice system.

The Components of Crime

Technically our society conceives of crime as having two distinct parts: the *act* itself and the *criminal intent*. Illustrations are given.

Types of Crime

Two major types of crime are recorded by the FBI in its statistical reports as "index crime." One, **crimes against the person**, or violent crimes, are defined as *crimes that direct violence or the threat of violence against others*. Examples are murder, rape, aggravated assault, and robbery. And two, **crimes against property**, or property crimes, defined as *crimes that involve theft of property belonging to others*. Examples are burglary, larceny-theft, auto theft, and arson. A third category, **victimless crime**, is defined as *violations of law in which there are no readily apparent victims*. Examples are gambling, prostitution and the use of illegal drugs.

Criminal Statistics

The FBI statistics indicate that crime dramatically rose during the 1970s, declined during the early 1980s, and since has been rising again. *Figure 8-2* (p. 222) shows the trends and relative frequencies for types of both violent and property crime between the years 1960-1993.

It is pointed out that these official statistics are far from accurate. First, they only include cases known by the police. People sometimes may not know they have been victimized, or may be reluctant to report a crime to the police. *Victimization surveys* suggest that the actual crime rate may be three times higher than official statistics show.

The "Street" Criminal: A Profile
Age

The likelihood of engaging in crime increases sharply during adolescence and declines thereafter. While only 14 percent of the population is between the ages of 15-24, this age group accounted for 43.6 percent of all arrests in 1993.

Gender

Statistics indicate crime to be predominantly a male activity. Males are four times more likely than women to be arrested. However, recent evidence suggests the disparity is shrinking.

Social Class

While most people believe that poor people simply commit more crime, the situation is actually more complex. Research suggests crime rates across social strata are relatively equivalent; it is the types of crimes committed which vary. Variation also exists in the victimization of people of different social strata by different types of crime.

Race and Ethnicity

The relationship between race and ethnicity and crime is also discussed as being very complex. While African-Americans, proportionally speaking, are arrested for "index crime" more than whites, three factors make this connection between race and crime very tenuous. First, arrest records are not statements of proven guilt. Second, race is closely related to social class. And third, white-collar and other crimes more representative of the white population are not counted in the statistics. Further, certain categories of our population, for example Asians, emphasize family solidarity and discipline, and very low arrests rates. Plus, they enjoy higher than average incomes and high educational achievement.

Crime in Global Perspective

Relative to European societies, the U.S. has a very high crime rate. For example, the homicide rate in the U.S. is five times that of Europe, the rape rate is seven times higher, and the property crime rate is twice as high. Several reasons for the relatively high rates in the U.S. have been offered. First, our culture emphasizes individual economic success. Second, families are weakened without guaranteed family incomes and child care. Third, the high levels of unemployment and underemployment create chronically poor categories of people. Finally, our society encourages private ownership of guns. *Figure 8-3* (p. 225) shows the United States leads the world by a significant margin in handgun deaths.

In the **Window on the World** box (p. 226) *Global Map 8-1* looks at prostitution worldwide. Rates for prostitution by society seem to vary with the relative status of women in the societies. Globalization is being experienced in many ways, including crime. Rape, terrorism, and the proliferation of illegal drugs are presented to illustrate this pattern.

THE CRIMINAL JUSTICE SYSTEM

The criminal justice system is comprised of three component parts. These are:

Police

The police represent the point of contact between the public and the criminal justice system. They are responsible for maintaining public order by uniformly enforcing the law. However, particularly because of the relatively small number of police in our population, they must exercise much discretion about which situations receive their attention. Seven "external clues" used by police to help them decide how to carry out their duties are discussed. The concentration of police across the U.S. is shown in the **Seeing Ourselves** box in *National Map 8-2* (p. 227).

Courts

It is within this component of the system where guilt or innocence is determined. *Plea bargaining* is a major practice in resolving cases. It is defined as *a negotiation in which the state reduces the charge against a defendant in exchange for a guilty plea.* This saves both time and expense, but it is a very controversial element within our court system.

Punishment

Iraqi television showed viewers in Baghdad special coverage of a man convicted of theft having his hand severed. Barbaric? Why do governments punish? How should it be carried out?

Four justifications for using punishment as part of our criminal justice system are given. These include:

Retribution

Retribution, or *moral vengeance by which society inflicts suffering on the offender comparable to that caused by the offense*, stands as the oldest justification for punishment. It remains a strong justification today in our society.

Deterrence

Deterrence, is *the attempt to discourage criminality through punishment*. It is based on the notion that people are calculating and rational beings. Two types are identified: *specific* and *general.*

Rehabilitation

Rehabilitation, refers to *a program for reforming the offender to preclude subsequent offenses*. The history of rehabilitation approaches in the U.S. is briefly discussed.

125

Societal Protection

Societal protection, or *a means by which society renders an offender incapable of further offenses temporarily through incarceration or permanently by execution*, is the fourth justification. These justifications of punishment are summarized in *Table 8-2* (p. 228). *Figure 8-4* (p. 229) shows that the United States incarcerates a larger share of its population than most other countries in the world.

While these justifications are widely recognized, demonstrating their consequences is very problematic. Their relative effectiveness is questioned given the high *criminal recidivism* rates, or *subsequent offenses committed by people previously convicted of crimes*. Reasons for the high recidivism rate are discussed.

Crime and other forms of deviance are more than simply the acts of "bad people." All deviance is bound up in the operation of society itself. This issue is discussed in the *Controversy and Debate* box (p. 231).

PART IV: KEY CONCEPTS

Define each of the following concepts in the space provided or on separate paper. Check the accuracy of your answers by referring to the key concepts section at the end of the chapter in the text as well as by referring to italicized definitions located throughout the chapter.

containment theory
conflict subculture
conformity
control theory
crime
crimes against property
crimes against the person
criminal justice system
criminal law
criminal recidivism
criminal subculture
deterrence
deviance
differential association
hate crime
index crime
juvenile delinquency
labeling theory
medicalization of deviance
plea bargaining
primary deviance
rebellion

Definition and Short-Answer

1. According to Travis Hirschi's *control theory* there are four types of social controls. What are these? Provide an example of each.
2. According to Robert Merton's *strain theory*, what are the four deviant responses by individuals to dominant cultural patterns? Provide an illustration for each. What are two criticisms of his theory?
3. What are the *functions of deviance* according to Emile Durkheim? Provide illustrations for each.
4. What characteristics are likely to have people labeled as being a member of a "problem population" according to Steven Spitzer?
5. How do researchers using the *differential association theory* explain deviance?
6. What is meant by the term *medicalization of deviance*?
7. What factors seem to be responsible for the relatively high crime rates in the U.S.?
8. What are the four *justifications* for the use of punishment against criminals? In your opinion, what evidence exists for the success of each type of justification?
9. What are the *social foundations* of deviance? Illustrate each.
10. Summarize the basic explanations of deviance using each of the following perspectives: *social-conflict*, *symbolic-interactionism*, and *structural-functionalism*.
11. Differentiate between the *biological* and *psychological* theories of deviance.
12. What are the two major parts or components of *crime*? Discuss how the criminal justice system is tied to this type of understanding of criminality.
13. What are the data reported in *Figure 8-2* on crime rates in the U.S. suggesting to us? What factors across the years covered in this figure might be related to the changes in the crime rate?
14. In what ways are the variables of *age, gender, race* and *ethnicity* related to arrest rates for alleged criminals?

PART VI: ANSWERS TO STUDY QUESTIONS

True-False

1.	T	(p. 203)	8.	F	(p. 211)
2.	F	(p. 205)	9.	F	(p. 213)
3.	T	(p. 205)	10.	T	(p. 215)
4.	T	(p. 207)	11.	T	(p. 223)
5.	F	(p. 209)	12.	T	(p. 224)
6.	F	(p. 210)	13.	F	(p. 226)
7.	T	(p. 211)	14.	T	(p. 228)

Multiple-Choice

1.	d	(p. 205)	7.	c	(p. 208)
2.	b	(p. 205)	8.	d	(p. 210)
3.	c	(p. 206)	9.	c	(p. 213)
4.	c	(pp. 207-09)	10.	d	(p. 214)
5.	a	(p. 207)	11.	d	(pp. 219-20)
6.	b	(p. 207)	12.	e	(p 229)

Fill-In

1. criminal justice system (p. 203)
2. physical attributes (p. 204)
3. containment (p. 205)
4. cultural norms, define, social power (p. 205)
5. structural-functional (p. 207)
6. ritualism, innovation, retreatism, rebellion (pp. 207-08)
7. primary, secondary (p. 210)
8. attachment, opportunity, involvement, belief (p. 213)
9. civil law, criminal law (pp. 215-16)
10. hate (p. 217)
11. act, criminal intent (p. 218)
12. victimization (p. 221)
13. police, courts, prison officials (p. 225)
14. retribution, deterrence, rehabilitation, societal protection (pp. 228-29)
15. criminal recidivism (p. 230)

PART VII: ANALYSIS AND COMMENT

Critical Thinking

"Date Rape: Exposing Dangerous Myths"

Key Points: Questions:

"Hate Crimes: Punishing Actions or Attitudes"

    Key Points: Questions:

Global Sociology

"Cockfighting: Cultural Ritual or Abuse of Animals?"

    Key Points: Questions:

Controversy and Debate

"What Can Be Done About Crime?"

    Key Points: Questions:

Seeing Ourselves

"National Map 8-1 Seeing Ourselves: Hate Crime Legislation Across the U.S."

Key Points: Questions:

"National Map 8-2 The Concentration of Police Across the U.S."

Key Points: Questions:

Window on the World

"Global Map 8-1 Prostitution in Global Perspective"

Key Points: Questions:

Social Stratification

PART I: CHAPTER OUTLINE

PART II: LEARNING OBJECTIVES

1.   To understand the four basic principles of social stratification.
2.   To differentiate between two systems of stratification: caste and class, and to be able to provide historical and cross-cultural examples of each.
3.   To know the relationship between culture, ideology, and stratification.
4.   To differentiate between the structural-functional and social-conflict perspectives of stratification.
5.   To understand the views of Karl Marx and Max Weber concerning the dimensions of social class.
6.   To know the synthesis approach to understanding social stratification put forward by the Lenskis.

PART III: CHAPTER REVIEW

WHAT IS SOCIAL STRATIFICATION?

Social inequality, referring to the unequal distribution of valued resources, is found in every society. Some of the inequality is the result of individual differences in ability and effort. However, it also relates to society. *Social stratification* refers to *a system by which a society ranks categories of people in a hierarchy*. This chapter opens with an illustration of the sinking of the *Titanic* to show the consequences of social inequality in terms of who survived the disaster and who did not. Four principles are identified which help explain why social stratification exists. First, *it is a characteristic of society, not simply a function of individual differences*. Second, *it persists over generations*. Related to this principle is the concept *social mobility* which refers to *change in one's position in a social hierarchy*. This change may be *upward* or *downward*. A third principle of social stratification is that *it is universal but variable*. Finally, *it involves not just inequality but beliefs*.

CASTE AND CLASS SYSTEMS

Sociologists distinguish between two general systems of social stratification based on the degree of social mobility representative of the system.

The Caste System

A *caste system* is *a system of stratification based on ascription*. Pure caste systems are "closed" with no social mobility. Two different stratification systems representing elements of a caste are discussed.

Two Illustrations: India and South Africa

The Hindu social system of rural India and racial apartheid in South Africa are used to illustrate caste systems. In such systems four factors underlie the fact that ascription determines virtually everything about a person's life. First, birth determines one's occupation. Second, marriage unites people of the same social standing, so they are *endogamous*. Third, powerful cultural beliefs underlie such systems. Fourth, caste systems constrain the contact members have with each other. The **Global Sociology** box (pp. 238-39) discusses the history of apartheid in South Africa.

Caste and Agrarian Life

Caste systems are typical of agrarian societies as discipline and duty are central in such cultures. In much of the world, as industrialization continues and spreads, the nature of stratification is changing.

The Class System

Representative of industrial societies, *class systems* are defined as *systems of social stratification based on individual achievement*. Social categories are not as rigidly defined as in the caste system. Individual ability, promoted by open social mobility, is critical to this system. Other factors characteristic of industrial economies which are central to such a system are high levels of migration to cities, democratic principles, and high immigration rates.

Status Consistency

Status consistency, or *the degree of consistency of a person's social standing across various dimensions of social inequality*, also distinguishes between caste and class systems. Class systems tend to have less status consistency.

Caste and Class Together: The United Kingdom

England represents a society where caste qualities of its agrarian past still are interwoven within the modern day industrial class system.

The Estate System

Great Britain's agrarian past, with deep historical roots, was based on a caste-like estate system. Three estates, the first (nobles), the second (primarily clergy), and the third (commoners) comprised this system. The law of *primogeniture* by which property of parents could only be inherited by the eldest son helped maintain this system.

The United Kingdom Today

Aspects of their feudal past persist today. For example, a monarch still stands as Britain's head of state, and descendants of traditional nobility still maintain inherited wealth and property. However, power in government resides in the House of Commons, which is comprised of people who have achieved their positions. Today, about 25 percent of Great Britain's population falls into the middle-class, and 50 percent into the working-class. Almost 25 percent are "poor." Their system reflects a class system, with an unequal distribution of wealth, power, and prestige. Though opportunities for social mobility are present they are not as numerous as those which represent the United States. Their class system is reflected in different linguistic patterns between social classes.

Another Example: Japan

Like Great Britain, Japan mixes both the traditional and contemporary in their social stratification system.

Feudal Japan

For many centuries of agrarian feudalism, Japan was one of the most rigidly stratified cultures in the world. An imperial family maintained a network of regional nobility *shoguns*, or powerful warlords of the nobility, who fought each other for control of the land. A warrior caste, called *samurai*, fell just below the nobility. The majority of people were commoners, like serfs in feudal Europe. However, there was an additional ranking, called *burakumin*, or outcasts, who were below the commoners.

Japan Today

Industrialization, urbanization, and intercultural contact have dramatically changed Japan over the last century. The nobility lost its legal standing after World War II. For many though, tradition is still revered and family background continues to remain important in determining social status. Male dominance, as an example, continues to be more extreme than in the West.

The Former Soviet Union

The "new Commonwealth," formally the Soviet Union, has experienced great changes during the last few years. We are perhaps seeing a second Russian revolution.

A Classless Society?

The Soviet Union, created through the 1917 revolution, has claimed itself to be a classless society because of the elimination of private ownership of the productive components of society. Yet, it remains socially stratified as occupations generally fall into four major categories: high government officials, the intelligentsia, manual laborers, and rural peasantry.

The Second Soviet Revolution

The reforms spurred by Mikhail Gorbachev's economic program known as *perestroika*, or "restructuring", have been significant. But, economic reform has been complicated by a number of factors, including the need to acquire advanced technology and to cut military spending. Interestingly, research has suggested that there has been more upward social mobility in the Soviet Union than in Japan, Great Britain, or the United States over the last century. A major reason for this is what sociologists call **structural social mobility**, or *a shift in social position of large numbers of people due more to changes in society itself than to individual efforts.*

Ideology: Stratification's "Staying Power"

Ideology refers to *cultural beliefs that serve to justify social stratification.* It is a key reason for the persistence of stratification in any society.

Plato and Marx on Ideology

For the ancient Greek philosopher Plato, a people's sense of stratification formed the basis of justice. For Marx, it created social injustice. In any event, social institutions ensure that systems of social stratification endure. Generally, members of society tend to accept their system of social stratification as fair. The role of culture in promoting values that support the system is critical in ensuring acceptance.

Historical Patterns of Ideology

However, over time people inevitably begin to question cultural "truths." Often changes in a society's economy and technology influence the change in ideas. The example of U.S. women questioning the assumptions of their "place in society" over the last three decades is evidence of this fact. The **Critical Thinking** box (p. 246) discusses the issues of justice and inequality by putting things into historical perspective.

THE FUNCTIONS OF SOCIAL STRATIFICATION

The Davis-Moore Thesis

The *Davis-Moore thesis asserts that social stratification has beneficial consequences for the operation of society*. They theorize that certain tasks in society are of more value than others, and in order to ensure the most qualified people fill these positions, they must be rewarded better than others.

Meritocracy

As society approaches a *meritocracy*, or a system of social stratification based on personal merit, it becomes more productive. Melvin Tumin, a critic of this view, argues that certain highly rewarded occupations seem no more intrinsically important than other less valued jobs. The **Critical Thinking** box (p. 248) discusses whether the "rich" are really worth what they earn. Tumin also points out ascribed statuses still remain as significant factors in our society. Further, social stratification creates conflict as well, so it is not merely functional.

STRATIFICATION AND CONFLICT

Karl Marx: Class and Conflict

Marx's view of social stratification is based on his observations of industrialization in Europe during the second half of the 19th century. He saw a class division between the *capitalists* (owners of the means of production) and the *workers* (proletariat). This resulted in separation and inevitable conflict. As influential as Marx's thinking has been for sociological understanding of social stratification, it does overlook its motivating value. The insight provided by the Davis-Moore thesis perhaps explains, in part, the low productivity characteristic of Eastern Europe under socialism.

Why No Marxist Revolution?

The overthrow of the capitalist system has not occurred for at least four central reasons: (1) *the fragmentation of the capitalist class*, (2) *white-collar work and a rising standard of living*, (3) *more extensive worker organization*, and (4) *more extensive legal protection*. Specifically relating to (2), a century ago the vast majority of workers in the U.S. had **blue-collar** *occupations*, or *lower-prestige jobs involving mostly manual labor*. Today, the majority of workers hold jobs classified as **white-collar occupations**, or *higher-prestige work involving mostly mental activity*. Most of this change has occurred through structural social mobility.

A Counterpoint

The value of Marx's perspective is still significant. There continues to be exploitation of workers, and a small percentage of people control the vast majority of wealth in our society.

Many social-conflict theorist defend Marx's analysis of capitalism, stressing four key points. These include: (1) *wealth remains highly concentrated,* (2) *white-collar jobs offer little to workers,* (3) *progress requires struggle,* and (4) *the law still favors the rich.*

Table 9-1 (p. 252) compares and contrasts the structural-functional and social-conflict explanations of social stratification.

Max Weber: Class, Status, and Power

Max Weber viewed Marx's ideas of social class as being too simplistic. Weber theorized that there were three dimensions of social stratification. The first, related to social inequality, which he termed *class* position. The second, or *status,* related to measures of social prestige. *Power* was the third dimension of social hierarchy these dimensions are continuous in quality such that a person's social prestige might be relatively higher or lower than another's. Weber also theorized that a single individual's rankings on the three dimensions might be quite different.

The Socioeconomic Status Hierarchy

Thus, a multi-dimensional aspect of social inequality was important to him. The term used today to reflect this idea is **socioeconomic status** (SES) referring to *a composite ranking based on various dimensions of social inequality.*

Inequality in History

According to Weber, each of his three dimensions of social inequality stands out at different points in history. In contrast to Marx, Weber did not believe that social stratification could be largely eliminated by abolishing capitalism.

STRATIFICATION AND TECHNOLOGY IN GLOBAL PERSPECTIVE

Gerhard Lenski and Jean Lenski developed a sociocultural evolutionary model of historical change concerning social stratification which combines both structural-functional and social-conflict perspectives.

Hunting and Gathering Societies

In technologically simple societies, age, and sex tend to be the only basis of social stratification. Survival in such societies depends upon sharing. No surpluses exist.

Horticultural, Pastoral, and Agrarian Societies

As technology advances and surpluses in valued resources occur, social inequality increases and social strata emerge.

Industrial Societies

They further propose that as technology continues to develop in industrial societies social inequality tends to diminish. Increasing productivity, a rising standard of living, and a more literate population further diminishes inequality. While at first industrialization increased inequalities between the sexes and between classes, as time has passed more equality has emerged.

The Kuznets Curve

The Kuznets curve, shown in *Figure 9-2* (p. 254), illustrates the pattern discussed by the Lenskis. The patterns of social inequality shown in *Global Map 9-1* (p. 255) as part of the **Window on the World** box, are also in accord with the Kuznets curve. This curve shows a pattern showing the following: *In human history, technological progress first increases but then moderates the intensity of social stratification.*

SOCIAL STRATIFICATION: FACTS AND VALUES

A quote from a Kurt Vonnegut novel describes a fictional America in the later 21st century represented by absolutely no social inequality. It highlights the significant social meaning social inequality actually has for us in our everyday lives.

Theoretical explanations contain both fact and position, or a statement of values. A comparison between the structural-functional and social-conflict paradigms illustrates how the same facts can be perceived and understood differently. It is a complex, but meaningful endeavor. This chapter concludes with a **Controversy and Debate** box (pp. 256--57) which focuses on a review of the basic propositions being set forth in the book *The Bell Curve*. The relationship between social stratification and intelligence is being addressed.

PART IV: KEY CONCEPTS

Define each of the following concepts in the space provided or on separate paper. Check the accuracy of your answers by referring to the key concepts section at the end of the chapter in the text as well as by referring to italicized definitions located throughout the chapter.

blue-collar occupations
burakumin
caste system
class system
Davis-Moore thesis
endogamous
ideology
Kuznets curve
meritocracy

perestroika
primogeniture
samurai
shoguns
socioeconomic status
social inequality
social mobility
social stratification
status inconsistency
structural social mobility
white-collar occupations

PART V: STUDY QUESTIONS

True-False

1. T F Social inequality is found in *all* societies.
2. T F *Ascription* is fundamental to social stratification systems based on castes.
3. T F *Endogamous* marriages tend to be more representative of caste systems than class systems.
4. T F The *working class* is the largest segment of the population in Great Britain.
5. T F In feudal Japan, *shoguns* were small agrarian villages where most commoners lived and worked.
6. T F The *Davis-Moore Thesis* is a component of the social-conflict perspective of social stratification.
7. T F *Structural-functionalists* argue that social stratification encourages a matching of talents and abilities to appropriate positions in society.
8. T F Max Weber developed a *unidimensional* model of social stratification which was very dominant in the early part of this century.
9. T F Gerhard and Jean Lenski argue that hunting and gathering societies have greater *social inequality* than agrarian or horticultural societies.
10. T F The *Kuznets curve* projects greater social inequality as industrial societies advance through technological change.

Multiple-Choice

1. A system by which entire categories of people within a society are ranked in a hierarchy is called:

    (a) social inequality   (c) meritocracy
    (b) social stratification   (d) social mobility

2. Which of the following principles is *not* a basic factor in explaining the existence of social stratification?

   (a) Social stratification is universal and variable.
   (b) Social stratification persists over generations.
   (c) Social stratification is supported by patterns of belief.
   (d) Social stratification is a characteristic of society, not simply of individuals.
   (e) All are basic factors in explaining social stratification.

3. *Apartheid* became law in South Africa in:

   (a) 1948   (b) 1916   (c) 1971   (d) 1875

4. Which of the characteristics that follow is true of *class systems*?

   (a) they are more clearly defined than castes
   (b) they have low status consistency
   (c) they have occupations based on ascription
   (d) all of the above
   (e) none of the above

5. In the text, contemporary Great Britain is identified as a(n):

   (a) neomonarchy   (d) caste system
   (b) estate system   (e) open estate system
   (c) class society

6. The social stratification system in Great Britain today still has vestiges of its feudal caste-like system of the past. Which of the following is true of Britain's feudal stratification system?

   (a) it was an estate system
   (b) it was based on the law of primogeniture
   (c) it consisted of nobility, clergy, and commoners
   (d) all of the above
   (e) a and c only

7. The former Soviet Union (now the Commonwealth of Independent States) is:

   (a) decidedly not classless
   (b) socially stratified
   (c) a society with greater extremes between the wealthy and the poor than U.S. society
   (d) more caste-like than U.S. society

8. Which society was identified as having experienced the *most* upward social mobility during this century?

(a) Japan   (c) Great Britain
(b) United States   (d) Soviet Union

9. "Ideas that support the interests of some category of a population" is part of the definition for:

(a) meritocracy   (c) ideology
(b) social stratification   (d) status inconsistency

10. Which *social institution* did Karl Marx believe had primary importance and had the greatest impact on the rest of society?

(a) religion   (d) government
(b) economy   (e) education
(c) family

11. According to Gerhard and Jean Lenski, social stratification is at its peak in:

(a) hunting and gathering societies
(b) postindustrial societies
(c) horticultural, pastoral, and agrarian societies
(d) industrial societies

12. The *Kuznets curve* has to do with:

(a) social stratification and technological development
(b) human intelligence and social stratification
(c) social class and standard of living
(d) status inconsistency
(e) the Davis-Moore thesis

Fill-In

1. _____ refers to a system by which society ranks categories of people in a hierarchy.
2. Social stratification is a matter of four *basic principles*. It is a characteristic of _____, not simply a reflection of individual differences, it _____ _____ _____, it is _____ but variable, and it involves not just inequality but _____.
3. A _____ is a system of social stratification based on *ascription*.
4. A system of social stratification in which *individual achievement* is of great importance is called a _____ system.

145

5. In feudal Great Britain, the law of _____ mandated that only the eldest son inherit property of parents.

6. In *Feudal Japan*, the emperor delegated much authority to a network of regional nobles, or _____, while the outcasts, or _____ were shunned by lord and commoner alike.

7. _____ _____ _____ refers to a shift in the social position of large numbers of people due more to changes in society than individual efforts.

8. _____ refers to cultural beliefs that, directly or indirectly, justify social stratification.

9. The idea that social stratification promotes a matching of talents and abilities to appropriate positions is from the _____ _____ paradigm.

10. A system of social stratification in which *personal merit* is related to the rewards one receives is termed _____.

11. The idea that social stratification systems reflect the interests of the more powerful members of society is from the _____ _____ paradigm.

12. Four reasons are given in the text as to why there has been no *Marxist revolution* in capitalist societies, including: The _____ of the capitalist class, _____ _____ work and a rising standard of living, more extensive _____ _____, and more extensive _____ _____.

13. The three *dimensions* of Max Weber's model of social stratification are termed _____, _____, and _____.

14. SES stands for _____ _____.

15. The Gerhard and Jean Lenski argue that the level of _____ representative of a society is a very significant factor in determining the nature of social stratification in that society.

Definition and Short-Answer

1. What are the four basic *principles* which help explain the existence of social stratification?

2. Briefly describe the social stratification system of the United Kingdom today. In what ways is it similar to the U.S.? In what way is it different?
    Review the history of stratification in Japan. In what ways is their history similar to that of the United Kingdom? How is it different?

3. According to information provided in the text, why hasn't the *Marxist revolution* occurred? What are the *counterpoints* being made by social conflict theorists?

4. What are the basic qualities of a *caste system*?

5. What is meant by the concept *structural social mobility*?

6. What are the *dimensions* of Max Weber's multidimensional model of social stratification?

7. What are the three criteria of the *Davis-Moore Thesis*?

8. How do *structural-functionalists* and *social-conflict* theorists differ in terms helping us understand social stratification?

9. How do the theories of Max Weber and Karl Marx differ in terms of their respective understanding of social stratification? In what ways did they envision the history of social stratification differently?
10. Review the history of *apartheid* in South Africa. What is the current policy in that nation regarding race?
11. Discuss the Lenskis *sociocultural evolution* perspective and how it relates to a global and historical understanding of social stratification.
12. What are the propositions being made in the book *The Bell Curve*? What are your reactions to the basic thesis being proposed in this book?

PART VI: ANSWERS TO STUDY QUESTIONS

True-False

1.	T	(p. 236)	6.	F	(p. 245)
2.	T	(p. 237)	7.	T	(p. 247)
3.	T	(p. 237)	8.	F	(p. 251)
4.	T	(p. 241)	9.	F	(p. 253)
5.	F	(p. 241)	10.	F	(p. 254)

Multiple-Choice

1.	b	(p. 236)	6.	d	(p. 240)	11.	c	(p. 253)
2.	e	(p. 236)	7.	b	(p. 242)	12.	a	(p. 254)
3.	a	(p. 238)	8.	d	(p. 244)			
4.	b	(p. 240)	9.	c	(p. 244)			
5.	c	(p. 240)	10.	b	(p. 249)			

Fill-In

1. social stratification (p. 236)
2. society, persists over generations, universal, beliefs (p. 236)
3. caste (p. 237)
4. class (p. 239)
5. primogeniture (p. 240)
6. Shoguns, Burakumin (p. 242)
7. social structural mobility (p. 244)
8. ideology (p. 244)
9. structural-functional (p. 245)
10. meritocracy (p. 257)
11. social-conflict (p. 247)
12. fragmentation, white-collar, worker organization, legal protection. (p. 250)
13. class, status, power (p. 252)
14. socioeconomic status (p. 252)
15. technology (p. 253)

PART VII: ANALYSIS AND COMMENT

Global Sociology

"Race and Caste: A Report Form South Africa"

Key Points: Questions:

Critical Thinking

"Ideology: When Is Inequality Unjust?"

Key Points: Questions:

"Big Bucks: Are the Rich Worth What They Earn?"

Key Points: Questions:

Controversy and Debate

"The Bell Curve Debate: Are rich People Really Smarter?"

Key Points: Questions:

Window on the World

"Global Map 9-1"

"Income Disparity in Global Perspective"

Social Class
In The United States

10

PART I: CHAPTER OUTLINE

I. Dimensions of Social Inequality
    A. Income
    B. Wealth
    C. Power
    D. Occupational Prestige
    E. Schooling
II. Ascription and Social Stratification
    A. Ancestry
    B. Race and Ethnicity
    C. Gender
    D. Religion
III. Social Classes in the United States
    A. The Upper Class
            1. Upper-Uppers
            2. Lower-Uppers
    B. The Middle Class
            1. Upper-Middles
            2. Average-Middles
    C. The Working Class
    D. The Lower Class
IV. The Difference Class Makes
    A. Class and Health
    B. Class and Values
    C. Class and Politics
    D. Class, Family, and Gender

PART II: LEARNING OBJECTIVES

1.   To understand the extent of social inequality in the United States.
2.   To understand the concept of socioeconomic status and its dimensions.
3.   To explain the role of economic resources, power, occupational prestige, and formal education in the U.S. class system.
4.   To identify and trace the significance of various ascribed statuses for the construction and maintenance of social stratification in the United States.
5.   To describe the general characteristics of the upper, middle, working, and lower classes in U.S. society.
6.   To be able to discuss the nature of social mobility in the U.S. over the last century.
7.   To explain the ways in which health, values, family life, and gender are related to the social class system in U.S. society.
8.   To distinguish between relative and absolute poverty.
9.   To explain the causes of absolute poverty.
10.   To describe the demographics of poverty in the United States.
11.   To understand the debate over who has responsibility for poverty.
12.   To understand how poverty is affected by politics and culture in U.S. society.

151

PART III: CHAPTER REVIEW

This chapter begins with a brief description of Camden New Jersey and its tragic decline as a place to live. In many ways it reflects in the extreme what is happening in many parts of the country given the changing nature of our economy.

DIMENSIONS OF SOCIAL INEQUALITY

We in the U.S. tend to underestimate the extent of social inequality in our society. Four reasons are identified for why this happens. First, U.S. society *embraces the legal principle of equality*. Second, *our culture celebrates individual autonomy and achievement*. Third, *we tend to interact with people like ourselves*. Fourth, *the U.S. is an affluent society*. Each of these points is briefly discussed. Various dimensions of social inequality are discussed, focusing on the SES (*socioeconomic status*) variable.

Income

An important dimension of economic inequality is ***income***, or *occupational wages or salaries and earnings from investments*. The median U.S. family income in 1994 was $38,808. *Table 10-1* (p. 262) presents the distribution of income among U.S. families by percentage for different levels of income in 1994. Reasons are discussed. *Figure 10-1* (p. 263) presents data regarding the distribution of income and wealth in the United States. *Figure 10-2* (p. 264) presents data on income disparities for selected industrial countries

Wealth

Wealth, *the total value of money and other assets, minus outstanding debts*, is distributed more unequally than income. In 1993, the typical wealth for a U.S. family was in the range of the median family income (about $40,000). The top 20 percent of U.S. families control 80 percent of this nation's wealth, while the bottom 40 percent have a net wealth of zero. The poorest 20 percent of the population lives in debt.

Power

Wealth is an important source of power in our society. An important question being raised is, Do the rich in our society dominate political and economic decisions in this country?

Occupational Prestige

In U.S. society, social prestige is accorded to individuals on the basis of several factors. Primary among these is one's occupation. *Table 10-2* (p. 265) presents the rank ordering of prestige scores for various occupational categories based on a random sample of U.S. adults. High income and advanced education and training requirements are positively correlated with higher prestige occupations. The occupations labeled white-collar tend to have higher prestige than those labeled blue-collar, though exceptions are noted. Women tend to be concentrated in "pink-collar" jobs (service and clerical), which tend to be low in prestige.

Schooling

The formal education a person receives significantly influences occupational opportunities and income. Education may be the right of everyone although great variation exists in terms of how much formal education different groups of people in our society receive. *Table 10-3* (p. 266) indicates this fact. While 80 percent of U.S. adults have a high school education, only 20 percent have a college degree.

ASCRIPTION AND SOCIAL STRATIFICATION

While individual talent and effort are important, several ascribed statuses influence our position in the U.S. social stratification system.

Ancestry

Nothing affects our social standing more than "the accident of birth." The family into which we are born significantly determines our future in terms of placement in the socioeconomic system.

Race and Ethnicity

Whites have significantly higher SES than African-Americans on average. African-American family income, for example, is only 54 percent of that for whites. The **Social Diversity** box (p. 267) focuses on differences between African-American and white affluence, suggesting that even controlling for SES, differences persist between blacks and whites.

Ethnic background also relates to social stratification. For example, the income of Hispanic families was about 60 percent of the comparable figure for all whites. *Figure 10-3* (p. 266) shows the differences in average wealth by race and ethnicity, of the U.S. population in 1993. Whites have approximately ten times more wealth on average than Hispanics and African-Americans.

Gender

On average, women have lower incomes, educational levels, and occupational prestige than men. *Table 10-3* (p. 266) shows data on the schooling of U.S. adults by sex, for 1993.

Religion

Religion influences social standing as well. Many upwardly mobile families actually convert to a "higher prestige" religion. Examples are discussed.

SOCIAL CLASSES IN THE UNITED STATES

Dividing our society up into distinct social classes is quite problematic. Many different criteria can be used to place an individual or family into a particular social class. Therefore, precise placement is not possible. Nevertheless, patterns of social structure do exist in our society. Four general social classes are identified.

The Upper Class

Approximately 5 percent of our society fall into this class. Even among this group there is stratification. Some statistics about the "rich" are presented.

Upper-Uppers

A difference is typically made between the upper-upper class, or "old money" rich and the lower-upper class, or "new money" rich. The former group (blue-bloods) represent about 1 percent of our population and obtain their standing through ancestry and inheritance.

Lower-Uppers

This group obtains wealth more typically through earnings. They also have tremendous power in society, controlling most of our nation's productive property. The caste-like quality of the upper-upper class is discussed in the **Critical Thinking** box (p. 270) on the *Social Register*.

The Middle Class

Roughly 40-45 percent of our population fall into this category. Given its size alone, the middle class has a significant influence on patterns of U.S. culture. Rather than exclusiveness and familiarity characterizing this group, an important quality in the middle class is a diversity of family backgrounds.

Upper-Middles

The upper half of this category is referred to as the *upper-middle*, being characterized by prestigious white-collar occupations, relatively high educations, nice homes, annual family incomes ranging from $50,000 to $100,000, and an accumulation of property and wealth during their lifetime.

Average-Middles

Commonly, household incomes for this category range from $35,000 to $50,000 a year. A small amount of wealth is accumulated by families in this category.

The Working Class

This category comprises about one-third of our population. This group has lower incomes, generally having household incomes between $15,000 and $35,000, and have virtually no accumulated wealth. They are characterized by *blue-collar* families. They are vulnerable to unemployment and illness to a greater extent than families in the middle and upper classes. The issues of fatalism, stratification, and pride are briefly pointed out.

The Lower Class

The remaining 20 percent of our population is identified as the lower class. Roughly 13% of the U.S. population (39 million people) are officially classified as being poor. The "marginal poor," while not falling below the official poverty line are not much better off and also live very insecure, unstable lives. Most poor people are white, but people of African and Hispanic descent are disproportionately represented among the poor. Most poor adults work; however, they are heavily concentrated in low prestige, minimal income jobs. Typically they have very low educational attainment. The poor tend to be very segregated from the rest of society, particularly in terms of housing. The socialization process for children tends to reinforce a sense of marginality.

THE DIFFERENCE CLASS MAKES

Class and Health

People with higher incomes are more than two times likely to describe themselves as healthy than poor people are. Social class is also positively correlated with life expectancy. Crucial links between health and social class are the cost of nutritional food, safe environments, and the cost of medical care. The poor simply cannot afford these things. Mental health patterns also vary with social class. Poorer people seem exposed more to stressful events leading to emotional distress.

Class and Values

The values and attitudes people support are closely associated with the types of lifestyles they live. Members of the upper-upper class value their sense of family history and hold attitudes regarding behavior consistent with maintaining this as an important element in their lives. People in the lower-upper and middle classes, who often desire to emulate the rich, are sensitive to their patterns of consumption. The pattern of *conspicuous consumption* is discussed. The working class has less security than the middle and upper classes and are more characterized as emphasizing conformity to conventional beliefs and practices. Members of different social classes also seem to vary in their orientation to time, with the upper class maintaining the past, the middle class being very future orientated, and the poor having a stronger orientation to the present.

Class and Politics

Political orientations vary by social class, though in a more complicated manner. Generally, however, conservative views on economic issues and liberal views on social issues are found among those of higher social standing.

Class, Family, and Gender

Who one marries, how many children are in the family, styles of childrearing, and spousal relationships are all influenced by social class.

SOCIAL MOBILITY

The U.S. is characterized by relatively high levels of social mobility. Social mobility, whether the result of personal achievement or societal change in the form of structural social mobility, is experienced as a transition. Social mobility can be *upward* or *downward*, and can be intragenerational or intergenerational. *Intragenerational social mobility* refers to *a change in social position occurring within a person's lifetime*. *Intergenerational social mobility* is defined as *upward or downward social mobility of children in relation to their parents*.

Social Mobility: Myth and Reality

Central to our sense of social mobility is that people have the opportunity to realize their own individual potential. Four general conclusions are made about social mobility in the U.S. These include:

(1)   Social mobility, at least among men,
       has been fairly high.
(2)   The long-term trend in social mobility
       has been upward.
(3)   Within a single generation, social
       mobility is usually incremental, not
       dramatic.
(4)   The short-term trend has been stagnation,
       with some income polarization.

Mobility by Income Level

Figure 10-4 (p. 275) shows how families faired between 1980-1994 according to their income level. Families are divided into quintiles according to income. Only the top fifth showed any real improvement.

156

Mobility by Race, Ethnicity, and Gender

African Americans showed a decline relative to white by income since 1980. On average, African-American households today earn about 58 percent of white households. Latino families have also dropped relative to whites since 1980. On average, Latino households earn 69 percent of white households. The earnings gap between men and women appears to be closing, however women earn only about 72 percent of what men earn.

The "Middle Class Slide"

Historically, our society and its economy has been characterized by growth and expansion. The depression years represent one exception. In the last generation though, optimism has been decreasing as structural social mobility has slowed. Four important trends are identified which suggest this middle-class slide. These include:

(1)   For many workers, earnings have stalled.
(2)   Multiple job-holding is up.
(3)   More jobs offer little income.
(4)   Young people are remaining at home.

Statistics for each of these patterns are provided to illustrate. In the **Seeing Ourselves** box (p. 276), *National Map 10-1* show national opinion on the issue of "Fear of Falling." Further, *Figure 10-5* (p. 277) shows the median income for U.S. families for the years 1950-1993 in constant 1993 dollars. The increases were dramatic between 1950-1968, but have been stagnant since.

The U.S. Class Structure in Global Perspective

Many of the industrial jobs which were the basis of our expanding economy have in recent decades been transferred overseas. Current patterns of change in our economy have undermined many people's expectations about improving their standard of living. This is so, even with over one-half of our families having more than one breadwinner. We are working harder and longer to just hold our positions. Twice as many families during the 1980s showed no improvement in their social standing, or lost ground as compared to the number that improved their positions. We are experiencing *downsizing* and *deindustrialization*.

POVERTY IN THE UNITED STATES

Two types of poverty are identified. ***Relative poverty*** is defined as *the deprivation of some people in relation to those who have more.* By definition this type of poverty is universal and inevitable. A more serious form of poverty is termed ***absolute poverty***, defined as *a deprivation of resources that is life threatening.* Roughly one-fifth of the world's population lives in such conditions.

The Extent of U.S. Poverty

The U.S. government began officially counting the poor in 1964 as part of its "war on poverty." The *poverty threshold* is the annual income level below which a person or family is defined as poor and, therefore, entitled to certain benefits. The poverty rate in the United States has generally decreased since 1960. However, during the 1980s there has been a slight increase. *Figure 10-6* (p. 278) shows the official poverty rate over the years since 1960. At present, about 39 million, or 15.1 percent of our population are classified as being poor. An additional 12.5 million people are identified as *marginally poor* (living within 25 percent of the poverty level). It is suggested that poverty means hunger in the U.S. and that federal government spending priorities could be easily changed to eradicate poverty and hunger. Currently about 10 percent of the federal budget is allocated for antipoverty programs. For an urban family of four the poverty threshold in 1993 was $14,763. The income of the typical poor family is some $6000 less than this amount.

Who are the Poor?

Age

Children are more likely to be poor than any other age group in our nation. About 22 percent of the children in the U.S. are poor. Some 40 percent of the people living in poverty are under the age of eighteen. The **Social Diversity** box (p 280) takes a closer look at the child poverty problem in the U.S. today. In the **Seeing Ourselves** Box, *Global Map 10-2* (p. 280) provides information on child poverty across the United States.

Race and Ethnicity

About two-thirds of all people living in poverty are white, but a disproportionate percentage of African Americans and Latinos are represented among the poor. While only about 11 percent of whites are poor, 33 percent of African Americans and 30 percent of Latinos are living in poverty. Rates are especially high for African American and Latino children.

Gender and Family Patterns

Poverty rates for women and men are considerably different. Of all poor people, about two-thirds are female. Over one-half of all poor families are headed by women. The widening gap in poverty rates between women and men has been labeled the *femininization of poverty*, referring to *the trend by which women represent an increasing proportion of the poor.*

Area of Residence

Though it may be hard to believe, poverty is more common in rural areas than in the cities. Though, the greatest concentration of poverty is found in central cities. Data is presented and discussed. In the **Seeing Ourselves** box (p. 282), *National Map 10-3* presents data from across the country on median family incomes.

Explaining Poverty

Sociologists agree that poverty is a product of social structure; however, two distinct views about who is responsible for poverty are debated. A recent national survey, the results of which are summarized in *Figure 10-7* (p. 283), suggests that adults in the U.S. are divided in terms of attaching responsibility. One view holds that the poor are primarily responsible for their own poverty. About 25 percent of U.S. adults tend to agree with this position.

One View: Blame the Poor

Edward Banfield is a proponent of the first view, He believes a subculture of poverty, with a "present-time" orientation, dominates the lives of the poor. He sees this to be particularly true in urban areas. This view is an extension of the *culture of poverty* theory developed by Oscar Lewis. Lewis argued in the early 1960s that resignation to their condition as being one of fate, perpetuated the condition of the poor.

Counterpoint: Blame Society

The idea that society is primarily responsible for poverty is held by about one-third of U.S. adults. William Ryan argues that the culture of poverty perspective leads people to "blame the victim." He suggests poverty results from the unequal distribution of resources in society. Lack of ambition is seen as a *consequence,* not as a *cause* of their lack of opportunity.

Weighing the Evidence

Empirical evidence exists to support both views. For example, while over one-half of the heads of poor families do not work, about one-fifth work full-time, but because of low wages cannot climb out of poverty. Further, inadequacies in child care programs make it difficult for many single-parent women to work. Our author agrees that, on balance, the poor are represented by categories of people who lack the same opportunities as others.

The Working Poor

In 1993, 16.6 percent of poor heads of households labored full time for the entire year. Another 25.8 percent remained poor despite part-time employment. Other data are discussed to highlight the "working poor."

159

Homelessness

Counting the Homeless

During the 1980s the public has become more aware of the plight of the homeless. Though no precise count of the homeless exists, estimates range from 500,000 to several million. The stereotype of the homeless population has been brought into question recently. It is a diverse population. One characteristic shared by the homeless though is poverty. Statistics for use of homeless shelters are discussed.

Causes of Homelessness

Both *personal traits* and *societal factors* are involved in creating the homelessness problem. Both of these must be considered. However, we must see homeless not simply as a housing problem, but also a *human* problem.

Our cultural values significantly affect our perception of the distribution of wealth and poverty in the United States. Our values support individual responsibility. For many, the idea of welfare programs undermine initiative. This attitude leads to the "hidden injury of class," a phenomenon which lowers the self-image of the poor person. All this is very interesting, particularly given the fact that "welfare for the rich" is such a major part of our value system. This chapter ends with a **Controversy and debate** box (pp. 286-87) that examines "welfare," discussing the dilemma of our current welfare system. Included in this box is *Figure 10-8* which show survey data on public opinion about the causes of poverty.

PART IV: KEY CONCEPTS

Define each of the following concepts in the space provided or on separate paper. Check the accuracy of your answers by referring to the key concepts section at the end of the chapter in the text as well as by referring to italicized definitions located throughout the chapter.

absolute poverty
conspicuous consumption
culture of poverty
femininization of poverty
income
intergenerational social mobility
intragenerational social mobility
lower-class
marginal poor
middle-class
middle-class slide
poverty threshold
prestige

10. What is the *culture of poverty*? What evidence is there for this condition?
11. Differentiate between Edward Banfield's and William Ryan's views on the causes for poverty in the U.S.
12. Review the general demographics of *homelessness* in the U.S.
13. What is the *femininization of poverty*? To what extent does it characterize the poor population in the United States?
14. Review *Figure 10-7* concerning attitudes toward government action to reduce income differences in the U.S. What are your reactions?

PART VI: ANSWERS TO STUDY QUESTIONS

True-False

1.	T	(p. 262)	8.	F	(p. 274)
2.	F	(p. 263)	9.	T	(p. 276)
3.	T	(p. 264)	10.	F	(p. 279)
4.	T	(p. 264)	11.	F	(p. 279)
5.	T	(p. 270)	12.	T	(p. 282)
6.	F	(p. 271)	13.	F	(p. 283)
7.	T	(p. 273)			

Multiple-Choice

1.	c	(p. 262)	6.	d	(p. 274)
2.	c	(p. 263)	7.	d	(pp. 275-79)
3.	a	(p. 266)	8.	a	(p. 277)
4.	c	(p. 269)	9.	b	(p. 279)
5.	e	(p. 271)	10.	d	(pp. 279-81)

Fill-In

1. income/wealth (pp. 262-63)
2. 20 (p. 264)
3. 6 (p. 267)
4. upper, middle, working, lower (p. 268)
5. conservative/liberal (p. 273)
6. intragenerational (p. 274)
7. fairly high, upward, incremental, stagnation, polarization (pp. 274-75)
8. stalled, multiple, little, home (p. 276-77)
9. 40 (p. 279)
10. 66 (p. 279)
11. culture of poverty (p. 282)
12. cause/consequence (p. 282)
13. hidden injury (p. 287)

PART VII: ANALYSIS AND COMMENT

Social Diversity

"Two Colors of Affluence: Do Black People and White People Differ?"

    Key Points: Questions:

"U.S. Children: Bearing the Burden of Poverty"

    Key Points: Questions:

Critical Thinking

"Caste and Class: The Social Register and Who's Who"

    Key Points: Questions:

Controversy and Debate

"The Welfare Dilemma"

     Key Points: Questions:

Seeing Ourselves

"National Map 10-1 Fear of Falling Across the U.S."

     Key Points: Questions:

"National Map 10-2 Median Household Income Across the U.S."

     Key Points: Questions:

Global Inequality

11

PART I: CHAPTER OUTLINE

PART II: LEARNING OBJECTIVES

1. To be able to define and describe the demographics of the three "economic development" categories used to classify nations of the world.
2. To be able to identify nations representative of each category and the characteristics they share.
3. To understand both the severity and extensiveness of poverty in the least-developed world.
4. To recognize the extent to which women are overrepresented among the poor of the world, and the factors leading to this condition.
5. To identify and understand the correlates of global poverty.
6. To identify and understand the two major theories used in explaining global inequality.
7. To identify and describe the stages of modernization.
8. To recognize the problems facing women as a result of modernization in the least-developed World.
9. To identify the keys to combating global inequality over the next century.

PART III: CHAPTER REVIEW

The extremes of poverty are emphasized in the account of a visit by an American to the Philippines, and to one of the poorest neighborhoods in the entire world--at Smokey Mountain, Manila's vast garbage dump.

GLOBAL ECONOMIC DEVELOPMENT

As we must recognize our place in our society to understand ourselves, so to understand our society we must explore how it fits into the larger global order. The interdependence of the world's nations is the focus of this chapter.

The Problem of Terminology

Citizens of the U.S. are very well-off relative to people in most other nations. Even our poor have a higher standard of living than most people living in the poorer countries around the world. Over the last half-century societies of the world have been classified into three broad categories based on their level of technological development and their political and economic system. However, this "three worlds" model has lost its validity in recent years. In this model the capitalist West was the First World, the communist East was the Second World, and the rest of the nations represented the Third World. This model lumped too many different types of poor nations in the Third World, and with the dramatic transformations in Eastern Europe the distinction between the First and Second World is less meaningful.

The new model also identifies three categories--*high-income, middle-income, and low-income* nations, but has two advantages to the "Three Worlds" system. First, it focuses on the variable of a nation's economic development, while ignoring the question of whether societies are capitalist or socialist. Second, a more precise picture of the relative economic development is possible. Differences do exist between societies being placed within each broad category. There are roughly 190 nations in the world, each with its own unique history and present way of life.

High-Income Countries

The term *high-income countries* refers to those nations which are industrialized and relatively rich. These nations were the first to go through the Industrial Revolution. Roughly 25 percent of the land surface of the globe and 15 percent of the world's population are identified as being part of this category. Because their economies are all market-driven, economic alliances with other such nations are often made. The roughly forty nations representing this economic level of development control more than one-half of the world's income. Per capita income in these nations range from $10,000-$20,000.

Middle-Income Countries

Middle-Income countries are composed of nations who have limited industrialization. About ninety of the world's nations fall at this level. Per capita income for these nations ranges from $2,500-$10,000. Relatively more people, about half, are involved in agricultural production. The old "eastern bloc" nations, who for many years had socialist economies, represent a large portion of this category. Another group of nations at this level are the oil-producing countries of the Middle-East. A third group includes Latin American nations and Western African nations. Taken together, these three groups of less-developed nations account for 40 percent of the world's land area and about 33 percent of humanity. *Figure 11-1 (p 292)* shows the distribution of world income by percentile of humanity.

Low-Income Countries

The *low-income countries* encompass primarily agrarian societies that are poor. Most people live in rural areas. Economically these societies are less productive than the rest of the world. These societies comprise about 35 percent of the earth's land area and 52 percent of the world's population. About 75 percent of the people in these countries live in rural areas.

Referencing back to **Window on the World:** *Global Map 1-1* (p. 7) will help organize your understanding of these three broad categories.

GLOBAL WEALTH AND POVERTY

Two important distinctions are being made by our author: that poverty in the least-developed countries is more *severe* and more *extensive* than in the United States.

The Severity of Poverty

The data presented in *Table 11-1* (p. 296) suggest why poverty is more *severe* in the low-income countries of the world. This table compares the GNP and per-person income between countries from around the world. Further, a *quality of life index* measure is suggested for each nation. Significant differences are indicated. It is pointed out that even beyond these general patterns of global inequality, every society has its own *internal* stratification.

Relative Versus Absolute Poverty

Every society experiences relative poverty. In wealthy nations poverty is often viewed as a *relative* matter. In the least-developed countries *absolute* poverty is much more critical. The people there typically lack the resources necessary to survive. *Figure 11-2* (p. 297) shows the relative share of income for the three categories of countries. The high-income countries have 15 percent of the world's population and 55 percent of the world's income, while the low-income countries have 52 percent of the world's population and 8 percent of the its income.

The Extent of Poverty

Poverty in the low-income countries is more *extensive* also. Most people in these nations live in conditions far worse than the bottom 15 percent of our population. These statistics boil down to one devastating fact, people are dying from a basic lack of nutrition. The magnitude of this tragedy is almost impossible to imagine with 40,000 people dying each day from starvation. In the **Window on the World** box (p. 298) *Global Map 11-1* puts life expectancy differences between nations in perspective. Other statistics are offered in this section to stress the extensiveness of this great problem. For example, the annual loss of life stemming from poverty is ten times greater than that resulting from all the world's armed conflicts.

Poverty and Children

Some 75 million children living in cities of poor countries work on the streets to assist their families. It is estimated that another 25 million children have abandoned their families altogether. The bloody act of "urban cleansing" in Rio de Janeiro is identified.

Poverty and Women

As in the United States, hardships of poverty fall harder on women than on men. Women are overrepresented in the poorest of the poor. Much of the work women engage in is "invisible," being out-side the paid labor force. Traditions of male dominance in kinship systems further subordinate women. Men in poor societies own 90 percent of the land. These male dominated traditions are illustrated clearly in the **Global Sociology** box (pp. 306-

171

301) in which infanticide and sexual slavery are discussed. Infanticide is something the males decide upon in poor societies. Most infants who are killed are female. Also, poverty forces many women into prostitution. About two-thirds of the poor people in the world today are women. *Figure 11-3* (p. 300) shows data concerning the percent of births attended by trained health professionals for different nations.

Correlates of Global Poverty

Several factors related to the severity and extent of global poverty are discussed. These include:

(1) *Technology*
(2) *Population growth*
(3) *Cultural patterns*
(4) *Social stratification*
(5) *Gender inequality*
(6) *Global power relationships*

The cultural patterns factor is discussed in the **Global Sociology** box (p. 303) in which India is focused upon as having a "different" kind of poverty. The Hindu concept of *dharma*, destiny and duty, dominates people's way of understanding their poverty.

In terms of global power relationships, two key concepts are introduced. First, is the historical factor of **colonialism**, or *the process by which some nations enrich themselves through political and economic control of other countries*. As a result of this, it is argued, many nations were exploited and remain under-developed. A second concept is **neocolonialism**, referring to *a new form of global power relationships that involves not direct political control but economic exploitation by multinational corporations*. The argument here is focused on **multinational corporations**, or *large corporations that operate in many different countries*.

GLOBAL INEQUALITY: THEORETICAL ANALYSIS

The two dominant explanations for the unequal distribution of the world's wealth and power are *modernization theory* and *dependency theory*. Both overlap to some extent, yet emphasize different factors.

Modernization theory

Modernization theory is *a model of economic and social development that explains global inequality in terms of differing levels of technological development among societies*.

Historical Perspective

A point made by these theorists is that until a few centuries ago all people in the world were poor. The development of cities during the middle ages and the trade and

172

exploration that emerged, coupled with the influence of the Industrial Revolution in the 18th and 19th centuries launched certain societies ahead in living standards. Therefore, *affluence*, not deprivation is what requires explanation.

The Importance of Culture

This theory suggests that new technology is likely to be exploited only in certain *cultural environments*. *Traditionalism* is the greatest barrier to economic development. This is consistent with Weber's theory of the influence of ideas on societal development. The Protestant Reformation in Europe toward the end of the middle ages transformed society with its focus on individualism and material affluence.

Rostow's Stages of Modernization

Modernization theorists argue that all societies are converging on one general form, the industrial model. According to W. W. Rostow, four general stages are followed by all societies. These include:

(1)   the *traditional stage*, which is strongly tied to kinship, family, and religion;

(2)   the *take-off stage* during which time a limited market economy emerges. Progressive influences like foreign aid and advanced technologies are critical for poor nations to move through this stage;

(3)   the *drive to technological maturity stage*, represented by India, Mexico, and the People's Republic of China, experience rapid economic development along with urbanization and specialization. Education becomes critical during this stage. The role of women begins to change and their status increases;

(4)   the *high mass-consumption* stage, characteristic of modern industrialized societies.

The Role of Rich Nations

Rather than seeing the First World as part of the cause for global inequality, modernization theorists see it as part of the solution. They see this to be so in the following respects:

(1)   *assisting in population control* through exportation of birth control technologies and the promotion of their use,

(2)   *increasing food production* by introducing "high-tech" farming methods (collectively referred to as the "Green Revolution"),

(3)   *introducing industrial technology* to increase productivity, and

(4)   *instituting programs of foreign aid*, particularly in the form of investment capital.

173

Modernization Theory

The modernization theory has helped provide perspectives for us in understanding how industrialization affects other dimensions of social life. These theorists point out that several societies have demonstrated significant economic developments with the help of the rich nations. However, others argue that modernization theory is just an attempt to defend and spread capitalism, and in many ways has fallen short in its own standards of success. Further, this approach tends to ignore historical facts that interfere with development. Other limitations involve a failure to make connections between rich and poor societies to see how the development of poor countries affects rich countries. Finally, the fact that this approach holds rich nations as the standard by which to judge all development is ethnocentric. Blaming the poor countries for their own poverty takes attention away from the negative effects of the rich nations.

Dependency Theory

Dependency theory is *a model of economic and social development that explains global inequality in terms of the historical exploitation of poor societies by rich ones.*

Historical Perspective

Dependency theorists argue that people in poor societies were better off in the past. They believe the economic positions of the rich and poor societies are interdependent.

The Importance of Colonialism

Colonialization in Africa, Asia, and the Americas by European societies gave countries like Great Britain and Spain great power and wealth. Colonialism is no longer a force in the world; however this *political liberation* has not meant *economic autonomy*. A neocolonialism has emerged. *Figure 11-4* (p. 309) presents information on Africa's colonial history.

Wallerstein's Capitalist World Economy

This model attempts to explain modern world inequality. A major point in this perspective is that the world economy, a global system, is beyond the control of traditional nations, and is dominated by capitalism. Rich nations are at the core of this world economy. This system perpetuates poverty in other parts of the world by creating and maintaining the dependency of other nations. This dependency is caused primarily by three factors:

(1) *Narrow, export-oriented economies,*
(2) *lack of industrial capacity,* and
(3) *foreign debt.*

174

The Role of Rich Nations

Dependency theorists argue that rich societies create new wealth through technological innovation. This leads to overdevelopment of some societies and underdevelopment of others. Rich nations then exploit poor nations in order to obtain profits. Further, dependency theorists believe capitalists encourage poor nations to believe poverty is a natural consequence of population increase. As opposed to highlighting the *productivity of wealth* as modernization theorists do, dependency theorists cast global inequality in terms of the *distribution of wealth*.

Dependency theory has demonstrated interdependence of all nations of the world. Critics argue however that there are weaknesses to this perspective. First, dependency theorists wrongly contend that the wealth of high-income nations resulted from stealing resources from poor societies. Second, if rich nations are to blame for global poverty, those nations with the strongest ties to rich societies would be among the poorest, but they are not. Third, while blaming world capitalism, dependency theorists ignore factors within the poor nations themselves which lead to poverty. Fourth, they underestimate the influence of the former Soviet Union on the poor nations. Finally, dependency theory does not produce clear policy-making alternatives.

GLOBAL INEQUALITY: LOOKING AHEAD

Table 11-2 (p. 313) summarizes the viewpoints of modernization and dependency theories in terms of how each provides perspective for understanding historical patterns, primary causes, and the role of rich nations in affecting global inequality. Those poor nations that have surged ahead economically seem to have two qualities in common: (1) they are *relatively small*, and (2) they have *traditions emphasizing individual achievement* and *economic success*.

Both theories are currently going through transformations given upheavals in the global economy (bringing socialism under fire and the tendency for poor nations recently seeing advantages to having more government control of their economies.)

These approaches however have uncovered two keys to success during the next century in combating global poverty. The first, offered by modernization theory, is understanding poverty as being in part a problem of *technology*. The second, derived from dependency theory, is to see poverty as a *political issue*. The **Controversy and debate** box (pp. 314-315) discusses the issue of global hunger and whether we have the technological means and political will to effectively address this critical problem.

PART IV: KEY CONCEPTS

Define each of the following concepts in the space provided or on separate paper. Check the accuracy of your answers by referring to the key concepts section at the end of the chapter in the text as well as by referring to italicized definitions located throughout the chapter.

absolute poverty
colonialism
dependency theory
high-income countries
low-income countries
middle-income countries
modernization theory
multinational corporations
neocolonialism
relative poverty
traditionalism
world economy

PART V: STUDY QUESTIONS

True-False

1.	T	F	The *high-income countries*, representing 15 percent of humanity, control over one-half of the world's income.
2.	T	F	About 50 percent of the world's people live in *low-income countries*.
3.	T	F	Approximately one-fourth of the population of *low-income countries* live in urban areas.
4.	T	F	*Low-income countries* are plagued by constant hunger, unsafe housing, and high rates of disease.
5.	T	F	*Modernization theory* suggests the greatest barrier to economic development is traditionalism.
6.	T	F	*Modernization theory* draws criticism for suggesting that the causes of global poverty lie almost entirely in poor societies themselves.
7.	T	F	Wallerstein's capitalist world economy model is used to illustrate and support *dependency theory*.
8.	T	F	According to *dependency theory*, global inequality must be seen in terms of the distribution of wealth, as opposed to highlighting the productivity of wealth.
9.	T	F	Poor nations that have surged ahead have two factors in common, including being *relatively large* and having a *strong traditional base*.
10.	T	F	The keys to combating global inequality during the next century lie in seeing it as partly a problem of *technology* and also a *political* issue.

1. The name of the Manila dump discussed at the beginning of the chapter in the text is:

   (a) Rohoolen Hollow
   (b) Svendoven
   (c) Veeshan Rue
   (d) Smokey Mountain
   (e) Shileen Heights

2. The *high-income countries*, representing 15 percent of the world's population, control over _____ percent of the world's income.

   (a) 25   (b) 35   (c) 50   (d) 80

3. What percentage of the world's population live in the *low-income countries*?

   (a) 50   (b) 60   (c) 77   (d) 85   (e) 95

4. The per-capita GDP of the United States is?

   (a) $10,033
   (b) $51,300
   (c) $105,400
   (d) $23,760
   (e) $75,028

5. Globally, how many people die *each day* from starvation?

   (a) 5,000
   (b) 100,000
   (c) 1,000,000
   (d) 15,000
   (e) 40,000

6. Which of the following is/are accurate concerning low-income countries?

   (a) men own about 90 percent of the land
   (b) over 60 percent of the people living in poverty are female
   (c) gender inequality is stronger in such countries as compared to high-income countries
   (d) all of the above are accurate
   (e) none of the above are accurate

7. Which of the following is *not* discussed as a correlate of global poverty?

   (a) cultural patterns
   (b) population growth
   (c) technology
   (d) social stratification
   (e) all are discussed

8. *Neocolonialism* is:

    (a) primarily an overt political force
    (b) a form of economic exploitation that does not involve formal political control
    (c) the economic power of the low-income countries is being used to control consumption patterns in the high-income countries
    (d) the exploitation of the high-income countries by the least-developed countries
    (e) none of the above

9. According to Rostow's *modernization model*, which stage is Thailand currently in?

    (a) traditional
    (b) take-off
    (c) drive to technological maturity
    (d) high mass consumption
    (e) residual-dependency

10. *Modernization theory* identifies _____ as the greatest barrier to economic development.

    (a) tradition   (c) lack of material resources
    (b) economic development   (d) lack of human resources

11. Which of the following is *not* a criticism of modernization theory:

    (a) it tends to minimize the connection between rich and poor societies
    (b) it tends to blame the least-developed countries for their own poverty
    (c) it ignores historical facts that thwart development in poor countries of the world today
    (d) it has fallen short of its own standards of success
    (e) all are criticisms of this theory

12. Which of the following is *not* mentioned in Wallerstein's capitalist world economy model as a reason for the perpetuation of the dependency of the least-developed nations?

    (a) narrow, export-oriented economies   (d) all are mentioned
    (b) lack of industrial capacity   (e) none are mentioned
    (c) foreign debt

13. Which of the following is *not* a criticism of dependency theory?

    (a)   it assumes that the wealth of the most-developed countries is based solely on appropriating resources from poor societies

    (b)   it tends to blame the least-developed countries for their own poverty

    (c)   it does not lend itself to clear policy making

    (d)   it simplistically assumes that world capitalism alone has produced global inequality

    (e)   all of these are criticisms of this theory

14. *High-income countries* give birth to _____ percent of the world's children.

    (a)   1   (b)   5   (c)   10   (d)   20   (e)   30

Fill-In

1. Compared to the older "three worlds" model, the new classification system used in this text has two main advantages, including a focus on the single most important dimension that underlies social life--_____ _____.

2. *Middle-income countries* are those with per-capita incomes ranging between _____ and _____.

3. The *middle-income countries* of the world represent about _____ nations and _____ percent of the world's population.

4. According to our author, poverty in *low-income countries* is more _____ and more _____ than it is in the United States.

5. The members of rich societies typically focus on _____ *poverty* of some members, highlighting how those people lack resources taken for granted by others.

6. _____ *poverty* refers to a lack of resources that is life threatening.

7. *Correlates of global poverty* include _____, population _____, _____ patterns, social _____, gender _____, and global _____ relationships.

8. _____ is a new form of economic exploitation that does not involve formal political control.

9. _____ *theory* suggests global inequality reflects differing levels of technological development among societies.

10. According to Rostow's stages of modernization, all societies are gradually converging to one general form: the _____ *model*.

11. _____ *theory* maintains that global poverty historically stems from the exploitation of poor societies by rich societies.

12. Poor nations that have surged ahead economically have two factors in common. One is they are *relatively* _____. Another is they have *cultural traditions* emphasizing _____ and _____.

13. Two keys to combating global inequality during the next century will be seeing it partly a problem of _____ and that it is also a _____ issue.

179

Definition and Short-Answer

1. Define the terms *high-income, middle-income,* and *low-income countries.* To what extent do you think this helps resolve the "problem of terminology" in relation to the terms First, Second, and Third Worlds?
2. How do the economies in each of the three levels or categories of countries differ from one another? Make specific reference to *Figure 11-1* and *Table 11-1* in your answer.
3. What factors create the condition of *women* being overrepresented in poverty around the world?
4. What are the *correlates* of global poverty? Describe each.
5. What is *neocolonialism*? Provide an illustration.
6. What are the four *stages* of modernization in Rostow's model of societal change and development?
7. What are the *problems* faced by women in poor countries as a result of modernization?
8. According to *modernization theory*, in what respects are rich nations part of the solution to global poverty?
9. Differentiate between how *modernization theory* and *dependency theory* view the primary causes of global inequality.
10. What are five *criticisms* of *modernization theory*?
11. What are five *criticisms* of *dependency theory*?
12. According to wallerstein's *world economy model*, dependency in low-income countries turns on what three factors? Describe or illustrate each of these factors.

PART VI: ANSWERS TO STUDY QUESTIONS

True-False

1.	T	(p. 293)	6.	T	(p. 307)
2.	T	(p. 295)	7.	T	(p. 309)
3.	T	(p. 295)	8.	T	(p. 310)
4.	T	(pp. 298-99)	9.	F	(pp. 312-13)
5.	T	(p. 305)	10.	T	(p. 313)

Multiple-Choice

1.	d	(p. 291)	8.	b	(p. 302)
2.	c	(p. 293)	9.	b	(p. 305)
3.	a	(p. 295)	10.	a	(p. 305)
4.	d	(p. 296)	11.	e	(p. 307)
5.	e	(p. 299)	12.	d	(pp. 309-10)
6.	d	(p. 300)	13.	b	(pp. 311-12)
7.	e	(pp. 300-02)	14.	c	(p. 315)

Fill-In

1. economic development (p. 292)
2. $2,500, $10,000 (p. 294)
3. 60/35 (p. 295)
4. severe/extensive (p: 296)
5. relative (p. 297)
6. absolute (p. 297)
7. technology, growth, cultural, stratification, inequality, power (pp. 301-03)
8. neocolonialism (p. 302)
9. modernization (p. 304)
10. industrial (p. 305)
11. dependency theory (p. 308)
12. small/individual achievement/economic success (p. 313)
13. technology/political (p. 313)

PART VII: ANALYSIS AND COMMENT

Global Sociology

"Modernization and Women: A Report From Rural Bangladesh"

    Key Points: Questions:

"A Different Kind of Poverty: A Report From India"

    Key Points: Questions:

"Infanticide and Sexual Slavery: Gender Bias in Poor Societies"

    Key Points: Questions:

Window on the World

"Global Map 11-1 Median Age at Death in Global Perspective"

    Key Points: Questions:

Controversy and Debate

"Will the World Starve"

    Key Points: Questions:

Race and Ethnicity 12

PART I: CHAPTER OUTLINE

I.   The Social Significance of Race and Ethnicity
     A. Race
     B. Ethnicity
     C. Minorities
II. Prejudice
     A. Stereotypes
     B. Racism
          1. Racism and Social Domination
     C. Theories of Prejudice
          1. Scapegoat Theory of Prejudice
          2. Authoritarian Personality Theory
          3. Cultural Theory of Prejudice
          4. Conflict Theory of Prejudice
III. Discrimination
     A. Institutional Prejudice and Discrimination
     B. Prejudice and Discrimination: The Vicious Circle
IV. Majority and Minority: Patterns of Interaction
     A. Pluralism
     B. Assimilation
     C. Segregation
     D. Genocide
V.   Race and Ethnicity in the United States
     A. Native Americans
     B. White Anglo-Saxon Protestants
     C. African Americans
     D. Asian Americans
          1. Chinese Americans
          2. Japanese Americans
          3. Recent Asian Immigrants

PART II: LEARNING OBJECTIVES

1. To understand the biological basis for definitions of race.
2. To distinguish between the biological concept of race and the cultural concept of ethnicity.
3. To identify the two major characteristics of any minority group.
4. To describe the two forms of prejudice: stereotyping and racism.
5. To identify and explain the four theories of prejudice.
6. To distinguish between prejudice and discrimination.
7. To provide examples of institutional discrimination.
8. To explain how prejudice and discrimination combine to create a vicious circle of persistent beliefs and practices.
9. To compare and contrast patterns of interaction between minorities and the majority.
10. To describe the history and relative status of each of the racial and ethnic groups identified in the text.

PART III: CHAPTER SUMMARY

The story of the 1954 Supreme Court decision in the Brown V. Board of Education of Topeka Kansas case opens this chapter. The Court's ruling struck down the historical doctrine of supposedly "separate but equal" education for African Americans and whites.

Ethnicity and race are important sources of group unity; however, their presence also causes conflict. This chapter investigates the meanings and consequences of race and ethnicity.

THE SOCIAL SIGNIFICANCE OF RACE AND ETHNICITY

Race

A **race** is *a category composed of people who share biologically transmitted traits that members of a society deem socially significant.* Common distinguishing characteristics include skin color, hair texture, shape of facial features, and body type. Over thousands of

184

generations, the physical environments that humans lived in created physical variability. In addition, migration and intermarriage spread genetic characteristics throughout the world. During the 19th century biologists developed a three-part scheme of racial classification, including *Caucasian, Negroid, and Mongoloid*. Research confirms however that no pure races exist. Cultural definitions of race are very important however.

Ethnicity

Ethnicity is *a shared cultural heritage*. While race is a biological concept, ethnicity is a cultural one. However, the two overlap. Ethnic characteristics are sometimes incorrectly believed to be racial by members of a society, but while ethnicity is subject to modification over time, racial identity persists over generations.

Minorities

A racial or ethnic *minority* is *a category of people, distinguished by physical or cultural traits, who are social disadvantaged*. *Table 12-1* (p. 322) presents 1990 data on the approximate sizes of different racial and ethnic groups in the United States. Minority groups have two distinctive characteristics: they maintain a *distinctive identity* characterized by endogamy, and are *subordinated* through the social stratification system. While usually being a relatively small segment of a society, there are exceptions, for example blacks in South Africa. The **Social Diversity** box (p. 323) discusses the increasing proportion of *people of color* in the United States. Some researchers are projecting that historical minorities, taken together, will constitute a majority of people in the U.S. during the coming century. The **Seeing Ourselves** box (p. 324) contains *National Map 12-1* showing the residence patterns of minority groups across the U.S.

PREJUDICE

Prejudice is *a rigid and irrational generalization about an entire category of people*. It can be positive or negative in nature. It is also a matter of degree.

Stereotypes

A *Stereotype* is *a prejudicial, exaggerated description of some category of people*. Stereotypes involve inaccurate descriptions of a category of people even when evidence would contradict the description. Because stereotypes involve strong, emotional attitudes, they are difficult to change.

Racism

A powerful form of prejudice is *racism*, or *the belief that one racial category is innately superior or inferior to another*.

Racism and Social Domination

Racism has a long and terrifying history. Examples are briefly discussed. Typical of racism is the assertion that innate inferiority justifies subjugation by the powerful. The **Critical Thinking** box (p. 326) addresses the question: Does race affect intelligence? Any disparity in measured intelligence between racial categories is argued to be the result of *cultural patterns* not biological differences

Theories of Prejudice

Scapegoat Theory of Prejudice

Scapegoat theory suggests that frustration leads to prejudice on the part of certain people. It also suggests prejudice is likely to be more common among people who themselves are disadvantaged. A **scapegoat** is *a person or category of people, typically with little power, whom people unfairly blame for their own troubles*.

Authoritarian Personality Theory

The *authoritarian personality* view, first suggested by T. W. Adorno at the end of World War II, holds that extreme prejudice is a personality trait linked to persons who conform rigidly to cultural norms and values. Such people typically have little education and were raised by harsh, inconsistent parents.

Cultural Theory of Prejudice

This view suggests that some prejudice takes the form of widespread cultural values. Emory Bogardus developed the concept of social distance to measure the attitudes of Americans toward different racial and ethnic groups. His findings conclude that prejudice is operative throughout society and not limited to "abnormal" people.

Conflict Theory of Prejudice

This approach argues that prejudice results from social conflict among categories of people. Prejudice is used as an ideology to legitimate the oppression of certain groups or categories of people. A different argument is also presented in this context, which focuses on the climate of *race consciousness* being created by minorities themselves as a political strategy to gain power.

DISCRIMINATION

Discrimination refers to *any action that involves treating various categories of people unequally*. While prejudice concerns attitudes and beliefs, discrimination involves behavior. The interrelationship between prejudice and discrimination is addressed by Robert Merton,

186

whose analysis is reviewed in *Figure 12-1* (p. 328). Four types of people are revealed: active bigots, timid bigots, all-weather liberals, and fair-weather liberals.

Institutional Prejudice and Discrimination

Institutional prejudice or discrimination refers to *bias in attitude or action inherent in the operation of a society's institutions.* Historically, legal discrimination has confronted many minority groups in our society and others. The 1954 Supreme Court Brown v. The Board of Education of Topeka decision reversing the "separate but equal" principle is an example. However, even with changes in the law and constitutional amendments, inequality between racial and ethnic groups continues. We may stand by the ideal of equality, but reaching this condition has not been achieved.

Prejudice and Discrimination: The Vicious Cycle

It is argued that these characteristics in our society persist because they are mutually reinforcing. The Thomas theorem, discussed in chapter 6, relates to this situation. The stages of the *vicious cycle* of prejudice and discrimination are outlined in *Figure 12-2* (p. 330).

MAJORITY AND MINORITY: PATTERNS OF INTERACTION

Four models can be used to describe patterns of interaction between minorities and the majority.

Pluralism

Pluralism is *a state in which racial and ethnic minorities are distinct but have social parity.* Distinct social identity provides pride in people. The U.S. takes pride in its racial and ethnic diversity; however, three barriers exist in our society, which results in only a limited pluralism. First, only a small proportion of our people maintain distinct racial or ethnic identity. Second, our tolerance for social diversity is limited. And third, racial and ethnic distinctiveness is sometimes forced on people. In global perspective, Switzerland may be the best example of pluralism for a nation.

Assimilation

Assimilation is *the process by which minorities gradually adopt patterns of the dominant culture.* The notion of the "melting pot" is linked to the process of assimilation. However, this characterization of the United States is a misleading idealism. Instead of a new cultural pattern emerging, minorities more often adopt the traits of the dominant culture. Herbert Gans argues that first generation immigrants retain their traditional culture to much greater degrees than subsequent generations.

The process of assimilation involves changes in ethnicity, but not race. Racial traits may diminish over the generations through *miscegenation*, or *the biological reproduction by partners of different racial categories*.

Segregation

Segregation is *the physical and social separation of categories of people*. It is generally an involuntary separation of the minority groups, although voluntary segregation occurs occasionally, such as in the case of the Amish. Racial segregation has a long history in the U.S. *De jure* segregation, or "by law" has ended, however *de facto*, or "by fact" segregation continues. Residential segregation is discussed as a particularly crucial problem in our society. Many blacks live in what researchers call "*hypersegregation*" conditions in inner city ghettos.

Most suburbs remain predominantly, if not virtually all, white. The inner cities, which are becoming more segregated as time goes on, are often characterized by internal colonialism, with many businesses and residential buildings owned by whites. Individuals can make significant differences though, as the case of Rosa Parks illustrates.

Genocide

Genocide is *the systematic annihilation of one category of people by another*. While being contrary to virtually every moral standard, genocide has existed throughout human history. Historical examples from around the world are discussed.

RACE AND ETHNICITY IN THE UNITED STATES

The words of Emma Lazarus, inscribed on the Statue of Liberty, provide us with a cultural ideal for opportunity in the U.S. What is the reality?

Native Americans

The term Native Americans refers to many distinct people who migrated from Asia to the Americas thousands of years ago. They were the original inhabitants of the Americas. Examples of Native Americans include the Cherokee, Sioux, and Inca. Several million Native Americans lived in the Americas when the Europeans began to arrive in the 1500s. The term Indian is traced back to Christopher Columbus who thought he was in India when he arrived in the Caribbean, and so he called the indigenous peoples "Indians." The relationship between European colonists and the Native Americans was violent and costly for the Native Americans who were subjected to disease and destruction introduced by the Europeans. The post-Revolutionary War government of the United States embarked on a pluralist strategy with the Indians but failed to achieve it in the face of their unfair payment for Indian land and discriminatory practices in relocating Indians. In the late 1800s assimilation with the Indians was sought. Yet, this also failed as Indians were made wards of the government on reservations. Today the remaining Native American territories are desired for their vast natural resources. Indians themselves are divided over how to utilize their lands. Citizenship was granted to Indians in 1924 yet their social standing is hampered by poverty and lack of education. Those who have been assimilated into the dominant culture still find prejudice and discrimination. *Table 12-2* (p. 334) reviews the social standing of Native Americans along the dimensions of income, poverty rates, and educational attainment. To reassert their rights control their own land, Indians have organized the Pan-Indian American Indian Movement.

White Anglo-Saxon Protestants

White Anglo-Saxon Protestants, or WASPS, have traditionally enjoyed the status of the dominant ethnic and racial category in U.S. society. Their ancestry is English, although the Scots and Welsh figure into the ancestry of some. They were the early, skilled, achievement-oriented settlers of American society. Their adherence to the Protestant work ethic motivated them to be productive. With the arrival of non-WASP immigrants to this society in the 19th century, socially powerful and wealthy WASPS tended to isolate themselves and form organizations to further their own causes. The influence of WASPs has continued to the present day. WASPS enjoy high income, high-prestige occupations and memberships in the culturally dominant Protestant churches.

African Americans

African Americans accompanied Spanish explorers to the New World in the 15th century and officially arrived in the United States in 1619. Twenty Africans were brought to Jamestown, Virginia and worked as slaves or indentured servants. Soon after, laws recognizing slavery were passed making slavery very profitable for white farm and plantation owners. Estimates put the number of Africans who were forcibly transported to the western hemisphere at 10 million. About half died in transit. Approximately 400,000 came to the United States. Social control exerted by whites barred slaves from receiving an education or becoming independent through other means. A small number of blacks in the North and South were legally free and worked as farmers, skilled workers, or small-business owners. The thirteenth Amendment to the Constitution outlawed slavery in 1865. This did not end racial segregation, however. Jim Crow laws perpetuated the racial division of blacks and whites. Many whites attributed an innate inferior status to African Americans in order to rationalize the majority's treatment of African Americans in the face of the principles of equality and freedom proclaimed in the Declaration of Independence. Gunnar Myrdal, a sociologist, later coined this contradiction the "*American dilemma.*" In the *Dred Scott* case of 1857, the Supreme Court answered the issue of whether blacks were citizens by saying no.

Important changes for blacks have occurred in the 20th century. Migration to northern cities brought greater work opportunities. A national civil rights movement won crucial battles that resulted in ending legal support for racially segregated schools and civil rights acts that improved the opportunities for African Americans in employment and use of public accommodations. Problems persist, though, in the social standing of blacks. The relative standing of African Americans in the U.S. in 1994 was summarized in *Table 12-3* (p. 336).

189

Their median income is significantly lower than whites and others. African Americans are more likely to be poor. African Americans continue to be overrepresented in low-paying jobs and unemployment has remained twice as high as for whites. Important gains have been made in education over the last generation. Blacks have made occupational gains but these have spawned additional problems such as the realization that education does not promote upward mobility for blacks in the same way it does for whites. Recently, African Americans have made strides in their acquisition of political power by increased registration of African American voters and increased numbers of African American elected officials.

Asian Americans

Asian Americans have great cultural diversity while sharing certain racial characteristics. Asian Americans constitute 3 percent of the U.S. population. Asian Americans of Chinese and Japanese ancestry began immigrating to the West over a century ago. Filipinos, Koreans, and Vietnamese have immigrated to this country in recent years. Immigration rates are increasing.

Chinese Americans

Chinese Americans have experienced interactions with the dominant culture that have at times been discriminatory and at times supportive of their ambitions. Prior to the economic depression of the 1870s their labor was highly valued in the expansion of the West. After 1870 the Chinese were barred from some occupations as a result of competition with whites for jobs. Violence and threats of violence were directed toward them. A legal end to immigration by Chinese created a sex-ratio imbalance among the Chinese population. Some Chinese moved to eastern cities and established urban Chinatowns protected by clans and kinship networks. In the 1940s, Chinese immigration was expanded and Chinese Americans moved out of Chinatowns and assimilated into the dominant culture. The 1950s brought upward social mobility. Outstanding educational and scientific achievements have been made by Chinese Americans in recent decades. Racial hostility has persisted while racial discrimination has lessened dramatically.

Japanese Americans

Japanese immigrants began to arrive in the United States in the 1860s. They worked in the Hawaiian Islands for low wages. The Japanese, perhaps due to their small numbers, escaped the prejudice and discrimination directed at the Chinese in the 1870s. Japanese immigrants later demanded high pay and experienced a curb on male Japanese immigration as a result. Japanese women were allowed to immigrate to adjust the sex-ratio imbalance. Immigration laws in the 1920s practically ended Japanese immigration. Overt prejudice and discrimination were directed toward Japanese. Two important differences between the Japanese and Chinese enhanced the position of the Japanese in the United States. First, the Japanese knew more about U.S. culture and were ready to assimilate. Second, the Japanese began to farm in rural areas as opposed to living and working exclusively in urban enclaves. However the purchase of farmland by noncitizens was legally outlawed in 1913. Since the Japanese of foreign birth (*Issei*) were not granted citizenship until 1953, efforts to purchase farmland earlier was accomplished in the names of their American-born children (*Nisei*). The Japanese also leased farmland. With World War II and the Japanese destruction of Pearl Harbor, the Japanese were treated with overt discrimination. With short notice, Japanese families were relocated inland to prison camps on the assumption that they might be disloyal to the U.S. The policy that led to the internment of the Japanese has been severely criticized in subsequent years. One profound consequence of it was to economically devastate the majority of the Japanese in the U.S. Even against this hardship, the Japanese recovered, entered a wide range of new occupations, and have been socially mobile within recent decades. *Table 12-4* (p. 338) reviews the relative social standing of Chinese and Japanese Americans.

Recent Asian Immigrants

Asian Americans are the fastest growing minority in the U.S., accounting for one-half of all immigration into this country. Along with Chinese and Japanese immigrants, the populations of both the Filipinos and Koreans are increasing in the U.S. The social history of Asians in the U.S. is described as being complex.

Hispanic Americans

Hispanic Americans are typically the descendants of a combination of Spanish, African, and Native American peoples. A few Hispanics have pure Spanish ancestry. Hispanic Americans represent three main cultures: Mexican American, Puerto Rican, and Cuban. Hispanic Americans represent roughly 10 percent of our population and this percentage is growing rapidly due to high immigration and birth rates. The relative social standing of these three groups is presented in *Table 12-5* (p. 341). Further, in the **Seeing Ourselves** box (p. 342) *National Map 12-2* locates counties across the U.S. favored by Hispanics, African Americans, and Asians for residence.

Mexican Americans

There are about 13 million Mexican Americans in the United States. Illegal entry into this country puts the actual figure higher. Prejudice and discrimination have marked the relationship of Mexican Americans and whites for several decades. Mexican Americans hold low-paying jobs for the most part and one-fourth of Mexican Americans are poor. A lack of education also inhibits a rise in their relative standing, although some increase in this sphere has been seen since 1980.

Puerto Ricans

Puerto Ricans became citizens of the United States in 1917 and many sought economic advantage by moving to cities like New York in the 1940s and later. Currently there are about three million Puerto Ricans living in the United States. They have not found the advantages they originally envisioned in the U.S., however. Strong ethnic identity is maintained because over three-quarters of them continue to speak Spanish in their homes, and they are able to move between the mainland and Puerto Rico easily. This has insulated them somewhat. Puerto Ricans have a lower social standing than other Hispanics as evidenced by more female-headed households, a fairly low median family income, and a high level of poverty.

Cuban Americans

Cubans immigrated to the United States after the 1959 socialist revolution. Currently about one million Cubans reside in the U.S. They are highly educated, have a higher median family income, and have less poverty than the other Hispanics. They have made significant contributions to the communities in which they live in large numbers, especially Miami and New York City. A recent immigration of 125,000 Cuban refuges has added a poorer and less educated component to the Cuban American population in the United States.

White Ethnic Americans

Many white Americans have traditionally been proud of their ethnic heritage. Those who are non-WASPS have been identified as *white ethnics*. Examples include German, Irish, Italian, and Jews. These immigrants, arriving mainly after 1840, faced hostility from the WASPs who had settled already. Overt discrimination was focused on the white ethnics during the height of immigration in the U.S.: 1880-1930. Immigration quotas restricted their immigration between 1921 and 1968 as a result of opposition by nativist elements. The white ethnics resisted the discrimination by forming ethnic enclaves. For many, economic prosperity and cultural assimilation followed. For others, relative social deprivation exists today. White ethnics and blacks sometimes find themselves on opposite sides of issues due to competition over valued resources in society.

RACE AND ETHNICITY: LOOKING AHEAD

Our society's great cultural diversity is the result of immigration. The pattern of immigration to the U.S. by decade between 1821 and 1990 is outlined in *Figure 12-3* (p. 345). Immigration rates today, roughly 1,000,000 annually, at about the same level as was representative of the great immigration era of a century ago. The countries from which the people are primarily coming is changing. They face prejudice and discrimination as did immigrants before them; however, they also share the hope of opportunity, and the hope that ethnic diversity will someday be viewed as a matter of difference rather than inferiority. This chapter concludes with a **Controversy and Debate** box (pp. 346-47) that focuses on the issue of affirmative action. The question being asked is whether it is a problem or solution.

Seeing Ourselves

"National Map 12-1 Where the Minority-Majority Already Exists"

    Key Points: Questions:

"National Map 12-2 Percent Hispanic/Latino, African American, and Asian American"

    Key Points: Questions:

Sex and Gender

13

PART I: CHAPTER OUTLINE

I.   Sex and Gender
      A. Sex: A Biological Distinction
            1. Primary and Secondary Sex Characteristics
            2. Hermaphrodites
            3. Transsexuals
      B Sexual Orientation
            1. Homosexuality and the Pursuit of Gay Rights
            2. Bisexuality
            3. Origins of Sexual Orientation
      C. Gender: A Cultural Distinction
            1. An Unusual Case Study
            2. The Israeli Kibbutzim
            3. Global Comparisons
      D. Patriarchy and Sexism
            1. The Costs of Sexism
            2. Is Patriarchy Inevitable?
II.   Gender Socialization
      A. Gender and the Family
      B. Gender and the Peer Group
      C. Gender and Schooling
      D. Gender and the Mass Media
      E. Gender and Adult Socialization

III. Gender Social Stratification
    A. Working Men and Women
        1. Gender and Occupations
    B. Housework: Women's "Second Shift"
    C. Gender, Income, and Wealth
    D. Gender and Education
    E. Gender and Politics
    F. Minority Women
    G. Are Women a Minority?
    H. Violence Against Women
        1. Sexual Harassment
        2. Pornography
IV. Theoretical Analysis of Gender
    A. Structural-Functional Analysis
        1. Talcott Parsons: Gender and Complementarity
    B. Social-Conflict Analysis
        1. Friedrich Engels: Gender and Class
V. Feminism
    A. Basic Feminist Ideas
    B. Variations within Feminism
        1. Liberal Feminism
        2. Socialist Feminism
        3. Radical Feminism
    C. Opposition to Feminism
VI. Looking Ahead: Gender In the Twenty-First Century
VII. Summary
VIII. Key Concepts
IX. Critical-Thinking Questions
X. Suggested Readings

PART II: LEARNING OBJECTIVES

1. To know the distinction between sex and gender.
2. To explain the biological distinction of sex and sexual orientation.
3. To explain the cultural component in gender and sexual orientation.
4. To know the various types of social organization based upon the relationship between males and females.
5. To begin to understand the causes of sexism and to know the arguments in the debate over whether patriarchy is inevitable.
6. To describe the role that gender plays in socialization in the family, the peer group, schooling, the mass media, and adult interaction.
7. To explain how gender stratification occurs in the workworld, home, economics, education, and politics.

8. To identify the key arguments in the debate over whether women constitute a minority.

9. To compare and contrast the two sociological analyses of gender: structural-functional analysis and social-conflict analysis.

10. To define and explain the central ideas of feminism, variations of feminism, and social resistance to feminism.

PART III: CHAPTER REVIEW

This chapter begins with a brief account of the *"beauty myth,"* in which, first, women are socialized to believe that their personal importance, accomplishment, and satisfaction be measured in terms of physical appearance. Second, women are taught to value relationships and how their beauty is tied to them. Third, women are to be seen as objects to be possessed by men. Through all of this the positions of men and women in society are established into a social hierarchy.

SEX AND GENDER

While women have made important gains relative to men during the last century and a half, in many ways the position of men remains privileged. The issue raised concerns the extent to which society and/or innate qualities construct these differences.

Sex: A Biological Distinction

Sex refers to *the biological distinction between females and males*. It is determined at the moment of conception. Each fertilized egg contains 23 chromosome pairs. One of these pairs determines sex. The female always contributes the X chromosome, and the male contributes either an X or a Y chromosome. If the male contributes an X, the embryo will develop into a female. If the male contributes a Y, the embryo will develop into a male. Sex differentiation occurs during the sixth week after conception. In the male embryo, the hormone testosterone is produced, which stimulates the development of male genitals.

Primary and Secondary Sex Characteristics

At birth, both males and females are distinguished by *primary sex characteristics, the genitals, used to reproduce the human species*. During adolescence, continued biological differentiation results in *secondary sex characteristics, bodily development, apart from the genitals, that distinguish biologically mature females and males*. Examples of these are reviewed. However, these are general differences, with a wide range existing for both sexes.

Hermaphrodites

Two variations from male and female sexes are discussed. *Hermaphrodite*, derived from Greek mythology, refers to *a human being with some combination of female and male internal*

202

and external genitalia. Our culture tends to be intolerant and even hateful of such people. However, their status in society varies cross-culturally.

Transsexuals

Another category is that of **transsexuals**, or *people who feel they are one sex though biologically they are the other.* Some of these people have surgery to alter their sex because of feeling "trapped" in the wrong body.

Sexual Orientation

Sexual orientation refers to *an individual's preference in terms of sexual partners: same sex, other sex, either sex, neither sex.* The meaning of different sexual orientations varies cross-culturally, but all societies endorse heterosexuality, by which a person is attracted to the opposite sex. However, *homosexuality*, or attraction to members of one's own sex, is not uncommon. *Bisexuality*, or attraction to either sex, or *asexuality*, or attraction to neither sex, also exist.

Homosexuality and the Pursuit of Gay Rights

Homosexuals, or gays, in the U.S. continue to be subjected to prejudice and discrimination, though tolerance is increasing. The term *lesbian* is used to refer to female homosexuals. In 1974 the American Psychiatric Association removed homosexuality from its list of mental disorders. *Homophobia*, or fear of gay people is still quite evident in our society. This has perhaps increased in recent years since the identification of the AIDS virus and its link to homosexuals.

The pioneering work of Alfred Kinsey during the middle of this century showed that exclusive homosexuality represented about 4 percent of our male population and 2 percent of our female population. A more recent survey, data from which is shown in *Figure 13-1* (p. 354), indicate 9 percent of men and 4 percent of women reported homosexual activity at some point in their lives.

Bisexuality

Twenty-five percent of our population have experienced at least one homosexual encounter. People who have combined homosexual and heterosexual orientations are called *bisexuals.*

The Origins of Sexual Orientation

Sexual orientation is determined by a combination of factors, including biological facts present at birth, hormonal influences, and social experiences. Further, sexual orientation is probably not established exactly the same for every person.

Gender: A Cultural Distinction

Gender, as introduced in Chapter 2, refers to the significance a society attaches to the biological categories of female and male. Typically they are differentiated into masculine and feminine traits. Involved here are all culturally learned differences between males and females, and the social inequality that results. Various statistics are reviewed in the text to illustrate.

Biologically, males and females reveal limited differences. Society dramatically affects the impact of these differences. The significance played by culture in the development of gender is illustrated by various types of research.

An Unusual Case Study

A case study of twin boys, one of whom had his penis severed during surgery at seven months of age, clearly reveals the significance of socialization. He was raised a girl, having further surgery to change his sex. The twins learned different **gender identity**, or *traits that females and males, guided by their culture, incorporate into their personalities.*

The Israeli Kibbutzim

The significance of culture is revealed using studies that focus on egalitarian gender role patterns in Israeli *kibbutzim*. However, close examination of the kibbutzim suggests that biology may undermine efforts to achieve complete gender equality.

Global Comparisons

Other cross-cultural evidence, for example the research by anthropologist Margaret Mead in New Guinea, again uncovers the variety of ways in which masculine and feminine traits are defined and experienced by males and females. Research by George Murdock involving over 200 preindustrialized societies reveals some general patterns about gender roles cross-culturally.

Significant variation in gender role patterns exists around the world, and these patterns are changing over history. An example of significant change presently occurring in Botswana on the continent of Africa is discussed in the **Global Sociology** box (p. 357).

Patriarchy and Sexism

While conceptions of gender vary cross-culturally and historically, there is an apparent universal pattern of **patriarchy**, *a form of social organization in which males dominates females.* **Matriarchy**, defined as *a form of social organization in which females dominate males*, has never known to have existed. The relative power of males over females does however vary significantly. Patriarchy is based on **sexism**, or *the belief that one sex is innately superior to the other.* Some researchers argue that sexism is very similar in form to racism. *Table 13-1* (p. 358) highlights the common characteristics or racism and sexism. *Institutionalized sexism*, or sexism built into the various institutions of our society, is evident. It is further argued that society itself, as well as men pay a price for sexism. It is not just women who are being rigidly defined.

The Costs of Sexism

Women suffer clear costs of sexism, but so to do men and society. The "A personality" type for men, their greater involvement in high-risk behaviors, and their greater isolation from others in terms of intimacy are discussed as examples.

Is Patriarchy Inevitable?

This discussion illustrates that patriarchy in societies with simple technology tends to reflect biological sex differences. In industrialized societies, technology minimizes the significance of any biological differences. Generally, the opinion of sociologists is that gender is principally a social construction and is subject to change.

GENDER SOCIALIZATION

Males and females are encouraged through the socialization process to incorporate gender into their personal identities. *Table 13-2* (p. 359) identifies the traditional gender identity characteristics along the dimensions of masculinity and femininity. Studies show that even with the cultural norms that script behavior, women and men don't exclusively exhibit gender appropriate attributes. Some score high on masculine characteristics, some high on feminine, some high on both, and some low on both. The pattern suggests however that scripts may be more imposing on males than on females.

Gender roles are *attitudes and activities that a society links to each sex*. They are the active expression of gender identity. Considerable social pressure is experienced by individuals to conform to gender role expectations.

Gender and the Family

Jesse Bernard, introduced in the **Profile** box (p. 360), suggests that girls and boys are born into different worlds, the "pink" and the "blue." She further argues that sociology, dominated by males, has not adequately studied females. The general pattern involves a female world revolving around passivity and emotion, and a male world involving action and independence.

Gender and the Peer Group

Janet Lever's research on peer group influences on gender suggests that the cultural lessons taught to boys and girls are very different. Boys are more likely to play in team sports with complex rules and clear objectives. Girls are more likely to engage in activities in smaller groups involving fewer formal rules and more spontaneity, and rarely leading to a "victory." The **Sociology of Everyday Life** box (p. 361) reviews one boy's sense of being socialized into masculinity.

Carol Gilligan, whose research on moral reasoning has demonstrated differences between boys and girls, suggests girls seem to understand morality in terms of responsibility and maintaining close relationships, and boys reason according to rules and principles.

Gender and Schooling

Research has shown that historically, males are the focus of attention in literature to a considerably greater extent than females. Further, females are more typically portrayed as "objects." In the last decade this pattern has begun to change. At the college level, females and males still tend to select different majors and extracurricular activities.

Gender and the Mass Media

The mass media has portrayed males as the dominant category of U.S. culture. Women have tended to be shown as less competent than men, and often as sex objects. Children's programs also reinforce gender stereotypes. While changes are occurring, they are doing so very slowly. This is particularly true in advertising, which has clung to traditional cultural views of women. Erving Goffman's research on how men and women are presented in photos for advertisements is discussed and reveals many subtle examples of sexism.

Gender and Adult Socialization

The two sexes seem to perceive different meaning in a wide range of everyday experiences. This is all reinforced by the surrounding culture. Feminine and masculine patterns are therefore typically followed by women and men respectively.

GENDER SOCIAL STRATIFICATION

Gender stratification refers to *society's unequal distribution of wealth, power, and privilege between the two sexes.* The general conclusion is that women around the world have fewer of their society's valued resources than men.

Working Men and Women

In the U.S. most adult men and women are in the labor force. *Figure 13-1* (p. 363) presents statistics on labor force participation rates for women and men from 1950-1993. The participation rate for women is increasing significantly. Several different categories of women, married, single, married with children, and divorced are discussed. In 1994 66.6 percent of people in the U.S. over the age of sixteen were working for income (75.1 percent of men and 58.8 percent of females). In the **Window on the World** box (p. 364) *Global Map 13-1* shows 1994 data on women's paid employment around the world. Throughout the industrialized world, at least one-third of the labor force is made up of women.

Gender and Occupations

However impressive the inclusion of women in the work force may be, women are still positioned in the lower-paying, traditionally female occupations. Almost one-half of working women fall into one of two broad occupational categories--clerical or service. *Table 13-3* (p. 365) reviews the jobs with the highest concentration of women. Men dominate virtually all other job categories. Even within a given occupational category (i.e., teaching), the higher prestige jobs and higher paying jobs are usually held by males.

Housework: Women's "Second Shift"

Housework is a domain of activity that almost exclusively falls on women to complete. The significance of housework is discussed as a cultural contradiction: essential, yet carrying minimal reward and prestige. The burden of this type of work is further increased by the monotony of the tasks involved. The increasing role of women in the labor force has not affected men's involvement in housework. The areas where responsibility is shared only seems to include the disciplining of children and finances. In the **Window on the World** box (p. 366) *Global Map 13-2* puts housework in global perspective, showing that as societies industrialize, household labor is divided more evenly than in poor societies.

Gender, Income, and wealth

Income tends to reinforce women's disadvantaged position in society. Women working full-time earn only 72 percent of what their male counterparts earn. In global perspective the earnings gap between men and women is greater in the U.S. than in most other industrial nations. Over time this disparity is narrowing.

Research shows that two-thirds of this difference can be attributed to the type of work in which males and females are employed, and family related factors. Still, one-third is attributable to discrimination. The issues of "comparable worth" and the "mommy-track" are discussed. *Table 13-4* (p. 368) presents statistics on earning differences between women and men for several different types of occupations.

Some evidence is presented to suggest that even though women out-live men, they do not control as much of the wealth in the U.S.

Gender and Education

Higher education was traditionally the domain of males. However, this pattern has been changing in recent decades. Over one-half of all college students today are females, with 55 percent of all associate and bachelor's degrees going to women in 1994. Females earn 52 percent of all M.A. degrees conferred, but only 33 percent of all doctorates. Further, females are pursuing programs traditionally dominated by males. However, significant differences still exist, particularly in the percentage of Ph.Ds granted, and in the areas of law and medicine.

Gender and Politics

U.S. political history reveals a significant pattern of male dominance. Key events in the history of women in U.S. politics are placed in chronological order in *Table 13-5* (p. 369). While the political power of women has increased dramatically during the last century, at the highest levels of government women's roles are still minimal compared to men.

Minority Women

Income statistics indicate that minority women are doubly disadvantaged, earning less than men of their own minority group. The femininization of poverty is evident by the fact that over 50 percent of households headed by African American or Hispanic women are living in poverty.

Are Women a Minority?

Our author argues that as a category women must be viewed as a minority group because of being socially disadvantaged, and identifiable by physical traits. However, subjectively, most women do not perceive themselves as such because they live within families that are distributed across the social class structure of society, and are socialized to accept their position.

Violence Against Women

Because violence is commonplace in our society, and closely linked to gender, it is often found where men and women interact most intensively (i.e., dating and the family). Sexual violence, it is argued, is mostly about *power*. A 1995 Justice Department report estimated 500,000 sexual assaults against women annually, with perhaps an additional 2 million nonsexual assaults.

Sexual Harassment

Sexual harassment is defined as *comments, gestures, or physical contact of a sexual nature that are deliberate, repeated, and unwelcome.* Sexual harassment is discussed as being inherently ambiguous in many instances, though often creating a *hostile environment*.

Pornography

The definition of pornography is very ambiguous as well. Current law requires different jurisdictions to decide for themselves what violates "community standards" of decency and lacks any redeeming social value. The point is made that there seems to be a pattern in our society of now seeing pornography as a *political* issue as well as a *moral* one. Like sexual harassment, pornography raises complex and conflicting concerns.

208

THEORETICAL ANALYSIS OF GENDER

Structural Functional Analysis

Theorists using this perspective understand gender role patterns over history and cross-culturally to be the result of the functional contributions these patterns make to the survival of the society within its social and physical environments. Industrial technology has allowed greater variation in gender roles, however gender roles still reflect long-standing institutionalized attitudes.

Talcott Parsons: Gender and Complementarity

Talcott Parsons theorized that gender plays a part in maintaining society in industrial times by providing men and women with a set of complementary roles (*instrumental* and *expressive*). Through socialization males and females adopt these roles. The primary societal responsibility of women, in this view, is child-rearing. Thus, they are socialized to display expressive qualities. Men are responsible for achievement in the labor force and therefore are socialized to exhibit instrumental traits.

Criticisms of this approach include the lack of recognition that many women have traditionally worked outside the home, the over-emphasis on only one kind of family, and the neglect of the personal strains associated with such a family orientation.

Social-Conflict Analysis

Social-conflict analysis of gender stratification focuses on the inequality of men and women. This theoretical view holds that women are a minority group and men benefit by the unequal relationship that is perpetuated by sexism and sexist ideology.

Friedrich Engels: Gender and Class

Friedrich Engels identified the historical formation of social classes to the origins of gender inequality. The basis of social class and private property marked the point at which males gained dominance over women in Engel's view. William Goode's research suggests that men are less likely to see gender as a source of inequality given their advantageous position relative to women. The complexities of male and female relationships that interfere with objective understanding of the inequality present are discussed using Goode's insights.

One criticism of this approach is that it neglects the cooperation of females and males in the institution of the family. Another criticism is that capitalism is not the origin of gender stratification since socialist societies are patriarchal as well.

FEMINISM

Feminism is defined as *the advocacy of social equality for the sexes, in opposition to patriarchy and sexism*. Its "first wave" in this country occurred in the 19th century, culminating with the right to vote for women. The "second wave" began in the 1960s and continues today.

Basic Feminist Ideas

Feminism shares at least two qualities with the sociological perspective: First, the questioning of our basic assumptions about social patterns; and second, an awareness of the relationship between personal experiences and society. However, feminism is decidedly political and critical, seeing the division of the sexes as necessarily harmful to individuals and society. Further, feminists are concerned with the implications of the gender division for social stratification patterns and sexuality issues. Five ideas considered central to feminism are explained; these include:

(1) The importance of change
(2) Expanding human choice
(3) Eliminating gender stratification
(4) Ending sexual violence
(5) Promoting sexual autonomy

Variations within Feminism

Three distinct forms of feminism are identified. These include: (1) *liberal feminism*, which accepts the basic organization of society, but seeks the same rights and opportunities for women and men, (2) *socialist feminism*, which supports the reforms of liberal feminists but believes they can be gained only though the elimination of the capitalist economy and socialist revolution, and (3) *radical feminism*, which advocates the elimination of patriarchy altogether by organizing a gender-free society.

Opposition to Feminism

Feminism has been resisted by both men and women. Reasons for this opposition include a preference for traditional gender and family definitions, a concern that our self-identity will be subject to change, and a fear or ignorance of what feminism is in actuality. A final issue concerns opinions about how change should occur.

The ERA; first proposed in Congress in 1923, has had considerable support, however the failure to formally enact the ERA suggests resistance is still strong.

LOOKING AHEAD: GENDER IN THE TWENTY-FIRST CENTURY

While sociologists differ in their projections (speculations) about the future of gender roles in our society, certain general observations are being made in the text. First, the trend over the last century or so in our society has been toward greater equality between the sexes. Second, while strong opposition to the feminist movement remains, deliberate policies

PART VII: ANALYSIS AND COMMENT

Window on the World

"Global Map 13-1: Women's Paid Employment in Global Perspective"

Key Points: Questions:

"Global Map 13-2: Housework in Global Perspective"

Key Points: Questions:

Seeing Ourselves

"National Map 13-1 Attitudes Toward Feminism Across the U.S."

Key Points: Questions:

Profile

"Jesse Bernard"

    Key Points: Questions:

Sociology of everyday Life

"Masculinity as Contest"

    Key Points: Questions:

Global Sociology

"Patriarchy Under Fire: A Report From Botswana"

    Key Points: Questions:

Controversy and Debate

"Men's Right! Are Men Really So Privileged?"

    Key Points: Questions:

Aging And The Elderly

14

PART I: CHAPTER OUTLINE

PART II: LEARNING OBJECTIVES

1. To define and explain the development of the graying of the U.S.
2. To describe the interrelationship and respective roles of biology and culture in growing old.
3. To explain the role of the elderly in global and historical perspectives.
4. To describe the relationship between adjusting to old age and personality type.
5. To describe the problems and transitions involved in growing old.
6. To describe, compare and contrast the three sociological explanations of aging.
7. To explain ageism and its impact on the elderly.
8. To identify the key arguments in the debate over whether the elderly constitute a minority group.
9. To describe the changing character of death throughout history and into modern times.
10. To describe the process of bereavement.

PART III: CHAPTER REVIEW

This chapter begins with a discussion about the best-selling book *Final Exit*. It is a book about dying, more specifically, a "how-to book" on suicide. The author of the book, Derek Humphrey, is the founder and executive director of the *Hemlock Society*, an organization that offers support and practical assistance to those who wish to die.

THE GRAYING OF THE UNITED STATES

It is pointed out that a powerful revolution is occurring in our society. It is referred to as the graying of the United States. The aged population is growing twice as fast as the general population. Currently the elderly account for 12.7 percent of the population. *Figure 14-1* (p. 384) portrays the extent to which the age structure of U.S. society is changing. The two major causes identified for this pattern are the aging of the baby boom generation and the increasing life expectancy in our society. *Figure 14-2* (p. 385) gives a brief global snapshot of the graying of society. In Italy, for example, almost 16 percent of the population is over 65 years of age.

These changes are affecting our society in many significant ways. The demands placed on social resources, particularly the federal budget, are becoming critical. Social security and health-care costs for our society are dramatically increasing as our population ages. The proportion of the federal budget supporting people over the age of 65 has increased threefold. The elderly account for one-fourth of all medical expenditures. Other social changes of great importance include the changes in interaction patterns between different age groups as the proportion of the aged increases, and the increased responsibility of adult children for their aged parents. Specifically, the concept of the *old-age dependency ratio*, or the ratio of elderly people to working-age adults, is discussed. The **Seeing Ourselves** box (p. 386) presents information on the residence patterns of the elderly across the U.S. in *National Map 14-1*.

GROWING OLD: BIOLOGY AND CULTURE

Gerontology is *the study of aging and the elderly*. This field provides great insight for us in understanding aging. Biological changes that are part of the aging process are indeed significant. However, so are the changes in social definitions that structure a person's everyday experiences.

Biological Changes

Biology by itself does not necessarily create social distinctions. However, we are a youth oriented-society. Changes that accompany old age are typically viewed more negatively than positively. Our general view seems to be that people reach a point when they "stop growing up and start growing down."

Cultural stereotypes of problems that complicate aging exaggerate differences between young and old. Gerontological research suggests differences do exist. For example, older people show declines in vitality and strength, suffer more chronic illnesses, are at a greater risk of many illnesses and diseases, and experience a decline in sensory abilities. However, patterns of change vary greatly between individuals and social groups. For example, the correlation between high social class and a sense of good or excellent health is very strong. Over 70 percent of white people over the age of 65 in the U.S. report their health as "good" or "excellent." In contrast the corresponding figure for African Americans is less than 50 percent.

Psychological Changes

Most elderly people do not suffer from mental or psychological problems. To more adequately assess mental functioning, psychologists have more precisely defined the concept of intelligence. Research suggests that measures of intelligence focusing on sensorimotor coordination do show decline in aged persons. Intelligence tests focusing on knowledge show no decline. Verbal and numerical skills even show rising ability with age. Psychological research has also shown that personality changes little as we grow old.

Aging and Culture

The significance of age comes from social constructs. Age is a relative term. Life expectancy shows significant cross-cultural variation. The **Window on the World** box (p. 389) contains in *Global Map 14-1* which shows life expectancy in a global perspective. Technological advances in medicine and health are important, but the critical role played by social relationships is perhaps even more significant. The **Global Sociology** box (p. 390) provides an illustration from Abkhasia in the Commonwealth of Independent States.

Age Stratification: A Global Assessment

Age stratification is defined as *the unequal distribution of wealth, power, and privileges among people at different stages in the life course.* This varies cross-culturally, and the old seem to generally have more power in societies in which they can accumulate wealth.

Hunting and Gathering Societies

These people are nomadic. At this technological level no surpluses of food exist. Aged people are less active and often seen as a burden.

Pastoral, Horticultural, and Agrarian Societies

Pastoral, horticultural, and agrarian societies have the technological capabilities to produce surpluses to enable accumulation to occur. Such societies tend toward **gerontocracy,** *a form of social organization in which the elderly have the most wealth, power, and prestige.* Industrialization tends to create a decline in the relative power and prestige of the aged as the prime source of wealth shifts away from the land and geographical mobility undermines the strength of families. The rapid change in technology also diminishes the expertise of the elderly. Many elderly are pushed toward nonproductive roles as the productivity of industrial society increases.

Industrial Societies

The rising living standards and medical technology of such societies brings an increase in life expectancy. At the same time, though, these forces diminish the power and prestige of the elderly. Geographic mobility, rapid social change, and increased productivity change the status of both the very young and old as their roles in production are not necessary. The *elders* (positive) become the *elderly* (negative) in society.

Japan: An Exceptional Case

Japan is discussed as an example of a culture in which the productive role and status of the elderly in the family and labor force have remained intact, providing the aged with greater prestige.

TRANSITIONS AND PROBLEMS OF AGING

It is argued that old age, as a stage in the human life cycle, presents the greatest of personal challenges. Recognizing one's own mortality and maintaining self-esteem during a period of physical decline are central to this challenge. Bernice Neugarten identified five different personality types and their differing adjustments to old age. From most successful to least successful they are: *integrated, defended, passive-dependent, disintegrated* and *disorganized.* A major point being made is that negative stereotypes of old age are misleading, and the experience of old age varies greatly from individual to individual.

222

Social Isolation

Central among the adjustments an individual must make during old age is the accommodation to increased social isolation. Negative stereotypes, retirement, and physical problems diminish social interaction. The most profound social isolation however occurs with the death of a significant other, particularly a spouse.

Table 14-1 (p. 391) outlines the living arrangements of the elderly. Critical differences between males and females are discussed. It is further pointed out that many elderly people live close to adult relatives. Contact with their children is more frequent than most of us might think, with only 10 percent reporting no visit with any of their children in the last month. Families are a meaningful cushion in lessening social isolation.

Retirement

Historically, particularly for men, occupational identity has been critical for a sense of self. Retirement is discussed as being a recent phenomenon. Before the Social Security Act of 1935 the vast majority of men had to continue their participation in the labor force out of economic necessity. Retirement has been promoted because of advanced technology reducing the need for labor and placing such importance on up-to-date skills. Congress phased out mandatory retirement policies in 1987; however most people still retire at age 65.

Aging and Poverty

Aging is typically associated with a decline in income. While poverty rates rise somewhat for people over the age of 65, relative to the entire population their poverty rate is below the average. Social Security, pensions, occupational and interest income are all important sources of income for the elderly. *Figure 14-3* (p. 393) shows the proportion of different age groups in the U.S. living in poverty. Children under the age of 15 years top the list. Gaps between racial and ethnic groups, and between men and women continue. Differences in median household incomes vary greater by the age of the householder.

Abuse of the Elderly

The government estimates that 3 percent of the aged in our society are victimized by some type of maltreatment each year. Perhaps one in ten suffers abuse at some time during old age. Much of the abuse is attributed to the stress resulting from the elderly person's child caring for him or her.

Ageism

Ageism refers to *prejudice and discrimination against the elderly*. Over time it becomes institutionalized in society. This can often take very subtle forms. Ageism causes unwarranted generalizations about the aged which creates stereotypes that perpetuate inequalities between the aged and the young. Some research suggests that such negative stereotyping has diminished in recent years, particularly in the mass media. Examples are discussed. The **Social Diversity** box (p. 396) focuses on research by Betty Friedan that shows how society ignores the aged in our society.

The Elderly: A Minority? ·

Sociologists vary in their opinions concerning the classification of the aged as a minority group. Certain general characteristics of the aged population seem consistent with such a status, however the social disadvantages faced by the elderly are less substantial than those experienced by other categories of people labeled as minorities. The situation of the elderly is labeled as an open status, not permanent or exclusive. Our author concludes that, while being a distinctive segment of the U.S. population, the aged should not carry the status of minority group.

THEORETICAL ANALYSIS OF AGING

Structural-Functional Analysis: Aging and Disengagement

Disengagement theory is *the proposition that society enhances its orderly operation by disengaging people from positions of responsibility as they reach old age.* This theory is based on Talcott Parson's structural-functional analysis. An orderly transfer of various statuses and roles from the old to the young provides benefits for both society and individuals. A problem with this view is that many older people do not want to relinquish their statuses and roles and are quite capably functioning within them.

Symbolic-Interaction Analysis: Aging and Activity

Activity theory is *the proposition that a high level of activity enhances personal satisfaction in old age.* Disengagement is viewed as diminishing satisfaction and meaning in life. While disengaging from certain statuses and roles, the elderly shift to new ones based on their own distinctive needs, interests, talents and capabilities. The diversity of the aged population is emphasized. This approach may however underestimate the degree of health restrictions present among the aged.

Social-Conflict Analysis: Aging and Inequality

Using this approach one sees different age categories across the life cycle competing for scarce resources. The status of the elderly relative to younger people is viewed as being disadvantaged. This is the result of the emphasis in capitalist societies on valuing people for what they do rather than for who they are. While focusing our attention on the age stratification that does exist in society, this approach tends to ignore the improvement in social standing of the elderly in recent decades. Another issue, even if inequality for the elderly exists, concerns whether *capitalism* is the culprit, or is it *industrialization*?

DEATH AND DYING

The Bible tells us of two certainties: the fact of birth and the inevitability of death. The character of death is discussed in this section as being variable over history.

Historical Patterns of Death

Throughout much of human history death was a part of everyday life. Disease and natural catastrophes were widespread. In preindustrial societies, less productive people (infants and the aged) were sometimes put to death (infanticide/geronticide) for the sake of preserving the group. As societies began to gain some measure of control over death through technological advances, attitudes about death changed. It was no longer an everyday experience in the lives of people. The **Controversy and Debate** box (p. 399) discusses some ethical and economic issues being raised given the longer life expectancy and larger aged population in our society.

The Modern Separation of Life and Death

Death is now looked at as something unnatural. Death is becoming, in a sense, separate from life. Death and dying are now *physically* removed from the rest of life. Dying now typically occurs away from the family, in a hospital. Fear and anxiety dominate our feelings about death.

This sense of dying may not be quite so representative of the aged who are sick, who may see it as being more a release from suffering. Many ethical issues are being raised concerning the extent to which a life should be prolonged by artificial means.

Bereavement

Elizabeth Kubler-Ross's stages of death are briefly discussed, and it is argued that the bereavement process parallels these stages of dying. The stages through which she believes individuals go include: *denial, anger, negotiation, resignation,* and *acceptance.* One program, *hospice,* is discussed as an attempt to provide support for dying people and their families. Bereavement may last a long period of time and cause social isolation and disorientation.

LOOKING AHEAD: AGING IN THE TWENTY-FIRST CENTURY

The "graying" of the United States is a remarkable trend. By the year 2050 the elderly population alone will exceed the population of the entire country in 1900. The reshaping of the age structure of our society raises many serious concerns. However, there re positive consequences as well.

PART IV: KEY CONCEPTS

Define each of the following concepts in the space provided or on separate paper. Check the accuracy of your answers by referring to the key concepts section at the end of the chapter in the text as well as by referring to italicized definitions located throughout the chapter.

activity theory
ageism
age stratification
defended personality
disengagement theory
disintegrated and disorganized personality
integrated personality
geronticide
gerontocracy
gerontology
Hemlock Society
hospice
old-age dependency ratio
open status
passive-dependent personality

PART V: STUDY QUESTIONS

True-False

1. T F Given the recent rise in the birth rate in the U.S., the *median age* in our society is decreasing.
2. T F The aged account for two-thirds of all *medical expenditures* in the U.S.
3. T F The *sensory abilities* of people tend to diminish in old age.
4. T F Most psychological research shows that *personality characteristics* of a person change considerably as they grow old.
5. T F A *gerontocracy* is a form of social organization in which elderly people have the most wealth, power, and prestige.
6. T F Most elderly women live *alone*.
7. T F Most U.S. workers *retire* at age 65 or earlier.
8. T F Children are more likely to be *poor* in the U.S. than are the aged.
9. T F Females working full-time past the age of 65 *earn more* than their male counterparts.
10. T F Our author argues that the elderly clearly represent a *minority group*.
11. T F In 1900, about one-third of all deaths in the United States occurred before the age of five, while in 1995, eighty-five percent of deaths involved people over the age of fifty-five.

1. Currently, the aged represent about _____ *percent* of our population.

   (a)   6   (b)   13   (c)   17   (d)   21

2. Between now and 2050 *median age* in the U.S. will rise to _____ and the *percent* of our population over the age of 65 will be _____.

   (a)   40/20   (c)   50/50
   (b)   30/15   (d)   25/40

3. The share of the *federal budget* directed toward the aged is:

   (a)   10   (b)   21   (c)   33   (d)   50   (e)   less than 5

4. The Abkhasian society exhibits exceptional *longevity* due to:

   (a)   a healthy diet
   (b)   regular exercise
   (c)   positive self-image of the elderly in society
   (d)   all of the above

5. Which of the following is *not* a personality type identified by Neugarten in her study of adjustment to old age?

   (a)   disintegrated and disorganized   (d)   integrated
   (b)   residual-active   (e)   defended
   (c)   passive-dependent

6. Most elderly males:

   (a)   live alone
   (b)   live in nursing homes
   (c)   live with extended family members
   (d)   live with their spouse

7. Approximately what percentage of the aged population in the U.S. live in poverty?

   (a)   less than 5   (d)   33
   (b)   18   (e)   13
   (c)   25

8. Some sociologists argue that the elderly constitute a minority group while others disagree. Which of the following reasons is an argument against the elderly being a minority group?

   (a) the status of being elderly is an open status
   (b) the elderly think of themselves in terms of sex, race, and ethnicity
   (c) the social disadvantages of the elderly are not as great as for other categories of people
   (d) all of the above

9. *Activity theory* is a sociological theory of aging that is based upon:

   (a) structural-functional analysis
   (b) social-conflict analysis
   (c) symbolic-interaction analysis
   (d) social-exchange analysis

10. In modern U.S. society *death* has become:

   (a) more common to everyday experience
   (b) less of an ethical issue
   (c) an event that occurs often in the home of the dying person
   (d) easier to accept
   (e) defined as an unnatural event

Fill-In

1. The _____ *society* founded in 1980, offers support and practical assistance to people who wish to die.
2. _____ is the study of aging and the elderly.
3. In her study on the transitions of aging Bernice Neugarten found the most aged people 70 years of age or older to have what she labeled a _____ *personality*.
4. Approximately _____ percent of elderly women in the U.S. live with a spouse.
5. _____ *theory* is an analysis linking disengagement by elderly people from positions of social responsibility to the orderly operation of society.
6. _____ refers to prejudice and discrimination against the elderly.
7. Our author believes the aged should not be identified as a minority group, but rather be considered a _____ segment of the U.S. population.
8. Betty Freidan suggests an *aging* _____ exists in our society.
9. One criticism of *social-conflict theory* is that rather than blaming capitalism for the lower standing of the elderly, the real culprit is _____.
10. It is estimated that *health care costs* for the aged in the year 2000 will reach _____ annually.

Definition and Short-Answer

1. What is the *Hemlock Society*? What are your thoughts and feelings about this organization and its purposes? What are some of the broader concerns relating to this issue?
2. Define *gerontology*. Further, many different demographic facts concerning the aged in our society are presented on pages 388-389. Select the two which most interest or surprise you and discuss their significance using your own opinions.
3. Define *age stratification*. How does it vary between hunting and gathering, horticultural, agrarian, and industrial societies?
4. What are the four *types of personalities* identified by Bernice Neugarten? In what ways are they different in terms of helping a person adjust to old age?
5. Differentiate between *activity theory* and *disengagement theory* in terms of how each helps us understand the changing status of the aged in society.
6. Why is *elder abuse* so common in the U.S.?
7. Discuss the relative economic condition of the aged in our society today?
8. According to *social-conflict theorists*, why is the status of the aged diminished in capitalist societies?
9. What are the arguments in the debate concerning whether the aged are a minority group?
10. What are Daniel Callahan's points concerning how much old age can the U.S. afford?
11. Review the points being made by Betty Friedan concerning the aged in our society. What are your reactions to her views?

PART VI: ANSWERS TO STUDY QUESTIONS

True-False

1.	F	(p. 384)	6.	F	(p. 391)	11.	T	(p. 397)
2.	F	(p. 385)	7.	T	(p. 392)			
3.	T	(p. 386)	8.	T	(p. 393)			
4.	F	(p. 387)	9.	F	(p. 393)			
5.	T	(p. 388)	10.	F	(p. 394)			

Multiple-Choice

1.	b	(p. 383)	6.	d	(p. 391)
2.	a	(p. 384)	7.	e	(p. 392)
3.	d	(p. 385)	8.	d	(p. 394)
4.	d	(p. 390)	9.	c	(p. 395)
5.	b	(p. 391)	10.	e	(p. 397)

1. Hemlock (p. 384)
2. gerontology (p. 386)
3. integrated (p. 391)
4. 40 (p. 395)
5. disengagement (p. 398)
6. ageism (p. 394)
7. distinctive (p. 394)
8. mystique (p. 396)
9. industrialization (p. 397)
10. 200 billion (p. 399)

PART VII: ANALYSIS AND COMMENT

Controversy and Debate

"Setting Limits: Must We "Pull the Plug" on Old Age?"

Key Points: Questions:

Global Sociology

"Growing (Very) Old: A Report From in Abkhasia"

Key Points: Questions:

Social Diversity

"The Fountain of Aging"

    Key Points: Questions:

Seeing Ourselves

"National Map 14-1 The Elderly Population of the U.S."

    Key Points: Questions:

Window on the World

"Global Map 14-1 Life Expectancy in Global Perspective"

    Key Points: Questions:

The Economy and Work

PART I: CHAPTER OUTLINE

I.   The Economy: Historical Overview
     A. The Agricultural Revolution
     B. The Industrial Revolution
     C. The Postindustrial Society and the Information Revolution
     D. Sectors of the Modern Economy
     E. The Global Economy

II.   Comparative Economic Systems
     A. Capitalism
     B. Socialism
         1. Socialism and Communism
     C. Democratic Socialism and State Capitalism
     D. Relative Advantages of Capitalism and Socialism
         1. Economic Productivity
         2. Economic Inequality
         3. Civil Liberties
     E. Changes in Socialist Countries

III.   Work in the Postindustrial Economy
     A. The Decline of Agricultural Work
     B. From Factory Work to Service Work
     C. The Dual Labor Market
     D. Labor Unions
     E. Professions
     F. Self-Employment
     G. Unemployment
     H. The Underground Economy
     I. Social Diversity in the Workplace
     J. Technology and Work

IV. Corporations
    A. Economic Concentration
    B. Conglomerates and Corporate Linkages
    C. Corporations and Competition
    D. Corporations and the Global Economy
V.   Looking Ahead: The Economy of the Twenty-First Century
VI. Summary
VII. Key Concepts
VIII. Critical-Thinking Questions
IX. Suggested Readings

PART II: LEARNING OBJECTIVES

1. To identify the elements of the economy
2. To explain the history and development of economic activity from the agricultural revolution through the industrial revolution to the postindustrial society.
3. To identify and describe the primary, secondary, and tertiary sectors of the economy.
4. To compare and contrast the economic systems of capitalism and socialism.
5. To identify the differences between democratic socialism and capitalism.
6. To explain the difference between socialism and communism.
7. To identify the advantages and disadvantages of capitalism and socialism on productivity, income, economic, and political factors.
8. To describe the general characteristics and trends of work in U.S. postindustrial society.
9. To compare and contrast corporations and conglomerates and analyze competition in the U.S. economy.
10. To explain the impact of multinational corporations on the world economy.

PART III: CHAPTER REVIEW

This chapter focuses on the economy as a social system that is operating within a complex global market. A report from Saigon, Vietnam and its changing economy opens the chapter.

THE ECONOMY: HISTORICAL OVERVIEW

The *economy* is *the social institution that organizes the production, distribution, and consumption of goods and services.* Goods range from basic necessities to luxury items. Services include various activities that benefit others. Modern complex societies are the result of centuries of technological development and social change.

The Agricultural Revolution

Being over ten times more productive than hunting and gathering societies, agrarian societies produce considerable surpluses. The four factors of agricultural technology, productive specialization, permanent settlements, and trade have been important in the development of the economy. There was no distinct economy in hunting and gathering societies, as production, distribution, and consumption all were dimensions of family life.

Economic expansion has also created greater inequalities. In agrarian economies like that which existed in medieval Europe, many people living in cities worked at home, referred to as the "*cottage industry*." An example from England three centuries ago is discussed.

The Industrial Revolution

Five revolutionary changes are identified as resulting from the industrial revolution of Europe beginning in the mid-18th century. These include: *New forms of energy, the spread of factories, manufacturing and mass production, specialization, and wage labor.* Greater productivity steadily raised the standard of living. The **Social Diversity** box (p. 405) illustrates however that their were special problems facing women who worked in factories.

The Postindustrial Society and the Information Revolution

By 1950, further changes created the beginning of the ***post-industrial society***, *an productive system based on service work and high technology. The Information Revolution* has brought about three key changes:

        (1)   From tangible products to ideas.
        (2)   From mechanical skills to literacy skills.
        (3)   The decentralization of work away from factories.

In the **Window on the World** box (p. 408) *Global Maps 15-1* and *15-2* put agricultural and industrial employment into global perspective. As discussed in the following section, developing countries are dominated by employment in the primary sector.

Sectors of the Modern Economy

Three parts, or sectors, of society's economy exist and their relative balance shifts over history. The ***primary sector*** is *the part of the economy that generates raw materials directly from the natural environment.* Today in the U.S. only 4 percent of the labor force is involved in this sector. The ***secondary sector*** is *the part of the economy that transforms raw materials into manufactured goods.* The ***tertiary sector*** is *the part of the economy that generates services rather than goods.* About 70 percent of our labor force is employed in such work.

The Global Economy

The ***global economy*** is defined as *economic activity spanning many nations of the world with little regard for national borders.* There are four main consequences of the trend toward a global economy. These include: (1) A global division of labor by which each region of the world specializes in a particular kind of economic activity, (2) More products passing through multiple national economies, (3) National economies not controlling economic activity within their own borders, and (4) A few businesses controlling the vast share of the world's economic activity.

COMPARATIVE ECONOMIC SYSTEMS

Capitalism

Capitalism is *an economic system in which natural resources and the means of producing goods and services are privately owned*. This system has three distinctive features: *private ownership of property, pursuit of personal profit*, and *free competition and consumer sovereignty*. A purely capitalist economy would operate with no government interference (a *laissez-faire* approach).

However, even in the leading capitalist society of the U.S., the government affects our economy very significantly. The government owns and operates specific parts of our economy, for example Amtrak and the postal service. It also assumes economic responsibility in bailout situations, as in the case of the Chrysler Corporation and the savings and loan industry. Many state and local governments also own and operate large businesses. Local, state, and federal governments employ 14 percent of the labor force in the U.S.

Socialism

Socialism is *an economic system in which natural resources and the means of producing goods and services are collectively owned*. Its distinguishing characteristics include: *collective ownership of property, pursuit of collective goals*, and *government control of the economy*.

Socialism and Communism

Communism is *a hypothetical economic and political system in which all members of a society are socially equal*. Karl Marx viewed socialism as a transitory stage on the way to communism. However, nowhere has this system been achieved. Such a society, even for Marx, is a *utopia*.

Democratic Socialism and State Capitalism

Several western European democracies have introduced socialist policies through elections. *Democratic socialism* is *an economic and political system that combines significant government control of the economy with free elections*. Sweden and Italy are examples.

Another blend of capitalism and socialism is *state capitalism*, or *an economic and political system in which companies are privately owned although they cooperate closely with the government*. This system is common in rapidly developing countries, for example, Asian countries along the Pacific Rim (e.g., Japan, South Korea, and Singapore).

Relative Advantages of Capitalism and Socialism

Precise objective comparisons are not possible. Many factors affect a society's economic performance, including historical and cultural patterns, variations in the size and composition of the labor force, available natural resources, different levels of technological development, and trade alliances. However, certain comparisons can be made keeping these factors in mind.

Economic Productivity

Comparisons are made concerning the economic performance for different capitalist and socialist economies using the per capita GDP as a gauge. The average figure for the capitalist systems was 2.7 times that of the socialist systems in the late 1980s.

Economic Inequality

Income inequality was twice as great in societies with capitalist economies in the mid-1970s. The conclusion is made that socialist economies create less income disparity, but offer a lower overall standard of living.

Civil Liberties

A society's economic system shapes its politics. In capitalist societies there are extensive civil liberties and political freedom. From the viewpoint of socialists, this market-based freedom translates into doing what you can afford. On the other hand, socialist societies attempt to maximize economic and social equality. This limits personal liberty.

Changes in Socialist Countries

The Solidarity Movement in Poland during the 1980s and the dissolving of the Soviet Union in 1992 are discussed to illustrate the significant changes occurring in these countries. Why the changes? Two reasons stand out, including the fact that socialist systems underproduced relative to capitalist economies, and the rigid control by the unresponsive governments caused problems.

WORK IN THE POSTINDUSTRIAL ECONOMY

The U.S. economic system has also been going through major changes during this century. In 1994 there were 131 million people, or two-thirds of those over the age of 16, in the labor force. *Table 15-1* (p. 412) shows the participation rates by sex and race. For white males the participation rate was 75.9 percent, for African American males 69.1 percent, for white women 58.8 percent, and for African American women 58.7 percent. Age also affects labor force participation.

The Decline of Agricultural Work

Currently, less than 3 percent of the U.S. labor force is involved in farming. In the **Seeing Ourselves** box (p. 413), *National Map 15-1* graphically illustrates the labor force participation rates across the country. U.S. agriculture is more productive now than it was in the past. More and more production is occurring in corporate agribusinesses.

From Factory Work to Service Work

As indicated in *Figure 15-2*, by 1994 about 70 percent of the labor force were in white-collar jobs. In 1900, more than 40 percent were in blue-collar jobs. Many of the white-collar occupations are lower paying service jobs.

The Dual Labor Market

One way to describe the change which is occurring in our economy is to divide work into two different labor markets. The ***primary labor market*** includes *occupations that provide extensive benefits to workers*, while the ***secondary labor market*** includes *jobs providing minimal benefits to workers*. A growing proportion of new jobs in postindustrial economies fall into the secondary labor market. The **Sociology of Everyday Life** box (p. 415) discusses the "temporary" status of many U.S. jobs today.

Labor Unions

In recent years there has been a significant decline in ***labor unions***, or *organizations of workers seeking to improve wages and working conditions through various strategies, including negotiations and strikes*. While union membership peaked during the 1970s, today only 16 percent of the non-farm labor force is unionized. Compared to other industrialized societies the United States has relatively low union membership. Several factors are related to this decline. First, the blue-collar sector of the economy has been experiencing massive layoffs in recent decades, in part due to the trends in the global economy. Second, most newly created jobs are found in the service sector, which is far less likely to be unionized. However, falling job security may make union membership a higher priority for more workers.

Professions

A ***profession*** is *a prestigious, white-collar occupation that requires extensive formal education*. Professions share the following characteristics: *Theoretical knowledge, self-regulated training and practice, authority over clients,* and *orientation to community rather than to self-interest*.

Besides traditional professions like medicine and law, *new professions* share these qualities, including accounting and architecture. There are many new service occupations seeking to *professionalize* their work. This process is initiated by members of an occupational category by labeling their work in a new way. This is followed by the development of a professional association, which develops a code of ethics, and perhaps, even schools to train members. In marginal cases, paraprofessional status may be obtained, denoting special training, but lacking extensive theoretical education.

Self-Employment

Self-employment refers to earning a living without working for a large organization. In the early 19th century, about 80 percent of the labor force was self-employed. By 1870, only about one-third was, and by 1940 only one in five. Today, about 9 percent of the labor force are classified as self-employed.

While the potential for earning good incomes is present, about one in five small businesses survive for ten years. Another trend is for more women to own their own business. About 40 percent of small businesses are owned by women today in the U.S.

Unemployment

Some unemployment is found in all societies. In predominantly industrialized societies the unemployment rate rarely drops below 5 percent. Such a level is even viewed as natural. Currently, about 6 percent of the civilian labor force in the U.S. is unemployed. Unemployment is much more common in the secondary labor market than in the primary labor market. Rates vary by race, age, and sex also. *Figure 15-3* (p. 418) illustrates these patterns for 1994. African American unemployment is more than twice that for whites. While white males and females have comparable rates, African American males have considerably higher rates than African American females. Rates though are typically underestimated because by definition a person must be actively seeking employment and many people are "underemployed."

The Underground Economy

In violation of government regulations concerning the "free enterprise" system is the **underground economy**, or *economic activity involving income unreported to the government as required by law*. Such activity ranges from having garage sales and not reporting the money generated, to illegal drug trade. The single largest segment of this underground economy is legally obtained income unreported on income taxes.

Social Diversity in the Workplace

Major changes are occurring in the workplace in terms of its composition. Demographic shifts are dramatically increasing the proportion of minority group members in the work force. The **Social Diversity** box (p. 419) looks at the workforce of the 21st century.

Technology and Work

The technological nature of the workplace is also affecting who is working. For example, with the rise of information technology, more women are working. Four ways in which the computer has changed the nature of work are discussed. These include: *Computers are deskilling labor, computers are making work more abstract, computers limit workplace interaction,* and *computers enhance employer's control of workers.*

CORPORATIONS

A *corporation* is *an organization with a legal existence, including rights and liabilities, apart from those of its members.* Of the approximately 20 million businesses in the U.S., 4 million are incorporated. There are two primary benefits of incorporating, including the protection of owners from personal liability and providing advantages under tax laws that increase profits.

Economic Concentration

While one-half of U.S. corporations are small, with assets of under $100,000, the largest corporations dominate the U.S. economy. Over this century there has been a tremendous concentration of national and international economic power. Several statistics are reviewed to illustrate this process.

Conglomerates and Corporate Linkages

A *conglomerate* is *giant corporation composed of many smaller corporations.* RJR-Nabisco, Coca-Cola, and Beatrice Foods are discussed as examples. Another type of linkage between corporations is called *interlocking directorates,* or social networks made up of people who simultaneously serve on the boards of directors of many corporations. This is an important part of the U.S. economic system. It is not necessarily against the public interest, but does tend to concentrate power.

Corporations and Competition

The competitive market in America is actually limited to smaller businesses and self-employed people. Large corporations are part of the noncompetitive sector. *Monopoly,* or *domination of a market by a single producer,* was declared a century ago by the government to be against the public welfare. Monopolies have been limited, but *oligopoly,* or *domination of a market by a few producers,* persists.

The government's role is to protect the public interest, yet capitalists ideally support minimal government intervention. Also, the government is the single biggest consumer of large corporations. Corporations and government really work together to help make the economy stable and profitable.

Corporations and the Global Economy

The largest corporations in the world, most of which are in the U.S., now span the globe. Beatrice Food, Exxon, and General Motors are discussed as examples. Such corporations are huge. Exxon, for example out-produces almost any low-income nation. Advantages and disadvantages of multinational corporations are discussed. *Figure 15-4* (p. 422) shows hourly wages of workers in manufacturing for several rich and poor nations.

LOOKING AHEAD: THE ECONOMY OF THE TWENTY-FIRST CENTURY

Today's rate of economic change is comparable to that which existed at the turn of the last century. Socialism, representing about one-fourth of all humanity, will likely be very variable over the next century.

A critical turning point occurred for the U.S. in 1990, when for the first time, foreign corporations owned more of the U.S. than U.S. corporations owned abroad. Events around the world are therefore critical to the U.S. economic system. Our economic future is no longer a matter of the performance of national economies, but rather a global economic system. Important transformations revolve around the Information Revolution and the global economy. Further, these recent changes have caused analysts to rethink conventional economic models (e.g., capitalism and socialism). The **Controversy and Debate** box (p. 424) addresses the issue of whether "the market" or "the government" better serves the public interest.

PART IV: KEY CONCEPTS

Define each of the following concepts in the space provided or on separate paper. Check the accuracy of your answers by referring to the key concepts section at the end of the chapter in the text as well as by referring to italicized definitions located throughout the chapter.

capitalism
communism
competitive sector
conglomerates
corporation
cottage industry
democratic socialism
economy
global economy
interlocking directorate
labor unions
monopoly
noncompetitive sector
oligopoly

postindustrial economy
primary labor market
primary sector
profession
professionalization
secondary labor market
secondary sector
socialism
state capitalism
tertiary sector
underground economy

PART V: STUDY QUESTIONS

True-False

1.	T	F	The *economy* includes the production, distribution, and consumption of both goods and services.
2.	T	F	In medieval Europe, people living in cities often worked at home, a pattern called *cottage industry*.
3.	T	F	Most workers in the New England textile factories in the early 19th century were *women*.
4.	T	F	The terms *primary*, *secondary*, and *tertiary*, referring to sectors in the economy, imply a ranking in importance for our society.
5.	T	F	Socialism is *both* a political and economic system.
6.	T	F	*Per capita GDP* tended to be significantly higher in capitalist as compared to socialist economies during the 1970s and 1980s.
7.	T	F	The *income ratio*, as a measure of the distribution of income in a society, tended to be higher in socialist systems as compared to capitalist systems during the 1970s and 1980s.
8.	T	F	Seventy percent of the entire labor force in the United States hold *white-collar jobs*.
9.	T	F	The secondary labor market includes jobs providing minimal benefits to workers.
10.	T	F	An *oligopoly* refers to domination of a market by a few producers.
11.	T	F	While the *global economy* is becoming very important, still, U.S. corporations currently own about 35 percent more overseas than foreign companies own in the United States.

Multiple-Choice

1.   That part of the economy that transforms raw materials into manufactured goods is termed the:

     (a)   primary sector   (d)   competitive sector
     (b)   secondary sector   (e)   basic sector
     (c)   manifest sector

2.   Which of the following is *not* a sector of the modern economy:

     (a)   primary   (c)   manifest
     (b)   secondary   (d)   tertiary

3.   An economic and political system in which companies are privately owned although they cooperate closely with the government is the definition for:

     (a)   communism   (d)   state capitalism
     (b)   democratic socialism   (e)   oligarchy
     (c)   socialism

4.   A political and economic system in which free elections and a market economy coexist with government efforts to minimize social inequality is termed:

     (a)   socialism   (d)   democratic socialism
     (b)   market communism   (e)   oligarchy
     (c)   world economy

5.   Socialist economies had about _____ as much *income inequality* as found in capitalist systems prior to the economic transformations of Eastern Europe in the late 1980s.

     (a)   one-half   (d)   one-tenth
     (b)   one-sixth   (e)   one and a half
     (c)   twice

6.   How many people in the United States were in the *paid labor force* in 1994?

     (a)   75 million   (d)   131 million
     (b)   50 million   (e)   90 million
     (c)   200 million

7. What percentage of women over the age of sixteen have *income-producing jobs*?

   (a) 31.7 (b) 44.6 (c) 58.8 (d) 67.5 (e) 81.5

8. What percentage of the U.S. labor force is *unionized*?

   (a) 75 (b) 32 (c) 3 (d) 54 (e) 16

9. In 1940, one-fifth of all U.S. workers were *self-employed*. Currently, what percentage of U.S. workers are self-employed?

   (a) less than 1   (d) 12.5
   (b) 3.1   (e) 20
   (c) 9

10. Which of the following is *most accurate*:

    (a) white males have higher rates of unemployment than white females
    (b) a higher proportion of African American females are unemployed than African American males
    (c) unemployment is more common in the secondary labor market than in the primary labor market
    (d) unemployment has risen significantly since 1982
    (e) all of the above are accurate

11. Giant corporations that are composed of many smaller companies are called:

    (a) megacorporations   (d) monopolies
    (b) multinational corporations   (e) conglomerates
    (c) oligarchies

Fill-In

1. _____ range from necessities like food to luxuries like swimming pools, while _____ include various activities that benefit others.
2. A _____ _____ is an economy based on service work and high technology.
3. The *Information Revolution* has unleashed three key changes, including--tangible products to _____, mechanical skills to _____ skills, and _____ of work way from factories.
4. The _____ _____ is the part of the economy generating raw materials directly from the natural environment.
5. The _____ _____ is the part of the economy generating services rather than goods.

6. _____ is a hypothetical economic and political system in which all members of society have economic and social equality.
7. During the decade before the dramatic transformation of Eastern European economies, the output of predominately capitalist countries (which averaged a *per-capita GDP* of about 13,500) was _____ times greater than that of socialist countries.
8. While _____ percent of males over the age of 16 in the U.S. have *income-producing jobs*, _____ percent of the females do.
9. _____ are giant corporations comprised of many smaller companies.
10. Four ways in which computers are altering the character of work are identified in the text, including: _____ labor, making work more _____, limiting workplace _____, and enhancing employers' _____ of workers.
11. The _____ sector of the economy is actually limited to smaller businesses and self-employed people. Large corporations fall within the _____ sector.

Definition and Short-Answer

1. What is meant by the term *cottage industry*?
2. What were the five revolutionary changes brought about by the *Industrial Revolution*?
3. Define the concept *postindustrial economy*. Be sure to identify its key characteristics and how they are represented in the U.S.
4. What are the basic characteristics of *capitalism* as reviewed in the text?
5. What are the basic characteristics of *socialism* as reviewed in the text? What two factors are identified as being reasons for why sweeping changes occurred in Eastern Europe in the late 1980s?
6. Differentiate between *socialism* and *communism*.
7. What is *democratic socialism*? How is it different from state capitalism?
8. Comparing *productivity* and economic *equality* measures for capitalist and socialist economic systems, what are their relative advantages and disadvantages.
9. Differentiate between the *primary* and *secondary* labor markets.
10. What are the basic characteristics of a *profession*?
11. What is the differentiation between the *competitive* and *noncompetitive* sectors of the economy?

PART VI: ANSWERS TO STUDY QUESTIONS

True-False

1.	T	(p. 403)	7.	F	(p. 411)
2.	T	(p. 404)	8.	T	(p. 413)
3.	T	(p. 405)	9.	T	(p. 414)
4.	F	(p. 406)	10.	T	(p. 422)
5.	F	(p. 409)	11.	F	(p. 424)
6.	T	(p. 411)			

Multiple-Choice

1.	b	(p. 406)	7.	c	(p. 412)
2.	c	(p. 406)	8.	e	(p. 414)
3.	d	(p. 410)	9.	c	(p. 416)
4.	d	(p. 410)	10.	c	(pp. 417-18)
5.	a	(p. 411)	11.	e	(p. 420)
6.	d	(p. 412)			

Fill-In

1. goods, services (p. 403)
2. postindustrial economy (p. 404)
3. ideas, literacy, decentralized (pp. 405-06)
4. primary sector (p. 406)
5. tertiary sector (p. 406)
6. communism (p. 410)
7. 2.7 (p. 411)
8. 75.1/58.8 (p. 412)
9. conglomerates (p. 420)
10. deskilling, abstract, interaction, control (p. 420)
11. competitive/noncompetitive (p. 421)

PART VII: ANALYSIS AND COMMENT

Social Diversity

"Women in the Mills of Lowell, Massachusetts"

Key Points: Questions:

"The Workforce of the Twenty-First Century"

Key Points: Questions:

Sociology of Everyday Life

"The Postindustrial Economy: The "Temping" of the U.S."

Key Points: Questions:

Controversy and Debate

"Does "The Market" Serve the Public Interest?"

Key Points: Questions:

Window on the World

"Global Maps 15-1 and 15-2 Agricultural and Industrial Employment in Global Perspective"

Key Points: Questions:

Seeing Ourselves

"National Map 15-1 Labor Force Participation Across the U.S."

Key Points: Questions:

Politics and Government 16

PART I: CHAPTER OUTLINE

I.   Power and Authority
    A. Traditional Authority
    B. Rational-Legal Authority
    C. Charismatic Authority

II.   Politics in Global Perspective
    A. Monarchy
    B. Democracy
        1. Democracy and Freedom: Contrasting Approaches
    C. Authoritarianism
    D. Totalitarianism
    E. A Global Political System?

III.   Politics in the United States
    A. U.S. Culture and the Growth of Government
    B. The Political Spectrum
        1. Economic Issues
        2. Social Issues
        3. Mixed Positions
        4. Party Identification
    C. Special-Interest Groups
    D. Voter Apathy

VI.   Theoretical Analysis of Power in Society
    A. The Pluralist Model
        1. Research Results
    B. The Power-Elite Model
        1. Research Results

V.   Power Beyond the Rules
    A. Revolution
    B. Terrorism

VI.   War and Peace
       A. The Causes of War
       B. The Costs and Causes of Militarism
       C. Nuclear Weapons
       E. Information Warfare
       E. The Pursuit of Peace
VII.   Looking Ahead: Politics in the Twenty-First Century
VIII. Summary
IX.   Key Concepts
X.   Critical-Thinking Questions
XI.   Suggested Readings

PART II: LEARNING OBJECTIVES

1.   To explain the difference between power and authority.
2.   To distinguish among the three types of authority: traditional, rational-legal, and charismatic.
3.   To describe the concepts of political state and nation state.
4.   To compare and contrast the four principal kinds of political systems.
5.   To describe the relationship between individualism and government in U.S. society.
6.   To identify what a political party is and the functions political parties serve in U.S. society.
7.   To distinguish between economic issues and social issues and their relationship to the political spectrum in U.S. society.
8.   To identify the composition and agenda of special-interest groups in U.S. society.
9.   To describe the ways in which people participate in the political system focusing on political socialization and voting patterns.
10. To compare and contrast the pluralist model of political power and the power-elite model of political power.
11. To describe the types of political power that exceed, or seek to eradicate, established politics.
12. To identify the factors that are involved in creating conditions that increase the likelihood of war.
13. To recognize the historical pattern of militarism in the U.S., and around the world.
14. To begin to understand the significance the impact of the Information Revolution on warfare.
15. To identify factors that can be used in the pursuit of peace.
16. To develop a sense about how politics around the world will change over the next century.

PART III: CHAPTER REVIEW

This chapter begins with an account of some events involving the bombing of the federal building in Oklahoma City in 1995. This savage attack was not perpetrated by some international terrorist group, rather it is a homegrown phenomenon.

The dynamics of power in and between societies is the focus of this chapter. *Politics* is the social institution that distributes, sets a society's agenda, and makes decisions.

POWER AND AUTHORITY

Max Weber defined **power** as *the ability to achieve desired ends despite resistance from others*. The most basic form is sheer force, physical or psychological coercion. History demonstrates that this type of power is difficult to maintain. **Authority** is defined by Max Weber as *power that people perceive as legitimate rather than coercive*.

The social context will determine to a large degree how power is perceived. Also, to be accepted it must be consistent with cultural norms. Authority demands obedience to norms from those who command as well as those who obey. Weber identified three general contexts in which power is commonly defined as authority.

Traditional Authority

Traditional authority is defined as *power legitimated through respect for long-established cultural patterns*. This type of power is very common in preindustrialized societies. It has a sacred character. The power of ancient Chinese emperors and nobility in medieval Europe are examples. As societies industrialize traditional authority declines, yet forms still exist in modern societies. Patriarchy and parental dominance over children are examples.

Rational-Legal Authority

Rational-legal, or bureaucratic authority, is *power legitimated by legally enacted rules and regulations*. Bureaucratic authority stresses achievement over ascribed characteristics, and underlies most authority in the United States today. This type of authority is closely linked to **government**, or *formal organizations that direct the political life of a society*.

Charismatic Authority

Charismatic authority is *power legitimated through extraordinary personal abilities that inspire devotion and obedience*. This type of power doesn't rest on a person's position or office. It is frequently used to move people away from the customary and established order in society. Examples of charismatic leaders from around the world throughout history are discussed. Societies have typically directed charismatic women to domains of life other than politics, while certainly a few exceptions exist.

Charismatic movements are very dependent on their leader. The long-term persistence of such a movement requires **routinization of charisma**, *the transformation of charismatic authority into some combination of traditional and bureaucratic authority*. Christianity is an example of this process.

POLITICS IN GLOBAL PERSPECTIVE

In hunting and gathering societies, leaders typically emerge as a result of having some unusual amount of strength, hunting skill or charisma. These leaders exercise only modest power over others, and while having special prestige, they do not have more wealth. In agrarian societies traditional authority develops. As political organization grows it leads to the formation of a *political state*, a formal government claiming the legitimate use of coercion to support its rule. The advance of technology significantly increases the power of the political state.

During the last several centuries political organizations have evolved toward nation-states. At the present time approximately 190 *nation-states* are recognized around the globe. Generally, four types of political systems which manage the affairs of contemporary nation-states are reviewed.

Monarchy

A **monarchy** is *a type of political system in which a single family rules from generation to generation*. It is legitimized primarily through tradition. Absolute monarchies dominated from England to China, and remained widespread until early in the 20th century. Historical examples are discussed.

Democracy

Democracy refers to *a political system in which power is exercised by the people as a whole*. In large societies it is not possible for everyone to directly be involved in politics. Therefore, a *representative democracy*, which places authority in the hands of elected officials who are accountable to the people develops. This type of system is most common in the relatively rich industrial societies of the world. They are characterized by rational-legal patterns of authority and function as bureaucracies. The United States, for example, has three million people working for the federal government (excluding the military). Fifteen million more people work for local governments across the country.

Democracy and Freedom: Contrasting Approaches

While the East and the West have had different political systems for most of this century, both claim to provide freedom for their people. In the capitalist West, political freedom means *personal liberty*, or personal freedom to pursue whatever they perceive as their self-interest. In the socialist nations of the old Soviet bloc, freedom was understood as "freedom from basic want." *Figure 16-1* (p. 434) and *Global Map 16-1* in the **Window on the World** box (p. 433) take a look at political freedom in global perspective. Evidence presented suggests that 40 percent of the world's population can be classified as "politically free."

Authoritarianism

Authoritarianism refers to *a political system that denies popular participation in government*. While to some degree this is true for all political systems, as used here, authoritarianism characterizes political systems that are indifferent to people's lives. Contemporary examples include the absolute monarchies in Saudi Arabia and Kuwait.

The **Global Sociology** box (p. 435) takes a look at an example of "soft authoritarianism," which exists today in the Asian nation of Singapore. Officials there view their system as one of "planned prosperity."

Totalitarianism

A more severe political control characterizes *totalitarianism*, or *a political system that extensively regulates peoples lives*. Such systems have emerged only within this century as technological means have enabled such leaders to rigidly regulate citizen's lives. Such systems bridge the political continuum from the far right, like Nazi Germany, to the far left, like the People's Republic of China. Socialism, an economic system, is not to be confused with totalitarianism, a political system.

POLITICS IN THE UNITED STATES

As a democracy, the U.S. system is distinctive given certain historical events, economic forces, and cultural traits.

U.S. Culture and the Growth of Government

These factors are forged in a complimentary fashion in U.S. society. Our tradition of valuing individualism is guaranteed in the Bill of Rights, and the self-reliance and competition that emerges supports our capitalist economy. While we in the U.S. do not like "too much" government, almost everyone thinks that government is necessary. The increasing size of the government in the U.S. (20 million workers), and the growing budget (1.5 trillion dollars in 1995) are discussed. *Figure 16-2* (p. 437) reviews data from several high-income societies concerning the size of government and tax revenues (as a share of their respective GDP).

The Political Spectrum

The *political spectrum* ranges from the extreme liberals on the left to the extreme conservatives on the right. Historically the Republican Party has been more conservative and the Democratic Party more liberal. However, within each Party there are both conservative and liberal wings.

Attitudes differ on two kinds of issues, *economic* and *social*. Public opinion on these is discussed. *Table 16-1* (p. 438) presents data from a national survey taken in 1994 on political attitudes. Many people in the U.S. consider themselves "moderates."

Economic Issues

The great depression caused Americans to see the reality of the economic insecurity of most of our population. The New Deal programs created by Roosevelt during the 1930s greatly expanded the role of government in economic matters in our society. Today, Democrats tend to support more extensive government involvement in the economy than the Republicans would support.

Social Issues

Social issues span many topics. The Democratic Party is more socially liberal than the Republican Party. Both parties, however, favor government action when it advances their aims. Examples of the death penalty, crime, abortion, and affirmative action are discussed.

Mixed Positions

Political attitudes vary by race, with African Americans being more liberal. Ethnicity does not seem to be an important factor today in affecting political attitudes. Social class is also identified as a factor related to political attitudes. For example, people who identify themselves as in the working class or lower-middle class tend to take liberal stances on economic issues and more conservative stances on social issues. This pattern is reversed for the affluent of our society.

Party Identification

Political party identification in the U.S. is relatively weak compared to European democracies. *Table 16-2* (p. 439) reviews the political party identification of U.S. adults. About 47 percent of the people identify themselves as Democrats and about 38 percent identify themselves as Republicans. In the **Seeing Ourselves** box (p. 440), *National Map 16-1* takes a look at voter turnout across the United States for the 1992 presidential election.

Special-Interest Groups

A *special-interest group* refers to *a political alliance of people interested in some economic or social issue.* Most voluntary associations would be examples. Many such groups employ lobbyists who represent their concerns to the government. Labor unions, the National Rifle Association, and the Sierra Club are examples.

Political action committees (PACs) are *organizations formed by special-interest groups, independent of political parties, to pursue political aims by raising and spending money.* They are often very controversial. Examples are discussed.

Voter Apathy

Despite socialization influences, formal and informal, many people in the U.S. express

252

indifference concerning politics. Voter apathy has recently been found to be worse in the United States than in 23 other industrialized democracies. The likelihood of voting increases with age and varies by race, ethnicity, and sex. While voter *eligibility* has been increasing over the years, the share of eligible citizens who *actually vote* has been dropping.

There are many causes for this apathy. Registration rules, physical disabilities, and illiteracy are all important factors. Being satisfied with social conditions as they are can also reduce voter participation.

THEORETICAL ANALYSIS OF POWER IN SOCIETY

The Pluralist Model

This approach is linked to the structural-functional paradigm. The *pluralist model* is *an analysis of politics that views power as dispersed among many competing interest groups.* Pluralists see politics as an arena of negotiation. Organizations operate as *veto groups.* Power, pluralists claim, has many dimensions as well, including wealth, prestige, charisma, etc.

Research Results

Research on the power structure operating in New Haven, Connecticut by Nelson Polsby during the 1950s supports this view. Research during the 1960s by Robert Dahl came produced similar conclusions.

The Power-Elite Model

The *power-elite model* is *an analysis of politics that views power as concentrated among the rich* an analysis of politics that views power as concentrated among the rich. The term power-elite was introduced by C. Wright Mills in 1956. He perceived U.S. society, its economy, government, and military, as being dominated by a coalition of families.

Research Results

Research by Robert and Helen Lynd suggests that this was true in a typical U.S. city they studied (Muncie, Indiana), which in their study was referred to as Middletown. Another study by Floyd Hunter in Atlanta, Georgia provided further support for this model.

How these models help us answer certain questions concerning the distribution and operation of power in U.S. society is reviewed in *Table 16-3* (p. 442).

POWER BEYOND THE RULES

Revolution

Political revolution is *the overthrow of one political system in order to establish another.*

253

While reform involves change within a system, revolution means change of the system itself. No political system is immune to revolution. Historical examples are identified to illustrate. Several general patterns characterize revolutions. These include: *Rising expectations, unresponsive government, radical leadership by intellectuals,* and *establishing a new legitimacy.*

Terrorism

Terrorism, or *violence or the threat of violence employed by an individual or a group as a political strategy,* has characterized the last two decades. Three insights are offered about terrorism. First, it elevates violence to a legitimate political tactic. Second, it is especially compatible with totalitarian governments as a means of sustaining widespread fear and intimidation. Third, extensive civil liberties make democratic societies vulnerable to terrorism. While many societies are targets, one-fourth of all acts of terrorism worldwide are directed against the U.S. What response should be made is difficult to decide upon. Exactly who is responsible is often difficult to determine.

An additional form of terrorism is **state terrorism**, or *the use of violence, generally without support of law, against individuals or groups by a government or its agents.* This type of terrorism has a long history. Examples are discussed.

WAR AND PEACE

War is defined as *armed conflict among the people of various societies, directed by their governments.* **Peace** is *a state of international relations devoid of violence. Figure 16-4* (p. 445) records the number of Americans killed in ten major wars from the American Revolution to date.

The Causes of War

War, according to research, is not the result of some natural human aggressive tendency. It is a product of society. The following factors are identified by Quincy Wright as ones promoting war: *Perceived threats, social problems, political objectives, moral objectives,* and *the absence of alternatives.* Each of this is discussed.

The Costs and Causes of Militarism

The cost of militarism runs far greater than actual war. To fund it, governments must divert resources away from social needs. Eighteen percent of our federal budget goes to fund our military. The *arms race,* a mutually reinforcing escalation of military might has developed. Globally, some 5 trillion dollars are spend annually for military purposes.

Certain analysts believe that the U.S. is dominated by a **military-industrial complex**, or a system involving the *close association among the federal government, the military, and defense industries.* Our economy is seen then as dependent on military spending.

Nuclear Weapons

The destructive capability of the 50,000 nuclear weapons in existence today is discussed. *Nuclear proliferation* refers to *the acquisition of nuclear-weapons technology by more and more nations*. The current list of nations possessing nuclear capability are identified, as well as those who are close to having such capability. The extent to which nuclear weapons capabilities have advanced since the end of World War II cannot be stressed to much.

Information Warfare

The impact of the Information Revolution on warfare is discussed focusing on military strategists term *virtual wars*.

The Pursuit of Peace

Several recent approaches have been used as means to reduce the danger nuclear war. These include: *Deterrence, high technology defense, diplomacy and disarmament,* and *resolving underlying conflict.* The first three of these have serious limitations. The *mutually assured destruction* logic of the arms race (MAD), the *strategic defense initiative* (SDI), and concession making are examples identified.

LOOKING AHEAD: POLITICS IN THE TWENTY-FIRST CENTURY

Several dilemmas and trends are identified to pay attention to over the next decades. Voter turnout is increasing in the short-term. Hopefully this will widen the range of issues included in national policy debate. There is also an expansion of the global political process, especially given the communications technology available now. Further, a global reformulation of political thinking is occurring; the case of state capitalism is an example. And finally, the danger of war remains great as nuclear technology escalates. Humanity must further develop a sense of political justice. The **Controversy and Debate** box (p. 450) focuses in part on the first dilemma or trend as it reviews issues regarding the new information technology's impact on public involvement in politics, and the greater power such technology gives government.

PART IV: KEY CONCEPTS

Define each of the following concepts in the space provided or on separate paper. Check the accuracy of your answers by referring to the key concepts section at the end of the chapter in the text as well as by referring to italicized definitions located throughout the chapter.

arms race
authoritarianism
authority

charismatic authority
democracy
government
military-industrial complex
monarchy
nuclear proliferation
peace
pluralist model
political action committee
political parties
political revolution
political state
politics
power
power-elite model
rational-legal authority
routinization of charisma
special-interest group
state terrorism
strategic defence initiative
terrorism
totalitarianism
traditional authority
voter apathy
war

PART V: STUDY QUESTIONS

True-False

1.	T	F	*Authority* is power widely perceived as legitimate rather than coercive.
2.	T	F	In hunting and gathering societies leaders tend to enjoy special prestige and have more wealth, and far more power than everyone else.
3.	T	F	*Monarchies* are more widespread today than they were at the turn of the 20th century.
4.	T	F	Per capita spending by the federal government has actually been *decreasing* since the late 18th century.
5.	T	F	More U.S. adults consider themselves *liberal* rather than *conservative*.
6.	T	F	Most *working-class* adults in the U.S. identify themselves *economically* conservative and *socially* liberal.
7.	T	F	Most adults in the U.S. claim identification with the *Republican Party*.
8.	T	F	*Political action committees* are organizations formed by special-interest groups, independent of political parties, to pursue political aims.

9. T F While *voter apathy* has been a problem in recent years in the United States, still, a greater percentage of U.S. adults vote than in virtually any other industrial democracy.

10. T F Research by Robert and Helen Lynd in Muncie, Indiana (the Middletown study) supported the *power-elite model* concerning how power is distributed in the United states.

11. T F More American soldiers lost their lives in the Civil War than in World War I and World War II combined.

Multiple-Choice

1. Who defined *power* as the ability to achieve desired ends despite resistance from others?

   (a) C. Wright Mills   (c) Max Weber
   (b) Alexis de Tocqueville   (d) Robert Lynd

2. Which of the following is *not* one of the general contexts in which power is commonly defined as authority?

   (a) traditional   (c) charismatic
   (b) rational-legal   (d) democratic

3. Power that is legitimated by respect for long-established cultural patterns is called:

   (a) traditional   (d) sacred
   (b) political   (e) charismatic
   (c) power-elite

4. The survival of a *charismatic movement* depends upon _____, according to Max Weber.

   (a) pluralism   (c) routinization
   (b) political action   (d) pluralism

5. According to the research cited in the text, the *majority* of U.S. adults:

   (a) hold mixed (or moderate) political views
   (b) are liberal on both economic and social issues
   (c) are conservative on both economic and social issues
   (d) are conservative on social issues and liberal on economic issues

6. With which general sociological paradigm is the *pluralist* associated?

   (a) exchange
   (b) social conflict
   (c) symbolic-interaction
   (d) structural-functional

7. Which idea below represents the *pluralist model* of power?

   (a) power is highly concentrated
   (b) voting cannot create significant political changes
   (c) the U.S. power system is an oligarchy
   (d) wealth, social prestige, and political office are rarely combined

8. In which *stage of a revolution* does the danger of counter-revolution occur?

   (a) rising expectations
   (b) nonresponsiveness of the old government
   (c) establishing a new legitimacy
   (d) radical leadership by intellectuals

9. Quincy Wright has identified which of the following circumstances as conditions which lead humans to go to *war*?

   (a) perceived threats
   (b) social problems
   (c) moral objectives
   (d) political objectives
   (e) all are identified

10. Which of the following was *not* identified in the text as a means of reducing the danger of nuclear war?

   (a) deterrence
   (b) high-tech defense
   (c) diplomacy and disarmament
   (d) resolving underlying conflict
   (e) all were identified as ways of reducing the danger of nuclear war

Fill-In

1. _____ is the social institution that distributes power, sets a society's agenda, and makes decisions.

2. Power widely perceived as *legitimate* rather than coercive is referred to as _____.

3. _____ *authority* is power legitimated through extraordinary personal abilities that inspire devotion and obedience.

258

4. While *democracies* have focused on the concept of _____ freedom, *socialist systems* have focused on freedom from basic _____.

5. _____ percent of the world's people are *politically free*.

6. _____ refers to a political system that extensively regulates people's lives.

7. _____ percent of U.S. adults identify themselves as *Republicans*.

8. Many *special-interest groups* employ _____ who earn their living by representing the concerns of one group or another to political officials.

9. _____ are organizations formed by special-interest groups, independent of political parties, to pursue political aims by raising and spending money.

10. The _____ *model*, closely allied with the social-conflict paradigm, is an analysis of politics that views power as concentrated among the rich.

11. *Defense* is the largest single expenditure of the U.S. federal government, accounting for _____ percent of all federal spending.

12. The _____ - _____ _____ is the close association among the federal government, the military, and defense industry.

13. _____ _____ refers to the acquisition of nuclear-weapons technology by more and more nations.

14. How can the world reduce the dangers of war? Four recent approaches mentioned in the text include: _____, _____-_____ defense, _____ and _____, and resolving _____ _____.

Definition and Short-Answer

1. Differentiate between the concepts of *power* and *authority*.

2. Differentiate among Max Weber's three *types* of authority.

3. Four types of *political systems* are reviewed in the text. Identify and describe these systems.

4. It is pointed out in the text that political views of U.S. differ on two kinds of issues. What are these issues? What are the general patterns of the attitudes of people in the U.S. on these issues?

5. What is *voter apathy*? What are its causes? To what extent is voter apathy a problem in the U.S. as compared to other industrialized democracies?

6. Differentiate between the *pluralist* and *power-elite* models concerning the distribution of power in the United States. Review research findings reported in the text concerning these two approaches to understanding the distribution of power in our society.

7. What are the five *general patterns* identified in the text concerning *revolutions*?

8. What are the five *factors* identified in the text as *promoting war*? Provide an illustration for three of these.

9. Several *approaches* for reducing the chances for nuclear war are addressed in the text. What are these approaches?

10. What are the four important *dilemmas* or *trends* that seem likely to command widespread attention as we approach the next century?
11. What is *information warfare*? What impact do you think the Information Revolution is going to have on war?
12. Review the data presented in the section on *the costs and causes of militarism*. What conclusions do you draw from this information?

PART VI: ANSWERS TO STUDY QUESTIONS

True-False

1.	T	(p. 429)	7.	F	(p. 439)
2.	F	(p. 431)	8.	T	(p. 439)
3.	F	(p. 432)	9.	F	(p. 440)
4.	F	(p. 437)	10.	T	(p. 442)
5.	F	(p. 438)	11.	T	(p. 445)
6.	F	(p. 438)			

Multiple-Choice

1.	c	(p. 429)	6.	d	(p. 441)
2.	d	(pp. 429-30)	7.	d	(p. 441)
3.	a	(p. 429)	8.	c	(p. 444)
4.	c	(p. 430)	9.	e	(p. 447)
5.	a	(pp. 438-39)	10.	e	(p. 449)

Fill-In

1. politics (p. 429)
2. authority (p. 429)
3. charismatic (p. 435)
4. personal, want (p. 432)
5. 20 (p. 433)
6. totalitarianism (p. 434)
7. 37.5 (p. 439)
8. lobbyists (p. 439)
9. political action committees (p. 439)
10. power-elite (p. 442)
11. 18 (p. 448)
12. military-industrial complex (p. 448)
13. nuclear proliferation (p. 449)
14. deterrence, high-technology, diplomacy, disarmament, underlying conflict (p. 449)

VII: ANALYSIS AND COMMENT

Global Sociology

"Soft Authoritarianism or Planned Prosperity? A Report From Singapore"

Key Points: Questions:

"Violence Beyond the Rules: A Report From Yugoslavia"

Key Points: Questions:

Controversy and Debate

"Here Comes "On-line" democracy"

Key Points: Questions:

Window on the World

"Global Map 16-1 Political Freedom in Global Perspective"

Key Points: Questions:

Seeing Ourselves

"National Map 16-1 Voter Turnout Across the United States"

Key Points: Questions:

Family

17

PART I: CHAPTER OUTLINE

I.   The Family: Basic Concepts
II.   The Family: Global Variety
      A. Marriage Patterns
      B. Residential Patterns
      C. Patterns of Descent
      D. Patterns of Authority
III.   Theoretical Analysis of the Family
      A. Functions of the Family: Structural-Functional Analysis
      B. Inequality and the Family: Social Conflict Analysis
      C. Micro-Level Analysis
           1. Symbolic-Interaction Analysis
           2. Social-Exchange Analysis
IV.   Stages of Family Life
      A. Courtship
      B. Settling In: Ideal and Real Marriages
      C. Child Rearing
      D. The Family in Later Life
V.   U.S. Families: Class, Race, and Gender
      A. Social Class
      B. Ethnicity and Race
           1. Latino Families
           2. African-American Families
           3. Mixed Marriages
      C. Gender

VI.   Transition and Problems in Family Life
       A. Divorce
              1. Who Divorces?
              2. Divorce as Process
       B. Remarriage
       C. Family Violence
              1. Violence Against Women
              2. Violence Against Children
VII.   Alternative Family Forms
       A. One-Parent Families
       B. Cohabitation
       C. Gay and Lesbian Couples
       D. Singlehood
VIII. New Reproductive Technology and the Family
       A. In Vitro Fertilization
       B. Ethical Issues
IX.   Looking Ahead: Family in the Twenty-First Century

PART II: LEARNING OBJECTIVES

1.   To define the basic concepts of kinship, family, family of orientation, family of procreation, and marriage.
2.   To cross-culturally compare and contrast marriage patterns, residential patterns, patterns of descent, and patterns of authority.
3.   To describe the four functions of the family from the structural-functional perspective.
4.   To explain the link between family and social inequality using the social-conflict perspective.
5.   To identify the contributions that symbolic-interaction analysis and social-exchange analysis have made to the sociological knowledge of the family.
6.   To describe the life course of the "typical" U.S. family.
7.   To explain the impact of social class, race, ethnicity, and gender socialization on the family.
8.   To describe the problems and transitions that seriously affect family life: divorce, remarriage, spousal and child abuse.
9.   To describe the composition and prevalence of alternative family forms: one-parent families, cohabitation, gay and lesbian couples, and singlehood.
10. To explain the impact, both technologically and ethically, of new reproductive techniques on the family.
11. To develop a sense about the important social forces likely to impact upon the family over the next several decades.
12. To identify four sociological conclusions about the family as we enter the twenty-first century.

PART III: CHAPTER REVIEW

The controversial story of the legal case involving Gregory, a twelve year-old boy who was granted a divorce from his biological mother by a Florida court, opens this chapter. This is only one of many issues that confront our traditional notion of the family.

THE FAMILY: BASIC CONCEPTS

The *family* is *a social institution that unites individuals into cooperative groups that oversee the bearing and raising of children*. *Kinship* refers to *a social bond, based on blood, marriage, or adoption, that joins individuals into families*. The functional significance of this institution tends to decline with industrialization. A *family unit* is *a social group of two or more people, related by blood, marriage, or adoption, who usually live together*. Two different types of families are differentiated. A *family of orientation* is the family into which a person is born and receives early socialization, while a *family of procreation* is a family within which people have or adopt children of their own. In most societies, families begin with *marriage*, or a legally sanctioned relationship, involving economic cooperation as well as normative sexual activity and child bearing, that people expect to be enduring. The significance of marriage for child bearing is evident in the labels *illegitimacy* and *matrimony*. Controversy exists today in terms of how the family, both structurally and functionally, is to be understood, and how it is to be defined officially. For instance, *families of affinity*, or people with or without legal or blood ties who feel they belong together and want to define themselves as a family, are becoming more common.

THE FAMILY: GLOBAL VARIETY

While all societies recognize families there are great cross-cultural variations in the structures and functions of this institution. In preindustrial societies the *extended family*, *a family unit including parents and children, but also other kin*, is common. This type is also known as the *consanguine family*, meaning based on blood ties. Industrial societies recognize the *nuclear family*, *a family unit composed of one or two parents and their children*. This is sometimes referred to as the *conjugal family*.

What does the future hold for the family? The **Global Sociology** box (pp. 458-59) looks at Sweden, a very progressive society, and addresses the issue of how strong their family is today.

Marriage Patterns

Norms identify categories of people suitable for marriage for particular individuals. *Endogamy*, refers to a pattern of marriage between people of the same social category. It is differentiated from the norm of *exogamy*, or marriage between people of different social categories. All societies enforce varying degrees of each type. *Monogamy* refers to a form of marriage involving two partners. *Serial monogamy* refers to a number of monogamous marriages over one's lifetime. *Polygamy* is *a type of marriage uniting three or more people*. It takes one of two forms. One type is called *polygyny*, by far the most common, referring to *a type of marriage uniting one male and two or more females*. The second type is called *polyandry*, or *a type of marriage joining one female with two or more males*. The **Window on the World** box (p. 457) looks at marital forms in global perspective. While monogamy is the rule in the Americas and in Europe, polygamy is very common in many preindustrialized societies in Africa and Southern Asia.

Residential Patterns

Where people live after they are married also varies cross-culturally. *Neolocality, a residential pattern by which a married couple lives apart from the parents of both spouses*, is the most common form in industrial societies. In preindustrial societies residing with one set of parents is more typical. *Patrilocality* is *a residential pattern by which a married couple lives with or near the husband's family*. *Matrilocality* is *a residential pattern by which couples live with or near the wife's family*. This latter pattern is rare.

Patterns of Descent

Descent refers to *the system by which members of a society trace kinship over generations*. Industrial societies follow the **bilateral descent** system of *tracing kinship through both men and women*. Preindustrial societies typically follow one of two patterns of unilineal descent. The more common, *patrilineal descent,* is *a system of tracing kinship through males*. *Matrilineal descent* refers to *a system of tracing kinship through females*. Patrilineal systems are typically pastoral or agrarian societies, while matrilineal systems are common in horticultural societies.

Patterns of Authority

The universal presence of patriarchy is reflected in the predominance of polygyny, patrilocality, and patrilineal descent. No known society is clearly matriarchal.

THEORETICAL ANALYSIS OF THE FAMILY

Functions of the Family: Structural-Functional Analysis

The structural-functionalists focus on several important social functions served by the family. These include: (1) *Socialization*--The family serves as the primary agent in the socialization process during the entire life course of a person. (2) *Regulation of sexual activity*--Restrictions on sexual behavior is characteristic of every culture. Every society has some type of *incest taboo, a cultural norm forbidding sexual relations or marriages between certain kin*. However, the specific kinship members who are subject to the taboo varies greatly around the globe. The significance of the incest taboo is most basically social rather than biological. It minimizes sexual competition, creates alliances between families through exogamous marriages, and establishes specific linkages of rights and obligations between

266

people. (3) *Social placement*--Many ascribed statuses are determined at birth through the family. Transmission of social standing through the family is universal. And (4) *Material and emotional security*--Families are to provide for the physical and financial support of its members. Self- worth and security are established within the intense and enduring relationships characteristic of the family.

Structural-functionalists tend to underemphasize problems in families, and underestimate the great diversity of family forms.

Inequality and the Family: Social-Conflict Analysis

The focus of the social-conflict approach to the study of the family is how this institution perpetuates patterns of social inequality. Such analysis tends to focus on: (1) *Property and inheritance*--Social class divisions are preserved by the inheritance of wealth. Racial and ethnic inequalities are maintained through endogamy. (2) *Patriarchy*-- Patriarchal values and patterns have established and maintained the subordinate status of women. The fact that women still bear most of the responsibility for childrearing, even given their increased participation in the paid labor force is a critical issue. And, (3) *race and ethnicity*-- Endogamy is seen as shoring up the racial and ethnic hierarchy of a society.

A criticism of this view is that all societies, not just industrialized capitalist societies, have family problems.

Micro-Level Analysis

The structural-functional and social-conflict paradigms provide a macro-level perspective from which to understand the institution of the family.

Symbolic-Interaction Analysis

Symbolic-interaction analysis is used to study how specific realities are constructed within specific families. Varying experiences and perceptions of different family members are stressed.

Social-Exchange Analysis

Social-exchange theory draws attention to the power of negotiation within families. People are seen as exchanging socially valued resources with each other. As gender roles are converging, so is what males and females have to exchange.

While providing a meaningful counterbalance to the macro-level approaches, the micro-level is limited in its ability to allow us to see the cultural forces impacting upon the family.

STAGES OF FAMILY LIFE

Family life is viewed as dynamic, consisting of changing patterns over the life cycle.

Courtship

Preindustrial societies typically are characterized by *arranged marriages* where the kinship group determines marriage partners. Marriages are viewed as alliances between different kinship groups for economic and political purposes. *Personal* compatibility is not the important factor, but what is involves *cultural* compatibility.

In industrial societies personal choice in mate selection dominates, with tremendous emphasis on *romantic love*. This is particularly true in the U.S. Romantic love is a less stable foundation for marriage than are social and economic considerations. *Figure 17-1* (p. 463) shows a comparative look at the importance of romantic love in different countries. Economic patterns in society affect the average age at first marriage. **Homogamy**, or *marriage between people with the same social characteristics*, is very common.

Settling In: Ideal and Real Marriages

The institutions of marriage and family tend to be idealized by most people, with real life experiences never quite meeting expectations. The realities of marriage and its responsibilities and routines are often very different from courtship relationships. Changing patterns of sexual experiences and norms have affected courtship and marriage as well. *Table 17-1* (p. 470) presents data on the frequency of sexual activity among married couples. Research on extramarital sex suggests that this phenomenon is a reality in a fairly significant percentage of marriages.

Child Rearing

Child rearing creates major transitions for families. Child rearing presents significant changes for family relationships, some very problematic for marriage. *Table 17-2* (p. 465) presents statistics concerning U.S. adults' ideas about the ideal number of children for a family. Most people desire two or three children. Several factors have brought about a decline in the birth rate in the U.S. Children are no longer economic assets for families as they were in the past. Birth control technology has also affected birth rates. Further, with most women over the age of fifteen in the labor force (58.8 percent in 1994), this creates difficulties in having larger families.

As vital as parenthood is, we do very little officially to prepare people for its responsibilities. With most women in the labor force and also having to maintain their traditional domestic responsibilities, many other challenges and problems have been created. For instance, there are many *latchkey kids*--children of working parents who are left to care for themselves for portions of the day. The dilemma facing working parents is highlighted in the **Critical Thinking** box (p. 466), which discusses the importance of child care facilities.

The Family in Later Life

With life expectancy increasing, the number of years a couple live together without children during what is known as the "empty-nest" years is increasing. Many new challenges are faced by couples during these years. The departure of children and the maintenance of relationships with them, the increased value of companionship in marriage, retirement, and death of one's spouse are major events in later life.

U.S. FAMILIES: CLASS, RACE, AND GENDER

Social Class

Social class has a major impact on the family, including determining a family's standard of living, economic security, and likelihood of unemployment. Further, research by Lillian Rubin suggests that differences in the lifestyles of working-class and middle-class families affect relationships within a family and typical concerns of its members. Research also illustrates how social class also affects the relationship of spouses, with middle-class couples being more open and expressive with each other. Differences in socialization patterns are also discussed.

Ethnicity and Race

Latino Families

The traditional extended family system remains strong among this segment of our population. Conventional gender role patterns are also maintained. *Machismo*, masculine strength, daring, and sexual prowess, along with the resulting double-standard are also strong. Assimilation is gradually changing traditional patterns.

African-American Families

A critical fact concerning this segment of our population is the reality of their economic disadvantage. African-American families earn only 60 percent of the average for all U.S. families. Given these conditions maintaining family stability is very difficult.

The Moynihan Report of 1965 generated a controversy of opinion over the extent to which African-Americans were responsible for their high poverty rates. Moynihan emphasized the "pathological" black family as a cause of a cycle of poverty. Critics of this view, such as William Ryan, argue instead that African-Americans suffer economic disadvantages. Ryan sees the unstable family structure as a consequence, not a cause of poverty.

Figure 17-2 (p. 468) shows the differences in family structure between whites, African-Americans, Asians, and Hispanics.

Mixed Marriages

During the course of this century, ethnicity has meant less to white people in terms of marital partners. Race remains a more formidable consideration. While African Americans,

Asians, and Native Americans represent 16 percent of the U.S. population, the proportion of "mixed" marriages is less than 4 percent.

Gender

Cultural views regarding gender in U.S. society significantly affect the family. Jesse Bernard suggests every marriage is actually *two* different ones, "his" and "hers." Cultural values tend to promote the idea that marriage is more beneficial for women than for men. Marriage apparently provides many advantages for men.

Research has identified four different types of marriages related to different levels of depression in men and women. These include: (1) the *conventional* marriage in which the husband is the sole breadwinner and the wife is responsible for all housekeeping and childrearing, (2) a marriage where both spouses are in the labor force, the wife out of economic necessity, or a *strained conventional*, where once again the wife is responsible for all household chores and childrearing, (3) a marriage similar to (2), however, here the wife works for the psychological benefits of employment, or a *strained egalitarian* marriage and (4) an *egalitarian* marriage where both are happy to be working outside the home and both share household and childrearing responsibilities. *Figure 17-3* (p. 470) show how depression levels vary for women and men by type of marriage.

TRANSITION AND PROBLEMS IN FAMILY LIFE

Divorce

The divorce rate in the U.S. during this century has fluctuated dramatically with changing conditions in society. *Figure 17-4* (p. 471) illustrates these patterns. The U.S. has one of the highest marriage rates in the world. However, while the marriage rate has remained stable over the century, the divorce rate has risen significantly. A number of broad societal changes have influenced the increase on divorce rates. These factors include: *Individualism is on the rise, romantic love often subsides, women are now less dependent on men, many of today's marriages are stressful, divorce is more socially acceptable,* and *divorce is legally easier to accomplish.*

Over the last decade the divorce rate has eased downward. Two reasons for this trend are identified: (1) the large baby boom cohort is now reaching middle age, and (2) hard economic times discourage people from living alone.

Who Divorces?

Divorce is more common among young couples (especially teen and young marriages resulting from an unexpected pregnancy), the lower classes, couples with alcohol problems, couples with dissimilar social backgrounds, the geographically mobile, and in marriages in which women have successful careers. Further, people who have divorced once are more likely to divorce again than people in their first marriages. In the **Seeing Ourselves** box (p. 472), *National Map 17-1* indicates that 11 percent of the U.S. population over the age of fifteen are divorced or separated. Residence patterns of these people are illustrated.

Divorce as Process

Paul Bohannan has suggested divorce involves different adjustments for men and women, including *emotional, legal, psychic reorganization, community reorganization, economic reorganization,* and *parental reorganization.* Effects on children are also discussed. *Figure 17-5* (p. 473) shows data concerning payment of child support following divorce. Only about one-half of the children who are entitled to court-ordered support receive full payment.

Remarriage

About 80 percent of people who divorce in the U.S. remarry. Remarriage rates are higher for men than for women. The chances of the remarriage being successful are less than first marriages. Ann Goetting links the same transitions to remarriage as Bohannan does to divorce (emotional, legal, etc.).

Remarriage often creates a *blended family* consisting of a biological parent and stepparent, along with children of their respective first marriages and any children of the blended marriage. This provides a context in which stress and conflict are often greater than in other families.

Family Violence

Many families are characterized by **family violence**, or *emotional, physical, or sexual abuse of one family member by another.* The family has been characterized as one of the most violent institutions in our society.

Violence Against Women

Violence transcends the boundaries of social class. Common stereotypes of abusers are brought into question using empirical data. Low reporting rates of family violence deflates the statistics. One-sixth of all couples have relationships characterized by at least some violence each year. The argument is made that the seriousness of abuse is greater for wives than for husbands.

Marital rape is a form of family violence that has gotten much attention in recent years in the mass media. The historical factor of wives as property has negatively influenced our understanding of this problem.

Traditionally, women have had few options and the violent marriage acts as a trap for many women. The traditional view of domestic violence as a private concern of families has also hindered programs and policies in terms of their effectiveness in dealing with this problem.

Violence Against Children

About three million children are victims of abuse each year, though this is only a rough estimate. Abuse is argued to be both physical and emotional. These children often feel guilt, self-blame, and psychological problems as a result of the abuse. Most abusers are men. Their abusive behaviors are often learned during their own childhoods.

ALTERNATIVE FAMILY FORMS

One-Parent Families

Over the last twenty years there has been a dramatic increase in the percentage of single-parent families. Twenty-six percent of U.S. families with children have only one parent in the household. Twenty-eight percent of children live with only one parent. Women head 88 percent of the single-parent households in the U.S. Distributions for whites, African-Americans, and Hispanic Americans are discussed. Single-parent families are not by themselves detrimental to children's development; however, economic hardships often occur in female-headed, single-parent families. *Figure 17-6* (p. 475) compares the U.S. with Japan and several western European societies in terms of percentage of births to unmarried mothers. Currently, over 30 percent of children born in the U.S. are born to an unmarried woman.

Cohabitation

Cohabitation is *the sharing of household by an unmarried couple.* There has been a five-fold increase in cohabitation over the last twenty years. This particular household structure is very common among college students. Most cohabiting couples do not marry, and only a small percentage have children. Commitment tends not to be as strong as in marriage.

Gay and Lesbian Couples

In 1989 Denmark became the first country to legalize homosexual marriages. However, even there, legal adoption is still not allowed for such couples. A few legal benefits of marriage for gays exist in some metropolitan areas in the U.S. Many gay couples form long-term relationships. Some of these couples are raising children. Their interpersonal relationships parallel heterosexual relationships in terms of communication, finances, and domestic division of labor. Many feel they must keep their relationships a secret to avoid prejudice and discrimination. This situation can place considerable strain on relationships.

Singlehood

Singlehood is rapidly increasing in the U.S. About one in four households contains a single adult. Singlehood is still primarily a transitory stage, although financially independent women now comprise a fast-growing component who choose singlehood rather than being resigned to it. As women reach their 30s and 40s unmarried, the availability of men relative to themselves decreases significantly.

NEW REPRODUCTIVE TECHNOLOGY AND THE FAMILY

The impact of new reproductive technology on the family in recent years has been significant, with many benefits having been realized. However, the new technology has brought with it many difficult ethical problems.

In Vitro Fertilization

In vitro fertilization involves the union of the male sperm and the female ovum in glass rather than in the woman's body. The benefits are twofold. First, about 20 percent of couples who otherwise could not conceive are able to using this technique. Second, the genetic screening of sperm and eggs reduces the incidence of birth defects.

Ethical Issues

Several ethical issues have been created with the new reproductive technology. One concerns the fact that the benefits are expensive and only available to those who can afford them. A second issue involves the control medical experts have over who the technology is made available to. Another problem concerns surrogate motherhood. Moral and cultural legal standards to guide this option remain ambiguous at this time.

LOOKING AHEAD: FAMILY IN THE TWENTY-FIRST CENTURY

Family life has dramatically changed in recent decades. Five general conclusions are proposed looking ahead to the next century. First, divorce rates will remain high. Second, family life will be highly variable, being represented by many family forms. Third, economic changes in society are having a great impact in terms of reforming marriage and the family. Fourth, men are playing less of a role in raising children, particularly as more children will be raised in single-families. And fifth, new reproductive technology will shape families in the next century. Marriage and family are likely to remain the foundation of our society.

PART IV: KEY CONCEPTS

Define each of the following concepts in the space provided or on separate paper. Check the accuracy of your answers by referring to the key concepts section at the end of the chapter in the text as well as by referring to italicized definitions located throughout the chapter.

bilateral descent
blended family
cohabitation

consanguine family
descent
endogamy
exogamy
extended family
family
family of orientation
family of procreation
family unit
family violence
homogamy
incest taboo
kinship
marriage
matrilineal descent
matrilocality
monogamy
neolocality
nuclear family
patrilineal descent
patrilocality
polyandry
polygamy
polygyny
serial monogamy

PART V: STUDY QUESTIONS

True-False

1.   T   F   The family into which one is born is referred to as the *family of procreation*.
2.   T   F   Norms of *endogamy* are found in every society.
3.   T   F   *Patrilocality* is common in societies that engage in frequent, local warfare, while *matrilocality* is more likely to be found in societies that engage in more distant warfare.
4.   T   F   Every known culture has some type of *incest taboo*.
5.   T   F   Our society places less of an emphasis on *romantic love* than most other societies around the world.
6.   T   F   While the actual number is smaller, the "ideal" number of children to have for most married U.S. adults is *three or more*.
7.   T   F   Most U.S. children under the age of five whose mothers are working receive child care in a formal *day care center*.

8.	T	F	Lillian Rubin's research focuses on the interaction between *social class* and *marital relationship*.
9.	T	F	The typical African American family earns more than the typical Latino family in the United States.
10.	T	F	The *divorce rate* in the U.S. is lower than it is for most other modern industrialized societies.
11.	T	F	Men and women who divorce once are more likely to *divorce again*.
12.	T	F	According to the text, most *child abusers* are men.
13.	T	F	The percentage of households with single adults has actually been *decreasing* over the last two decades.
14.	T	F	Test-tube babies are, technically speaking, the result of the process of in vitro fertilization.

Multiple-Choice

1. The consanguine family is also known as the:

(a) conjugal family
(b) nuclear family
(c) extended family
(d) family of orientation
(e) family of procreation

2. A family unit composed of one or two parents and their children, and which is based on marriage, is the:

(a) nuclear family
(b) consanguine
(c) exogamous
(d) extended

3. *Exogamy* and *endogamy* are cultural norms relating to:

(a) marriage patterns
(b) descent regulations
(c) beliefs about romantic love
(d) residence patterns
(e) authority patterns

4. A *marriage form* that unites one woman with two or more men is termed:

(a) monogamy
(b) polygyny
(c) polyandry
(d) endogamy

5. Which of the following is *not* a descent pattern?

(a) matrilineal
(b) patrilineal
(c) bilateral
(d) neolocal
(e) all are descent patterns

6. Preindustrial societies that are agrarian or pastoral in nature typically exhibit:

(a) neolocality
(b) bilateral descent
(c) patrilineal descent
(d) matrilineal descent

7. The type of sociological analysis of the family that holds that the family serves to perpetuate patriarchy is:

(a) social-exchange analysis
(b) social-conflict analysis
(c) structural-functional analysis
(d) symbolic-interaction analysis

8. Sociologists have noted that *romantic love* as a basis for marriage:

(a) is reinforced by cultural values
(b) acts as a strong incentive to leave one's original family of orientation to form a new family of procreation
(c) is not as stable a basis for marriage as social and economic bases
(d) all of the above

9. Which of the following is *not* an accurate statement?

(a) 48 percent of African American families are headed by women
(b) African-American household income is only about 60 percent of white family income on average
(c) the divorce rate in the U.S. has increased ten-fold over this century
(d) 68 percent of African American children are born to single women
(e) egalitarian marriages tend to be happier for women, but are very frustrating and unfulfilling for men

10. Daniel Moynihan published a controversial interpretation of the African American in the 1960s. Which of the following is a criticism of Moynihan's analysis?

(a) Moynihan neglected to analyze the most commonly occurring African American family headed by two parents
(b) Moynihan implied that the female-headed, single-parent family was the cause of poverty among African Americans
(c) Moynihan claimed that female-headed African American families were pathological
(d) all of the above

11. Which of the following *types of marriage* does Jesse Bernard suggest tends to be happier for both wives and husbands?

(a) egalitarian   (d) blended
(b) emergent   (e) conventional
(c) traditional

12. Remarriage often creates families composed of both biological parents and stepparents and children. These are called:

(a) second families   (c) focal families
(b) blended families   (d) families of orientation

13. Which of the following is *incorrect*?

(a) most child abusers were abused themselves as children
(b) most child abusers are women
(c) approximately 3 million children are abused each year in the U.S.
(d) most states in the U.S. have marital rape laws

14. What percentage of children in the U.S. live with only *one parent*?

(a) 10   (b) 19   (c) 28   (d) 42   (e) 53

Fill-In

1. The family into which one is born and receives early socialization is termed the *family of* _____. A family within which people have their own children is termed the *family of* _____.
2. The _____ *family* is based on blood ties.
3. _____ is the normative pattern referring to marriage between people of the *same social group or category*.
4. _____ is a marriage that joins *one female* with *more than one male*.
5. Cultural norms that forbid sexual relations or marriage between specified kin are called _____ _____.
6. According to *structural-functionalists* the family performs several vital tasks, including: _____, _____ of sexual activity, social _____, and _____ and _____ security.
7. According to *social-conflict* theorists, the role of families in the social reproduction of inequality takes several forms, including: _____ and _____, _____, _____ and _____.
8. For children under the age of five years whose parents both work _____ percent are in *day care* or a *preschool* setting during the day.

277

9. Sociologist Jesse Bernard claims that compared to _____ women, _____ women have poorer mental health, evince more passive attitudes toward life, and report less personal happiness.

10. Several factors related to the high *divorce rate* in the United States include: _____ is on the rise, _____ _____ often subsides, women are now less _____ on men, many of today's marriages are _____, divorce is more socially _____, and divorce is _____ easier to accomplish.

11. Six *adjustments to divorce* (divorce as a process) include: _____ divorce, _____ divorce, _____ reorganization, _____ reorganization, _____ reorganization, and _____ reorganization.

12. Remarriage often creates _____ *families*, composed of children and some combination of biological parents and stepparents.

13. Today, approximately _____ percent of households in the U.S. are *single person* households.

14. The term for one woman biologically bearing another woman's child is _____ _____.

15. This chapter concludes with the sentence: Marriage and family life today may be more _____ than in the past, but both will likely remain the _____ of our society for some time to come.

Definition and Short-Answer

1. What are the four basic *functions* of the family according to structural-functionalists?
2. Define and describe the three patterns of *descent* outlined in the text.
3. What were the basic conclusions of the *Moynihan Report* of 1965? What are some criticisms of this report?
4. Why has the *divorce rate* increased in recent decades in the U.S.? Why has it begun to level off or even decline in recent years?
5. What are the four *stages of the family life cycle* that are outlined in the text? Describe the major events which occur during each stage.
6. Six *adjustments to divorce* are identified by Paul Bohannan. Identify and describe each.
7. Four *types of marriages* are described that are related to depression in men and women. what are these?
8. In what ways are *middle-class* and *working-class* marriages different according to research cited in the text?
9. Review the statistics in *Figure 17-2*. What are the implications of this pattern of household forms in the U.S.
10. Review the key demographic facts concerning *family violence* in the U.S.
11. What are the four types of *alternative family forms* discussed in the text? Briefly describe each and their demographic pattern in our society today.
12. What are the five *conclusions* being made about marriage and family into the twenty-first century?

PART VI: ANSWERS TO STUDY QUESTIONS

True-False

1.	F	(p. 456)	8.	T	(p. 467)
2.	T	(p. 457)	9.	F	(p. 467)
3.	T	(p. 459)	10.	F	(p. 471)
4.	T	(p. 460)	11.	T	(p. 472)
5.	F	(p. 463)	12.	T	(p. 474)
6.	F	(p. 465)	13.	F	(p. 476)
7.	F	(p. 466)	14.	T	(p. 476)

Multiple-Choice

1.	c	(p. 456)	8.	d	(p. 463)
2.	a	(p. 456)	9.	e	(pp. 468-71)
3.	a	(p. 457)	10.	d	(p. 468)
4.	c	(p. 458)	11.	a	(p. 470)
5.	d	(p. 460)	12.	b	(p. 473)
6.	c	(p. 460)	13.	b	(p. 474)
7.	b	(p. 461)	14.	c	(p. 474)

Fill-In

1. orientation, procreation (p. 456)
2. consanguine (p. 456)
3. endogamy (p. 457)
4. polyandry (p. 458)
5. incest taboos (p. 460)
6. socialization, regulation, placement, material, emotional (p. 460)
7. property, inheritance, patriarchy, race, ethnicity (p. 461)
8. 23 (p. 466)
9. single, married (p. 470)
10. individualism, romantic love, dependent, stressful, acceptable, legally (p. 471)
11. emotional, legal, psychic, community, economic, parental (pp. 472-73)
12. blended (p. 473)
13. 25 (p. 476)
14. surrogate motherhood (p.477)
15. controversial, foundation (p. 479)

PART VII: ANALYSIS AND COMMENT

Global Sociology

"The Weakest Families on Earth? A Report From Sweden"

    Key Points: Questions:

Critical Thinking

"Who's Minding the Kids"

    Key Points: Questions:

Controversy and Debate

"Should We save the Traditional Family?"

    Key Points: Questions:

Window on the World

"Global-Map 17-1 Marital Forms in Global Perspective"

Key Points: Questions:

Seeing Ourselves

"National Map 17-1 Divorced People Across the U.S."

Key Points: Questions:

Religion

18

PART I: CHAPTER OUTLINE

I.   Religion: Basic Concepts
       A. Religion and Sociology
II.   Theoretical Analysis of Religion
       A. Functions of Religion: Structural-Functional Analysis
       B. Constructing the Sacred: Symbolic-Interaction Analysis
       C. Inequality and Religion: Social Conflict Analysis
III.   Religion and Social Change
       A. Max Weber: Protestantism and Capitalism
       B. Liberation Theology
IV.   Types of Religious Organization
       A. Church and Sect
       B. Cult
V.   Religion in History
       A. Religion in Preindustrial Societies
       B. Religion in Industrial Societies
VI.   World Religions
       A. Christianity
       B. Islam
       C. Judaism
       D. Hinduism
       E. Buddhism
       F. Confucianism
       G. Religion: East and West
VII.   Religion in the United States
       A. Religious Affiliation
       B. Religiosity
       C. Religion and Social Stratification
              1. Social Class
              2. Ethnicity and Race

PART II: LEARNING OBJECTIVES

1.   To define the basic concepts of religion, faith, profane, sacred, and ritual.
2.   To explain the aspects of religion that sociology addresses.
3.   To identify and describe the three functions of religion as developed by Emile Durkheim.
4.   To identify and describe the view that religion is socially constructed.
5.   To identify and describe the role religion plays in maintaining inequality.
6.   To compare and contrast the basic types of religious organizations: church (two types), sect, and cult.
7.   To distinguish between preindustrial and industrial societies in terms of religious beliefs and practices.
8.   To identify and describe the size, location, and type of belief system of the major world religions: Christianity, Islam, Hinduism, Buddhism, Confucianism, and Judaism.
9.   To explain the religious affiliation, religiosity, and the correlations of religious affiliation in the United States.
10. To describe the pattern of secularization and the development of civil religion in U.S. society.
11. To identify and describe religious revival in U.S. society.
12. To begin to critically think about the role of religion in the world as it will unfold over the next generation, and to consider the interesting relationship between religion and science.

PART III: CHAPTER REVIEW

A story of "divine sightings" in a small Georgia town opens this chapter. At issue, the distinction between the otherworldly and the ordinary, which lies at the heart of religion.

RELIGION: BASIC CONCEPTS

Religion primarily concerns the purpose and meaning of life. These are areas where scientific knowledge is inadequate. Durkheim suggested human beings distinguish between the **profane**, meaning *that which is an ordinary element of every day life*, and the **sacred**, or *that which is defined as extraordinary, inspiring a sense of awe, reverence, and even fear*. This differentiation, according to Durkheim, is the key to religious belief. **Religion** is therefore *a social institution involving beliefs and practices based upon a conception of the sacred*. Because it transcends everyday experience its truth cannot be tested by science. The sacred is approached through **ritual**, or *formal, ceremonial behavior*.

Religion and Sociology

Sociology is concerned with the analysis of the consequences of religion, not with passing judgments on its validity. Religion is a matter of **faith**, or *belief anchored in conviction rather than scientific evidence*. Examples of "faith" are presented.

THEORETICAL ANALYSIS OF RELIGION

Functions of Religion: Structural-Functional Analysis

Emile Durkheim argued society has an existence of its own, beyond the lives of the people who create it. Society and the sacred are inseparable in Durkheim's view. Durkheim believed that the power of society was understood by people through their creation of sacred symbols. In technologically simple societies a **totem** was *an object in the natural world collectively defined as sacred*. Ritual behavior with the totem provided unity for the community. He saw religion as providing major functions for society. These include: (1) *Social cohesion*--Religion unites members of a society through shared symbolism, values, and norms. (2) *Social control*--Every society promotes some degree of social conformity. Mores, for example, are justified using religious doctrine. And (3) *Providing meaning and purpose*--Religion provides people with a sense of meaning and purpose by addressing the ultimate issues of life.

A weakness in the structural-functional view is that it downplays the dysfunctions of religion, particularly its role in producing destructive social conflict.

Constructing the Sacred: Symbolic-Interaction Analysis

Peter Berger, operating from the symbolic-interaction view, theorized that religion is a socially constructed reality much as the family and economy are. The sacred can provide a permanence for society as long as society's members ignore the recognition that the sacred is socially constructed.

Inequality and Religion: Social-Conflict Analysis

The social-conflict view of religion draws attention to the social ills perpetuated by the existence of religion. Karl Marx theorized that the powerful in society benefit by religion because it defines the present society as morally just.

Religion can also promote social change and encourage greater social equality. Therefore, while providing meaning and insight, this approach does have limitations in helping us to understand religion in society. The **Social Diversity** box (p. 488) addresses the question of the extent to which religion favors males, fitting into the social-conflict view for the study of religion.

RELIGION AND SOCIAL CHANGE

Max Weber: Protestantism and Capitalism

Max Weber's basic argument is that new kinds of religious thought created the context for the Industrial Revolution in Europe. The Calvinist doctrine in *predestination* is identified as a key to beliefs in progress and investment, which were foundations to industrialization.

Liberation Theology

Liberation theology is *a fusion of Christian principles with political activism, often Marxist in character.* This view originated in the 1960s, and asserts that not only is the teaching of Christianity necessary for liberation from human sin, but the Church must help people liberate themselves from poverty in poor countries. Adherents tend to follow the basic principles that global inequality contradicts Christianity, and global poverty is preventable.

TYPES OF RELIGIOUS ORGANIZATION

Church and Sect

A *church* is *a type of religious organization well integrated into the larger society.* Two types of church organization are the *ecclesia*, *a church formally allied with the state*, and a *denomination*, or *a church, independent of the state, that accepts religious pluralism.* The Catholic Church of the Roman Empire and the Anglican Church of England are examples of ecclesia. The Methodist, Presbyterian, and Catholic churches in the U.S. are examples of denominations.

A *sect*, distinct from a church, is *a type of religious organization that stands apart from the larger society.* Sects tend to lack the formal organization of a church. They exalt personal experience. Leaders are often those people who manifest *charisma*, or, *extraordinary personal qualities that can turn an audience into followers.* Proselytizing is important to obtain new members through *conversion*, a personal transformation or rebirth resulting from new adopting religious beliefs. Sects tend to reject the established society. These terms church and sect are ideal-type concepts with any religious organization having qualities of each to some degree.

Cult

A *cult* is *a religious organization that is substantially outside a society's cultural traditions.*

It represents something almost completely new. Cults often arise from the diffusion of religious ideas cross-culturally. They tend to be more extreme than sects, requiring members to change their entire lifestyle and self-concepts.

RELIGION IN HISTORY

Religion in Preindustrial Societies

Archaeological research suggests religious ritual has existed for at least 40,000 years. Among hunting and gathering societies religion typically takes the form of **animism**, or *the belief that elements of the natural world are conscious life forms that affect humanity*. In such cultures, a *shaman*, or religious leader may be recognized, however not as occupying a full-time position as a specialist. With technological development religion moves out of the family and emerges as a distinct social institution, often closely tied to politics.

Religion in Industrial Societies

With industrialization, science begins as a force that diminishes the scope of religious power and thinking. Yet science has not caused religion to be eliminated as science cannot answer certain fundamental questions. The relationship between religion and science has been uneasy. Recent debate focuses on the issue of the origin of humanity. The **Controversy and debate** box (pp. 504-05) addresses the issue of *creationism*, and the extent to which science threatens religion.

WORLD RELIGIONS

Religion is found virtually everywhere in the world. Many of the thousands of religions are highly localized, but a few may be termed *world religions* because they have millions of followers.

Christianity

Christianity is the world's largest religion with 1.6 billion followers. Christianity is based on **monotheism**, or *belief in a single divine power*. When this view first emerged it challenged the Roman Empire's tradition of **polytheism**, or *belief in many gods*. Eventually Christianity become the official religion of the Roman Empire. Over the centuries there have been several divisions within Christianity, each however shares the belief that Jesus of Nazareth was sent by God to provide salvation. **The Window on the World** boxes (p. 493 and p. 495), which contain *Global Maps 18-1* through *18-4,* show us four major world religions in global perspective.

Islam

Islam is the world's second largest religion with almost one billion followers called

Muslims. This religion is based on the life of Muhammad, born in Mecca in 570. He is seen as a prophet, not a divine being. Allah is the God of Islam. Islam means "submission and peace." While divisions exist, there are five pillars of Islam: recognition of Allah as the one true God and Mohammed as God's messenger, ritual prayer, giving alms to the poor, regular fasting, and making at least one pilgrimage to Mecca.

Judaism

Like Confucianism, Judaism is historical in focus. The critical event in Jewish history is the Exodus from Egypt in the 13th century B.C.E. After this event, Judaism became monotheistic. The *Covenant*, a special relationship with God, is a distinctive element of this religion. The *Torah*, or first five books of the Bible, is of special importance for Jews. Judaism emphasizes moral behavior in this world as opposed to being concerned with salvation. There are divided interpretations of doctrine, but a keen awareness of their cultural history and historical endurance of prejudice and discrimination (antisemitism) are central to the Jews' understanding of their religious faith.

Hinduism

Hinduism is probably the oldest religion, coming into existence about 4500 years ago. It has about 700,000 to 800,000 followers. Hinduism and Indian society are closely fused, so unlike Islam Christianity it is not easily diffused. Also, it is not linked to the life of one person. Therefore, beliefs and practices vary greatly. All Hindus generally believe that a force confronts all people with moral responsibility termed *dharma*. *Karma*, a belief in the spiritual progress of a person's soul and involving reincarnation, is also a fundamental aspect of this religion. Hinduism is neither monotheistic nor polytheistic.

Buddhism

Buddhism emerged in India about 2500 years ago. Siddharta Gautama was its founder. After years of travel and meditation he reached "bodhi," or enlightenment. Followers began spreading his teachings, the *dhamma*. Buddhists see existence as suffering and reject the idea of wealth as a solution to human problems. Reincarnation is also a belief in this religion. The answer to world problems lies in personal transformation toward a spiritual existence.

Confucianism

Confucianism was the official religion of China from 200 B.C.E. until the beginning of this century. This religion was shaped by K'ung-Fu-Tzu (Confucius) who lived in the 6th and 5th centuries B.C.E. This religion is based on the concept of the *jen*, humaneness. Lacking a clear concept of the sacred, it is more a disciplined way of life than a religion.

Religion: East and West

Two general difference between the belief systems that predominate in Eastern and Western societies are identified in the text. First, Western religions are typically deity-based, with a clear focus on God. Eastern religions tend to be more like ethical codes, with less clear-cut distinction between the sacred and secular. Second, the operational unit of Western religious organization is the congregation, with people attending a specific place of worship with others. In the East, religious organization is more broadly tied to culture itself.

RELIGION IN THE UNITED STATES

Religious Affiliation

About 90 percent of U.S. adults identify with a specific religion, and some two-thirds have formal affiliation with one. *Table 18-1* (p. 498) outlines the religious identifications among people in the U.S. The U.S. is described as religiously pluralistic. The **Seeing Ourselves** box (p. 500) shows, *National Map 18-1,* which suggests however that certain religious affiliations predominate within certain regions of the country.

Religiosity

Religiosity is *the importance of religion in a person's life*. This concept can be measured in a number of different ways. Charles Glock has distinguished five distinct dimensions of religiosity: *experiential, ritualistic, ideological, consequential,* and *intellectual.*

The vast majority of people in the U.S. (95%) believe in a divine power of some kind. Some two-thirds of the people in the U.S. believe that God exists, without doubt. In ideological terms we in the U.S. seem less religious, with 70 percent believing in an afterlife, 50 percent praying each day, one-third attending church weekly or almost weekly. Religiosity is therefore a difficult concept to measure.

Religion and Social Stratification

Social Class

Jews, and among Protestants--Episcopalians and Presbyterians, have the highest social standing in our society on average. Catholics, and among Protestants, Lutherans and Baptists, are more representative of the lower social strata. Those Protestants who have the higher average social standing typically represent Northern European societies, making immigration to this country easier, with less prejudice and discrimination. Certain stereotypes, for example, Jews' success being linked to banking involvement, are confronted and rejected.

Ethnicity and Race

Religion is also closely related to ethnicity and race, with certain religions predominating particular geographic regions. Examples of patterns are provided, including a discussion of the historical importance of the church for African-Americans.

RELIGION IN A CHANGING SOCIETY

Secularization

An important and controversial pattern of social change is *secularization*, or *a historical decline in the importance of the supernatural and the sacred*. This is common among modern, technologically advanced societies. Advances in science have significantly influenced our relationship with the world of ideas and the world of nature. Yet, religion is still an important part of society and very significant in many people's lives. Two-thirds of the U.S. population maintains identification with a religious affiliation (two times higher than in 1900 and four times higher than in 1850). A decline in some aspects of religion may be accompanied by increases in others. Secularization cannot be viewed as a matter of moral advance or decline.

Civil Religion

Secularization has brought about a decline in certain traditional religious beliefs, but has also affected the advancement of new forms. *Civil religion*, *a quasi-religious loyalty binding individuals in a basically secular society*, is strong in U.S. society. Patriotic ties are an example. Civil religion involves much ritual behavior, like the celebration of Thanksgiving and the 4th of July. It is not related to a specific religious doctrine.

Religious Revival

Membership in established religions may be declining, however membership in other religious organizations is increasing. The human need for security seems to always give rise to some form of religious activity and commitment. The **Global Sociology** box, (p. 502) takes a look at the state of religious affiliation in Great Britain. As in the U.S., mainstream churches in England have lost members. The relative gains and losses for different religious organizations are summarized.

Religious Fundamentalism

Religious fundamentalism, or *a conservative religious doctrine that opposes intellectualism and worldly accommodation in favor of restoring traditional, otherworldly spiritually*, has been increasing in the U.S. over the last decade or so. Five characteristics identify Christian fundamentalists: *A literal interpretation of Scriptures, a rejection of religious pluralism, a pursuit of the personal experience of God's presence, an opposition to "secular humanism," and the en-*

dorsement of conservative political goals. About 20 percent of U.S. adults, for example, believe in the literal interpretation of the Bible. The **Controversy and Debate** box (pp. 504-05) addresses the question as to whether science threatens religion. The answer seems to be that science and religion do not necessarily contradict each other.

The Electronic Church

Fundamentalists have heavily used the mass media, particularly television and radio, to attract and maintain followers. About 5 percent of the U.S. population are regular viewers of televangelists, with 20 percent watching at least once a month. Several scandals, including those involving Jimmy Swaggart and Jim and Tammy Bakker, are noted.

LOOKING AHEAD: RELIGION IN THE TWENTY-FIRST CENTURY

The point is being made that secularization is not squeezing out religion from our society. Processes of change appear to be creating more need for religion.

PART IV: KEY CONCEPTS

Define each of the following concepts in the space provided or on separate paper. Check the accuracy of your answers by referring to the key concepts section at the end of the chapter in the text as well as by referring to italicized definitions located throughout the chapter.

animism
anti-semitism
charisma
church
civil religion
consequential religiosity
conversion
covenant
creationism
creation science
cult
denomination
dhamma
dharma
ecclesia
experiential religiosity
ideological religiosity

jen
karma
liberation theology
monotheism
nirvana
polytheism
profane
religion
religious fundamentalism
religiosity
ritual
ritualistic religiosity
sacred
sect
secularism
shaman
Torah
totem

PART V: STUDY QUESTIONS

True-False

1. T F A major component of Emile Durkheim's approach to the study of religion was to determine whether a divine power exists or not.
2. T F Two types, or forms, of *churches* identified in the text are the ecclesia and the denomination.
3. T F Whereas a *cult* is formed by a schism from established religious organizations, a *sect* represents something almost entirely new.
4. T F In hunting and gathering societies, a *shaman*, or religious leader may be recognized, but shamanism is not a full-time, specialized activity.
5. T F There are more followers of *Islam* around the world than of any other religion.
6. T F After Christianity and Islam, Judaism has the next most followers around the world.
7. T F Hindus generally believe that a force in the universe confronts everyone with moral responsibility termed *dharma*.
8. T F *Ideological religiosity* concerns an individual's degree of belief in religious doctrine, while consequential religiosity has to do with how much religious beliefs influence a person's daily behavior.
9. T F According to research on *religiosity* cited in the text, approximately one-third of U.S. adults say they attend religious services weekly, or almost weekly.

10. T　F　The distribution of the U.S. population by *religious affiliation* is very evenly distributed across the country.

11. T　F　A quasi-religious loyalty binding individuals in a basically secular society is called *civil religion*.

Multiple-Choice

1. _____, according to Emile Durkheim, is that which is defined as extraordinary, inspiring a sense of awe, reverence, and even fear.

   (a) the sacred   (c) religion
   (b) the profane   (d) jen

2. A *totem*--an object imbued with sacred qualities--is characteristically found within which of the following societies?

   (a) technologically simple   (c) heathen
   (b) modern advanced   (d) agrarian

3. Which of the following is a *function* of religion according to Emile Durkheim?

   (a) social cohesion
   (b) social control
   (c) providing meaning and purpose
   (d) all are functions identified by Durkheim
   (e) none are, as he saw religion as having negative consequences for society

4. *Liberation theology*, developed in the later 1960s, advocates a blending of religion with:

   (a) family   (c) economy
   (b) education   (d) politics

5. Which of the following is *not* a feature of a sect?

   (a) charismatic leaders
   (b) membership through conversion
   (c) animism
   (d) result of a religious schism

6. Which religion has the *most* followers?

   (a) Islam   (c) Buddhism
   (b) Christianity   (d) Hinduism

7. The first five books of the Bible are known as the:

(a) Covenant   (d) Talmud
(b) Kadesh   (e) Torah
(c) Mesora

8. Which of the following world religions is the oldest, contains beliefs related to dharma, and is neither monotheistic nor polytheistic?

(a) Islam   (c) Buddhism
(b) Hinduism   (d) Confucianism

9. Buddha's teachings are known as:

(a) karma   (c) dhamma
(b) jen   (d) the covenant

10. Which of the following is the *largest* Protestant denomination?

(a) Baptist   (d) Presbyterian
(b) Methodist   (e) Episcopalian
(c) Lutheran

11. Which of the following is *not* accurate based on information provided in the text?

(a) in the U.S. religious preference is related to social class
(b) throughout the world, religion is tied to ethnicity
(c) secularization refers to the historical decline in the importance of the supernatural and the sacred
(d) civil religion is a quasi-religious loyalty binding individuals in a basically secular society
(e) all of the above are accurate

12. The *fastest growing* organized religion in Great Britain is:

(a) Hinduism   (d) Jewish
(b) Fundamental Christianity   (e) Islam
(c) Mormon

Fill-In

1. Emile Durkheim labeled the ordinary elements of everyday life the _____.

2. A _____ is an object within the natural world that is imbued with sacred qualities.
3. _____ is belief anchored in conviction rather than scientific evidence.
4. According to Emile Durkheim the three major *functions of religion* are: Social _____, social _____, and providing _____ and _____.
5. _____ theology is a fusion of Christian principles with political activism.
6. An _____ is a church that is formally allied with the state.
7. While a _____ is a type of religious organization that stands apart from the larger society, a _____ refers to a religious organization that is substantially outside a society's cultural traditions.
8. _____ refers to extraordinary personal qualities that can turn audiences into followers.
9. _____ is the belief that natural objects are conscious forms of life that can affect humanity.
10. _____ is the second largest religion in the world, with one billion followers who are called _____.
11. Confucianism is based on the concept of _____, or *humaneness*.
12. Two major distinctions between Eastern and Western regions are (1) Western religions are typically _____-_____, with a clear focus on _____, and (2) Western religions are organized around the _____, while Eastern religious organizations are more broadly tied into the _____ itself.
13. Five distinctive qualities of *religiosity* are identified by Charles Glock, including: _____, _____, _____, _____, and _____.
14. A historical decline in the importance of the supernatural and the sacred is referred to as _____ *religion*.
15. A _____ religion is a quasi-religious loyalty binding individuals within a basically secular society.
16. *Religious fundamentalism* is distinctive in five ways, including: interpreting the _____ literally, not accepting religious _____, pursuing the _____ experience of God's presence, opposing _____, and endorsing _____ political goals.

Short-Answer

1. According to *structural-functionalists*, what are the three major *functions* of religion? Provide an example for each.
2. Discuss Max Weber's points concerning the historical connection between *Protestantism*, the Industrial Revolution, and capitalism.
3. Differentiate between the concepts *church*, *sect*, and *cult*.
4. How do theorists operating from the *social-conflict* perspective understand religion and how it operates in society? Provide examples to illustrate their points.

5.   In a one-page written discussion, debate the issue of whether *science* threatens or strengthens *religion* in modern industrialized societies.
6.   Discuss the issue concerning the extent of *religiosity* in the U.S. today. Why is it so difficult to determine a measure for religiosity in our society?
7.   Briefly describe the history and religious beliefs of two of the following religions: Christianity, Judaism, Islam, Buddhism, Hinduism, Confucianism.
8.   Differentiate between the concepts, *ecclesia*, and *denomination*.
9.   Differentiate between the nature of religion in preindustrial and industrial societies.
10. Differentiate between *civil religion* and religious *fundamentalism*.

PART VI: ANSWERS TO STUDY QUESTIONS

True-False

1.	F	(p. 484)	7.	T	(p. 496)
2.	T	(pp. 488-89)	8.	T	(p. 499)
3.	F	(p. 490)	9.	T	(p. 499)
4.	T	(p. 491)	10.	F	(p. 500)
5.	F	(p. 491)	11.	T	(p. 501)
6.	F	(p. 494)			

Multiple-Choice

1.	a	(p. 483)	7.	e	(p. 494)
2.	a	(p. 484)	8.	b	(p. 495)
3.	d	(p. 485)	9.	c	(p. 497)
4.	d	(p. 487)	10.	a	(p. 499)
5.	c	(p. 489)	11.	e	(pp. 499-501)
6.	b	(p. 491)	12.	b	(p. 502)

Fill-In

1.   profane (p. 483)
2.   totem (p. 484)
3.   faith (p. 484)
4.   cohesion, control, meaning, purpose (p. 485)
5.   liberation (p. 487)
6.   ecclesia (p. 488)
7.   sect, cult (pp. 489-90)
8.   charisma (p. 490)
9.   animism (p. 491)
10. Islam, Muslims (p. 492)
11. jen (p. 497)
12. deity-based, God, congregation, culture (p. 498)

13. experimental, ritualistic, ideological, consequential, intellectual (p. 499)
14. secularization (p. 501)
15. civil (p. 501)
16. Scriptures, pluralism, personal, secular humanism, conservative (p. 503)

PART VII: ANALYSIS AND COMMENT

Social Diversity

"Religion and Patriarchy: Does God Favor Males?"

    Key Points: Questions:

Controversy and Debate

"Does Science Threaten Religion?"

    Key Points: Questions:

Global Sociology

"The Changing Face of Religion: A Report From Great Britain"

Key Points: Questions:

Window on the World

"Global Maps 18-1 and 18-2 Christianity and Islam in Global Perspective"

Key Points: Questions:

"Global Maps 18-3 and 18-4 Hinduism and Buddhism in Global Perspective"

Key Points: Questions:

Seeing Ourselves

"National Map 18-1 The Religious Diversity of the U.S."

Key Points: Questions:

Education

19

PART I: CHAPTER OUTLINE

I.   Education: A Global Survey
      A. Schooling and Economic Development
      B. Schooling in India
      C. Schooling in Japan
      D. Schooling in Great Britain
      E. Schooling in the United States
II.   The Functions of Schooling
      A. Socialization
      B. Cultural Innovation
      C. Social Integration
      D. Social Placement
      E. Latent Functions of Schooling
III.   Schooling and Social Inequality
      A. Social Control
      B. Standardized Testing
      C. School Tracking
      D. Inequality Among Schools
           1. Public and Private Schools
           2. Inequality in Public Schooling
      E. Access to Higher Education
      F. Credentialism
      G. Privilege and Personal Merit
IV.   Problems in the Schools
      A. School Discipline
      B. Student Passivity
           1. Bureaucracy
           2. College: The Silent Classroom

PART II: LEARNING OBJECTIVES

1. To describe the role of education throughout history.
2. To compare and contrast schooling in Great Britain, Japan, India, and the United States.
3. To identify and describe the functions of schooling.
4. To explain how education supports social inequality through social control, testing, and tracking.
5. To distinguish between the quality of education between different public schools, and between public and private schools.
6. To describe the problems associated with unequal access to higher education and credentialism.
7. To identify and analyze the problems facing U.S. education today: school discipline, student passivity, and the decline of academic standards.
8. To describe and explain the reason for development of alternative types of schooling, such as magnet schools, schooling for students with disabilities, adult education, and the use of computers in schools.

PART III: CHAPTER REVIEW

We are introduced to the Masuo family of Yokohama, Japan. Education in Japan is very competitive, and rigorous application of oneself to its demands is critical through primary and secondary levels to even hope to achieve high enough scores on national tests to get into a national university. Many children go to the *Juku*, or "cram school," several days a week after their regular day at school.

Education refers to *the social institution guiding a society's transmission of knowledge-- including basic facts, job skills, and cultural norms and values--to its members.* **Schooling,** involves *formal instruction under the direction of specially trained teachers.*

299

EDUCATION: A GLOBAL SURVEY

Schooling and Economic Development

While today the Japanese and U.S. citizens live in advanced industrialized societies that rely heavily on a formal education system, the history of education reveals that preindustrial societies relied on the family to teach the young the necessary skills to survive. Most of the world's people today live in agrarian societies where limited schooling imparts practical knowledge needed to perform farming and other traditional tasks. The church provided schooling during the Middle Ages. In European societies of the West, school was an opportunity for the rich only. The English word school comes down to us from the Greek word for *leisure*.

Mass education was first adopted as a principle in the U.S. *Mandatory education laws*, or legal requirements that children receive a minimum of formal education, began to be enacted in the 1850s. The median number of years of schooling was 8.1 in 1910 and rose to 12.7 by 1993. *Table 19-1* (p. 510) summarizes the educational achievement levels of U.S. adults over the age of 25 years (by decade) from 1910-1993.

While all industrialized societies provide formalized schooling, each does so in its own particular and unique way. In the **Window on the World** box (p. 511), *Global Map 19-1* looks at illiteracy in global perspective. In Latin America and Africa illiteracy rates are extremely high.

Schooling in India

In a low-income country like India, people earn about 5 percent of the income standard in the United States. As a result, parents expect their children to work and earn money for the family. Less than one-half of Indian children attend secondary schools. Patriarchy is also still very strong in India, so significant educational differences exist between females and males.

Schooling in Japan

Mandatory education laws began in 1872. The cultural values of tradition and family are stressed in the early grades. In their early teens, students begin to face the rigorous and competitive exams of the Japanese system. Test scores determine whether a person will go to college, rich and poor alike. Some 90 percent of Japanese students graduate from high school, compared with 76 percent in the U.S. However, only 30 percent go on to college compared to 60 percent in the U.S. Japanese mothers of school age children participate in the labor force at considerably lower rates than U.S. mothers in order to devote themselves to the educational success of their children. The results of their system seem impressive, particularly in the areas of math and science.

Schooling in Great Britain

Schooling in Great Britain has long been associated with the elite. Traditional social distinctions still exist, with many children from wealthy families attending *public* schools, the equivalent of our private boarding schools. Expansion of the university system during the 1960s and 1970s has allowed all children to compete for Britain's government funded college system. However, graduates of the elite schools of Oxford and Cambridge have considerable economic and political power in Britain.

Schooling in the United States

As is true of the other educational systems discussed, the U.S. educational system has been shaped by distinctive cultural patterns. Democratic ideals have characterized our system, though the ideal of *equal opportunity* has not been fully achieved. Still, the U.S. has a higher proportion of its population attending college than any other industrialized society. *Figure 19-1* (p. 513) presents a *Global Snapshot* indicating the U.S. has an outstanding record of higher education for its people.

People in the U.S. also value *practicality*, and this fact has influenced the types of studies emphasized in schools. Earlier in this century, John Dewey was a foremost proponent of *progressive education*. While reflecting this view, George Herbert Mead, a symbolic-interactionist, stressed these same ideas. The **Sociology of Everyday Life** box (p. 514) shows recent trends in the types of Bachelor's degrees conferred and how these follow trends in jobs.

THE FUNCTIONS OF SCHOOLING

Structural-functional analysis focuses our attention on the functions that educational systems have for society.

Socialization

As societies become more technologically advanced, social institutions must emerge beyond the family to help socialize members of the society to become functioning adults. Important lessons on cultural values and norms are learned in schools at all levels.

Cultural Innovation

Education is not merely a transmission of culture, it is also a factor in the creation of culture through critical inquiry and research.

Social Integration

Through the teaching of certain cultural values and norms, people become more unified. This is a particularly critical function in culturally diverse societies.

Social Placement

Schooling serves as a screening and selection process. Performance is evaluated on the basis of achievement. It provides an opportunity for upward mobility; however ascribed statuses still influence people in terms of their success in our educational system.

Latent Functions of Schooling

Schools serve as babysitters for younger children, and by occupying the time of teenagers, keep them from engaging in higher rates of socially disruptive behaviors. Lasting relationships are also established in school.

The structural-functionalists stress the ways in which education supports the operation of the industrial economy. One weakness of this approach, however, is that it fails to focus on how the quality of education varies greatly for different groups of people.

SCHOOLING AND SOCIAL INEQUALITY

Social-conflict analysis views schooling as a perpetuation of social stratification in the United States.

Social Control

Using social-conflict analysis, social control is viewed as an outcome of schooling because youth are socialized to accept the status quo. The term *hidden curriculum* refers to *the subtle presentations of political or cultural ideas in the classroom.* Compliance, punctuality, and discipline are part of the hidden curriculum.

Standardized Testing

An example of a culturally biased question on an achievement test is reviewed. The argument is that standardized tests favor upper-middle class backgrounds. The validity of such tests is therefore being questioned.

School Tracking

Standardized tests are used for the basis of *tracking*, or *the assignment of students to different types of educational programs.* Proponents of this approach argue that students with superior innate abilities and high motivation should be placed in learning environments with similar students to maximize their learning experience. Critics argue that it perpetuates inequalities and labels certain people as inferior without giving them a chance to prove themselves. Tracking has a clear and strong impact on a student's self-concept, with those in the higher tracks being affected positively and those in the lower negatively.

Inequality Among Schools

Public and Private Schools

In 1992, almost ninety percent of the sixty-five million U.S. students in primary and secondary levels were in public schools. Most students in private educational institutions and the primary and secondary levels attend *parochial* schools. An increase in fundamentalism has caused some Protestants to send their children to Christian schools where academic and disciplinary standards are more to their liking. Desegregation policies have also caused some parents to place their children in private, more racially homogeneous schools. A small number of families send their children to prestigious preparatory schools. Higher rates of academic achievement are found among students attending private schools than among students attending public schools.

Inequality in Public Schooling

Funds available for public schools vary considerably across the United States. We have some 15,000 school districts in the United States, with annual per-student spending varying from over $8,000 in some areas to under $3,000 in others.

The 1966 Coleman Report revealed that racially segregated schools, officially illegal since 1954, provided inferior education. This report helped initiate *busing* policies. Coleman however found only a weak relationship between funding and academic qualities of schools. Families and peer groups, and the attitudes of teachers seemed to be most highly correlated with academic achievement.

Access to Higher Education

The vast majority of parents want their children to attend college, and most high school students what to go to college. Only 61 percent of graduating high school seniors attend college the following fall. Only one in five people over the age of twenty-five is a college graduate in the U.S. The most crucial factor affecting access to higher education is money. The cost is high and rapidly increasing. In many respects, however, equal access has improved in recent decades, though family income continues to affect chances of attending college. In the **Seeing Ourselves** box (p. 518), *National Map 19-1* shows where in the U.S. people are more or less likely to reach college. *Figure 19-2* (p. 519) shows the educational achievement levels for men and women and how these affect income. Regardless of educational level men earn significantly more than do women. For example, on average, a woman with a college degree earns almost 20 percent less than the average man with a high school education. Further, whites are more likely than minorities to complete high school, and the gap increases with each higher level in the educational system. Further, minorities, who are represented disproportionately in lower income families, are finding it more difficult to obtain a college degree. *Figure 19-3* (p. 519) shows the correlation between family income level and college attendance rates. The pattern clearly illustrates the significance of social class in determining who goes to college. Even those who make it to college do not neces-

303

sarily receive equivalent educations. People from lower income families are more likely to be attending community colleges or public universities. Equal opportunity policies and financial aid has certainly opened the doors of higher education for many people who in past decades would not have been able to attend. A college education certainly expands career opportunities and lifetime earning potential.

Credentialism

Sociologist Randall Collins refers to the U.S. as a *credential society*, meaning degrees and diplomas are used as a sign of a person's ability to perform a specialized occupational role.

Credentialism means *evaluating a person on the basis of educational degrees*. It acts as a gatekeeping strategy, say conflict theorists, who argue that often credentials bear little relation to the skills and responsibilities of specific jobs.

Credentialism has produced *overeducation*, a situation in which workers have more formal education than the performance of their occupation requires. In many respects educational attainment has outpaced the job market's demand for it.

Privilege and Personal Merit

An important theme of social-conflict analysis is that schooling turns social privilege into personal merit. College is seen as a rite of passage for children of wealthier families. In contrast, the **Social Diversity** box (p. 521) discusses the process of transforming social disadvantage into personal deficiency in the life of one bright but disillusioned boy.

The social-conflict approach focuses on education in terms of social inequality. However, it ignores how different kinds of schooling may actually meet the needs and talents of specific students and different categories of students.

PROBLEMS IN THE SCHOOLS

Attitudes of adults in the U.S. about education are mixed. This is illustrated in *Table 19-3* (p. 522) entitled "Grading Public Schools in the U.S., 1995." A lack of discipline and the presence of violence are viewed as major problems in many schools. Passivity of students is seen as another significant problem. Further, many argue that school standards have dropped recently.

School Discipline

Discipline is a problem in schools. The key to overcoming this problem appears to be firm disciplinary policies in schools, with support from parents and local law enforcement agencies. A school in Los Angeles is discussed as an example.

Student Passivity

Bureaucracy

There is perceived to be a lack of active student participation in the learning process. It is being referred to as *student passivity*. This seems to hold true in all types of schools. Students seem to view education as a series of hurdles rather than as a privilege. Theodore Sizer argues that our bureaucratic structure in schools, while necessary, causes five serious problems. These include: *Rigid uniformity* tending to ignore cultural variation within local communities, defining success by *numerical ratings* of performance while overlooking less quantifiable factors, forcing *rigid expectations* on all students regardless of their particular talents or situations, creating too *specialized* a division of labor, and giving students *little individual responsibility* for their own learning.

Suggested changes in the bureaucratic system include smaller classes, more broadly trained teachers, elimination of rigid class schedules, and basing graduation on what is learned rather than on the amount of time spent in school.

College: The Silent Classroom

What little research has been done in college classroom settings, for example research by David Karp and William Yoels, suggests that patterns of interaction are very predictable and involve little student initiative or creative thinking. Smaller classes seem to generate more student participation, but participation rates in these classes are still low.

Research on reasons why students believe their participation rates is low are reviewed in *Table 19-4* (p. 524). Students see passivity as mostly their own fault; however, this may be due to the bureaucratic process of which they are a part.

Dropping Out

Dropping out is defined as quitting school before earning a high-school diploma. The drop out rate has eased slightly in recent years. Currently the rate stands at about 12 percent. Rates vary significantly by family income and by racial and ethnic group. The consequences for drop outs are great, particularly in regard to employment opportunities.

Academic Standards

A 1983 report by the National Commission on Excellence in Education entitled "*A Nation At Risk*," found that education in the U.S. had deteriorated during the previous decade. This report points out lowering SAT scores as a major indicator of this decline. Further, it noted the extent of *functional illiteracy*, or *reading and writing skills insufficient for everyday living*. About one in eight U.S. students complete secondary school without learning to read or write. The extent of functional illiteracy is discussed in the **Critical Thinking** box (p. 530). The 1983 report recommends more stringent educational requirements including

305

raising standards, requiring certain courses, keeping students in school until they reach certain levels of achievement, increasing the salaries of teachers, and professional training. *Figure 19-3* (p. 532) shows length of the school year for different countries. The U.S. has a relatively short academic year.

RECENT ISSUES IN AMERICAN EDUCATION

School Choice

The essence of the *school choice* position is that education has failed to live up to expectations because of lack of competition. *Magnet schools* are schools that attract students through special facilities and programs promoting educational excellence. Purposes of this type of school include improving educational performance and making inner-city schools more attractive to more affluent people. Another proposal involves providing parents with *vouchers* and allowing them to choose any school-- public, private, or parochial for their children. Finally, *schooling for profit*, or schools operated by private profit-making companies, has also been suggested.

Schooling People With Disabilities

Our educational system requires our society to provide basic educational opportunities for everyone. However, in our bureaucratized system many physically and mentally handicapped children receive few if any services. Several obstacles are discussed that make providing educational services to these children difficult.

One recent trend had been toward **mainstreaming**, or *integrating special students into the overall educational program*. This approach is also known as *inclusive education*. Advantages of this policy include enabling these children the broadest range of educational experiences and to having other people learn to interact with the disabled. Costs of such programs and policies are very expensive. The issue of *political correctness* is discussed in the **Controversy and Debate** box (p. 528).

Adult Education

Twenty-five million adults are currently enrolled in educational programs; most are from the middle and upper classes. The motivation for them to return to school is generally work related.

LOOKING AHEAD: SCHOOLING IN THE TWENTY-FIRST CENTURY

The U.S. educational system is summarized as manifesting both outstanding and poor qualities. The technology revolution, particularly the use of computers, is having a tremendous impact on the nature of education. Not only are computers important to learn about for eventual application at work, but they also change the very nature of the learning environment at school.

PART IV: KEY CONCEPTS

Define each of the following concepts in the space provided or on separate paper. Check the accuracy of your answer by referring to the key concepts section at the end of the chapter in the text as well as by referring to italicized definitions located throughout the chapter.

"A Nation At Risk"
Coleman Report
credentialism
education
functional illiteracy
hidden curriculum
inclusive education
Juku
magnet schools
mainstreaming
mandatory education laws
overeducation
schooling
student passivity
tracking

PART V: STUDY QUESTIONS

True-False

1. T F The U.S. was among the first nations to embrace the principle of *mass education*.
2. T F A little more than twenty percent of U.S. adults have a *college degree*.
3. T F More U.S. students who graduate from high school then go on to college than do Japanese students.
4. T F John Dewey was the foremost advocate of the idea that schooling should have *practical* consequences.
5. T F Over the last decade or so, with our concern over the social problems confronting our society, the proportion of college students obtaining a degree in the *social sciences* has been increasing.
6. T F *Hidden curriculum* refers to categorically assigning students to different types of education programs.
7. T F Roughly seventy-five percent of U.S. primary and secondary school children attend *public schools*.

8.   T   F   The *Coleman Report* determined that educational funding was the most important factor in determining educational achievement.

9.   T   F   Male college graduates can expect to earn about 40 percent more in their lifetime than women college graduates.

10.   T   F   The argument is being made that an emphasis on *credentialism* in our society leads to a condition of undereducation as people seek the status of a career and its earnings over the completion of a degree program at college.

Multiple-Choice

1. The extra, intensive schooling received by Japanese elementary school children in the afternoon takes place within the:

   (a)   huanco   (b)   mitchou   (c)   taruko   (d)   juku

2. *Mandatory education laws* were found in every state in the U.S. by:

   (a)   1781   (d)   1894
   (b)   1822   (e)   1918
   (c)   1850

3. In 1993 the median number of years of schooling completed in the U.S. was:

   (a)   8.1   (d)   16.1
   (b)   11.2   (e)   12.7
   (c)   10.0

4. Who advocated the idea that schooling should have *practical* consequences?

   (a)   James Coleman   (c)   John Dewey
   (b)   Daniel Moynihan   (d)   Christopher Jencks

5. Which of the following *functions* of formal education helps to forge a population into a single, unified society?

   (a)   socialization   (c)   social placement
   (b)   social integration   (d)   cultural innovation

6. Compliance, punctuality, and discipline are an important part of the _____ in formal education.

   (a)   manifest functions   (c)   hidden curriculum
   (b)   tracking system   (d)   residual system

7. The *Coleman Report* focused on which educational issue?

   (a) inequality
   (b) mandatory education
   (c) private schools
   (d) job training
   (e) religious education

8. Karp and Yoels did a study of *student passivity* in college and concluded that, from the students' point of view, _____ was ranked as the number one source of their passivity.

   (a) the large size of classes
   (b) the possibility that other students might not respect their point of view
   (c) the chance they would appear unintelligent in the eyes of the teacher
   (d) the fact that they had not done the reading assignment

9. The National Commission on Excellence in Education (1983) issued a report called *A Nation At Risk* in which it recommended:

   (a) ending student passivity
   (b) increasing credentialism
   (c) more stringent educational requirements
   (d) reducing the length of time students spend in school
   (e) reducing our educational focus on reading, writing, and arithmetic

10. *Functional illiteracy* refers to:

   (a) an inability to read and write at all
   (b) an inability to read at the appropriate level of schooling one is in
   (c) an inability to write
   (d) an inability to read and write well enough to carry out everyday activities

Fill-In

1. Formal instruction under the direction of specially trained teachers is the definition for: _____.
2. In India, _____ percent of females and _____ percent of males attend secondary schools.
3. Many wealthy families in England send their children to what the British call _____, the equivalent of U.S. private boarding schools.
4. Which country has the highest percentage of its adult population with a college degree.

5. The term _____ refers to the content of schooling that is often unrecognized.

6. _____ refers to the assignment of students to different types of educational programs.

7. A general rule in U.S. education is that the more _____ the county, the better the schools.

8. The *Coleman Report* cautioned that _____ alone does not magically bolster academic quality.

9. _____ is evaluating a person on the basis of educational degrees.

10. A key theme of _____ _____ analysis is that schooling transforms social privilege into personal merit.

11. Five ways in which large *bureaucratic* schools undermine education includes: rigid - _____, numerical _____, rigid _____, _____, and little individual _____.

12. The 1983 report by the National Commission on Excellence in Education was entitled _____.

13. Three alternatives for *school choice* discussed in the test include: _____, _____ schools, and schooling for _____.

14. The government acknowledges that _____ million U.S. adults have eighth-grade language skills or less.

15. _____ refers to the integration of special students into the overall educational program.

Definition and Short-Answer

1. Describe the four basic *functions* of education as reviewed in the text. What are the latent functions of education?

2. What were the basic methods and findings of the *Coleman Report*?

3. How do lifetime *earnings* differ for men and women given different levels of educational achievement?

4. What are the five serious problems with the *bureaucratic* nature of our educational system?

5. What recommendations were made in the report *A Nation At Risk*?

6. Review the data reported in *Table 19-4*. What are your reactions to the findings?

7. Discuss the similarities and differences between schooling in Japan, Great Britain, India, and the United States.

8. Discuss the issue of *testing* and *inequality* within our educational systems.

9. What are the major *problems* confronting schools in the United States today? What is being done about these problems? What do you think we should be doing?

PART VI: ANSWERS TO STUDY QUESTIONS

True-False

1.	T	(p. 510)	6.	F	(p. 515)
2.	T	(p. 510)	7.	F	(p. 517)
3.	T	(p. 512)	8.	F	(p. 518)
4.	T	(p. 513)	9.	T	(p. 519)
5.	T	(p. 514)	10.	F	(p. 520)

Multiple-Choice

1.	d	(p. 509)	6.	c	(p. 515)
2.	e	(p. 510)	7.	a	(pp. 517-18)
3.	e	(p. 510)	8.	d	(pp. 523-24)
4.	c	(p. 513)	9.	c	(p. 525)
5.	b	(p. 514)	10.	d	(p. 525)

Fill-In

1. schooling (p. 509)
2. 30/45 (p. 510)
3. public schools (p. 512)
4. the United States (p. 513)
5. hidden curriculum (p. 515)
6. tracking (p. 516)
7. affluent (p. 517)
8. money (p. 518)
9. credentialism (p. 520)
10. social-conflict (p. 520)
11. uniformity, ratings, expectations, specialization, responsibility (pp. 522-23)
12. A Nation At Risk (p. 525)
13. vouchers, magnet, profit (pp. 525-27)
14. 50 (p. 526)
15. mainstreaming (p. 528)

PART VII: ANALYSIS AND COMMENT

Sociology of Everyday Life

"Following the Jobs: Trends in Bachelor's Degrees"

    Key Points: Questions:

Social Diversity

"Cooling Out The Poor: Transforming Disadvantage into Deficiency"

    Key Points: Questions:

Critical Thinking

"Functional Illiteracy: Must We Rethink Education?"

    Key Points: Questions:

Controversy and Debate

"Is Political Correctness Undermining Education?"

Key Points: Questions:

Window on the World

"Global Map 19-1 Illiteracy in Global Perspective"

Key Points: Questions:

Seeing Ourselves

"National Map 19-1 College Attendance Across the U.S."

Key Points: Questions:

Health and Medicine

20

PART I: CHAPTER OUTLINE

I.   What is Health?
     A. Health and Society
II. Health: A Global Survey
     A. Health in History
     B. Health in Low-Income Countries
     C. Health in High-Income countries
III. Health in the United States
     A. Social Epidemiology: The Distribution of Health
          1. Age and Sex
          2. Social Class and Race
     B. Health and Society: Three Examples
          1. Cigarette Smoking
          2. Eating Disorders
          3. Sexually Transmitted Diseases
     C. Ethical Issues: Confronting Death
IV. The Medical Establishment
     A. The Rise of Scientific Medicine
     B. Holistic Medicine
     C. Paying for Health: A Global Survey
          1. Medicine in Socialist Societies
          2. Medicine in Capitalist Societies
     D. Medicine in the United States

V. Theoretical Analysis of Health and Medicine
    A. Structural-Functional Analysis
        1. The Sick Role
        2. The Physician's Role
    B. Symbolic-Interaction Analysis
        1. The Social Construction of Illness
        2. The Social Construction of Treatment
    C. Social-Conflict Analysis
        1. The Access Issue
        2. The Profit Motive
        3. Medicine as Politics
VI. Looking Ahead: Health and Medicine in the Twenty-First Century
VII. Summary
VIII. Critical-Thinking Questions
IX. Key Concepts
X. Suggested Readings

PART II: LEARNING OBJECTIVES

1. To show the ways in which the health of a population is shaped by society's cultural patterns, its technology and social resources, and its social inequality.
2. To know the differences in health among early societies, agrarian societies, and industrial societies.
3. To know the challenges that face the world in confronting the poor health of the low-income counties of the world.
4. To explain how age, sex, race, and social class affect the level of health of individuals in our society.
5. To identify and describe the issues of environmental pollution, cigarette smoking, and sexually transmitted diseases to world health today.
6. To explain the ethical issues related to dying and death.
7. To distinguish between health care and medicine.
8. To compare and contrast scientific medicine with holistic medicine.
9. To compare and contrast medical care in socialist and capitalist societies.
10. To describe, compare, and contrast the three sociological paradigms and their contributions to understanding health and medicine.

PART III: CHAPTER REVIEW

A story of a female college student with *anorexia nervosa* opens this chapter. This health problem (a disorder characterized by "severe caloric restriction") is both a biological and sociological issue. Many women with eating disorders are pressured by their parents to be high achievers. About 95 percent of people with this disease are female. Most are white and from affluent families. Cultural pressure is very much involved in creating this disease. It is an illustration of how social forces shape health in the U.S.

WHAT IS HEALTH?

Health is defined by the World Health Organization (WHO) as *a state of complete physical, mental, and social well-being*. Therefore, it is viewed as much a *social* as a *biological* issue.

Health and Society

Health in any society is shaped by several important factors. These include: (1) *People judge their health relative to others*, (2) *People pronounce as "healthy" what they hold to be morally good*, (3) *Cultural standards of health change over time*, (4) *Health relates to a society's technology*, and (5) *Health relates to social inequality*. Each of these is reviewed.

HEALTH: A GLOBAL SURVEY

Health in History

Health as a social issue is demonstrated by the significant increase in well-being over the course of history. The simple technology of hunting and gathering societies made it difficult to maintain a healthful environment. As many as one-half of the people in such societies died by age twenty, and few lived passed the age of forty.

The agricultural revolution increased surpluses, but also inequality, so only the elite enjoyed better health. Urbanization during medieval times created horrible health problems. Life expectancy was no better in Europe during medieval times than it was thousands of years earlier.

Health in Low-Income Countries

Health in poor countries today is much worse than in industrial societies. The World Health Organization estimates 1 billion people worldwide to be in poor health, mostly due to hunger. Infectious disease is very widespread. The **Global Sociology** box (p. 536) discusses hunger in West Africa. Focus is given to a disease known in West Africa as *Kwashiorkor*. The **Window on the World** box (p. 537) presents *Global Map 20-1* which focuses on medical care in global perspective, showing the scarcity of medical doctors in poor societies.

Improving health in these poor countries is very problematic due to the vicious circle of poverty and disease, and the fact that the introduction of medical technology, while reducing the deaths from infectious diseases also is related to a population growth which hinders development in such areas.

Health in High-Income countries

Initially, there was little improvement in health due to industrialization. The increase in health conditions, often believed to be attributable to medical advances, were actually related to the rising standard of living with its better nutrition and safer housing. It was not until the second half of the 19th century that medical advances had any significant impact on health. *Table 20-1* (p. 538) shows the 10 leading causes of death in the U.S. for the years 1900 and 1994. Significant differences appear. Medical advances have significantly changed the patterns, but so have lifestyles. About 60 percent of the deaths in the U.S. are attributable to heart disease, cancer, and cerebro-vascular diseases. Chronic illnesses, rather than infectious diseases are the major threat today.

HEALTH IN THE UNITED STATES

Social Epidemiology: The Distribution of Health

Social epidemiology is *the study of how health and disease are distributed throughout a society's population.*

Age and Sex

The health of people in the U.S. of all ages has improved during this century, with the exception of young adults, who are victims of more accidental deaths. Most white and African American females (86 percent and 78 percent respectively) and most white and African American males (76 percent and 58 percent respectively) born in 1991 can expect to live to at least age 65. Gender distinctions explain significant differences in longevity than race.

Social Class and Race

There is a strong relationship between social class and health. *Table 20-2* (p. 539) shows the perceptions people in the U.S. have concerning their own health by family income level categories. A strong positive correlation between income and health is illustrated. Health also affects income, given missed school and work resulting from illness. *Table 20-3* (p. 539) shows the life expectancy for U.S. children by race and sex. Significant differences again emerge. Factors related to the relationship are again economic, with African-Americans being overrepresented among the poor, placing them in conditions of poorer diet and greater stress. Further, the homicide rate among African-Americans, particularly for males, is extremely high. While wealth is no cureall, affluent people live longer and healthier lives on average than other people in the U.S.

Health and Society: Three Examples

Cigarette Smoking

Cigarette smoking is the leading preventable cause of illness and death in the U.S. It has recently begun to be labeled as deviant, as laws mandating smoke-free environments have been enacted in many parts of the country.

Evidence of the health risks of smoking first appeared in the 1930s. It was not for another thirty years until the government actually began systematic research. Currently, about 450,000 people die each year as a result of the effects of cigarette smoking.

Today, 25 percent of our adult population smokes. The figure was 37 percent in 1970, and 45 percent in 1960. A further reduction over the next decade is expected. Some smokers become addicted to the nicotine. Smoking varies by social class, with blue-collar workers more likely to smoke than white-collar workers. African-Americans smoke in greater proportions than whites. A greater percentage of males smoke than females.

As sales in the U.S. and other industrialized societies drop, tobacco companies have begun to sell more products in poor countries of the world. Tobacco remains a 30 billion dollar industry in the U.S. alone.

Eating Disorders

An **eating disorder** is *an intense involvement in dieting or other forms of weight control in order to become very thin.* The evidence suggests there is a strong cultural component to eating disorders, as suggested in the opening story to this chapter. The issue of the "gendered image" of women's bodies is discussed as a key element in this problem.

Sexually Transmitted Diseases

Increased concern about *venereal diseases* occurred during the 1960s at the beginning of the "sexual revolution." They are viewed by many as not just an illness, but also a punishment for immorality.

Sexually transmitted diseases (STDs) represent an exception to the general decline in infectious diseases during this century. About one-half million cases of *gonorrhea* are reported each year in the U.S., although the actual number is probably much higher. Approximately 78 percent of the cases reported involved African-Americans. Untreated gonorrhea can lead to sterility.

Syphilis is much more serious. There are about 110,000 cases reported in the U.S. annually. It can lead to damage of major organs, and result in blindness, mental disorders, and death. About 76 percent of the cases reported involve African-Americans.

Both diseases cannot be easily cured with penicillin. Neither then currently carries the label of a serious health problem in the U.S.

It is estimated that between 20 to 30 million people in the U.S. are carriers of the virus *genital herpes*. The infection rate among African-Americans is about three times higher than it is for whites. Although not as serious as gonorrhea or syphilis, there is currently no cure available.

AIDS, or acquired immune deficiency syndrome, is a health problem which could potentially become the most serious epidemic of modern times. AIDS is incurable and fatal. AIDS is caused by a human immunodeficiency virus (HIV). The virus attacks white blood cells, the core of our immune system. About 100,000 new cases were reported in the U.S. during 1995. The presence of the virus does not necessarily generate AIDS. About 205,000 people had AIDS in the U.S. in 1995. Globally there are some 15 million people infected with HIV. By the year 2000 this figure could be between 45-60 million.

Transmission of HIV almost always occurs through blood, semen, or breast milk. AIDS is not spread through casual contact. There are specific behaviors identified which put people at high risk for getting AIDS. The first is anal sex. Two-thirds of the people with AIDS are homosexual or bisexual males. Other risk factors include *sharing needles*, *having multiple sex partners*, and *using any drugs*. In the **Window on the World** box (p. 542) *Global Map 20-2* shows the distribution pattern of HIV infection of adults worldwide. *Figure 20-1* (p. 543) illustrates the type of transmission for reported U.S. AIDS cases in 1995. Fifty-five percent involved homosexual sex and 24 percent involved intravenous drug use.

AIDS has been a major financial problem as well, costing over 4 billion dollars in 1992. During the early 1990s the economic cost will likely triple. The government was slow to respond to the crisis because intravenous drug users and homosexuals were the first groups identified as having the disease. Money for research has increased rapidly in recent years. One drug AZT has shown the ability to slow the progression of the disease. Educational programs remain the best method to fight the spread of the AIDS virus as right now the only cure is prevention. AIDS is identified as both a medical and social problem.

Ethical Issues: Confronting Death

Ethical issues permeate health and medical concerns. Questions addressed include: When is a person dead? Do people have a right to die? And, what about mercy killing?

Medical and legal experts presently define death as an *irreversible* state involving no response to stimulation, no movement or breathing, no reflexes, and no indication of brain activity.

The Nancy Cruzan case, concerning a young woman who went into an irreversible coma after an automobile accident in 1990 is reviewed. The U.S. Supreme Court has ruled in this case that a patient has the right to die.

A presidential commission in 1983 issued guidelines outlining the rights of people in permanent vegetative states. Included is the suggestion that physicians honor a patient's *living will*, or a statement of personal intention regarding heroic treatment of terminal illness.

Euthanasia, commonly known as *mercy killing*, is *the assisting in the death of a person suffering from an incurable disease*. It can take two forms, *passive* and *active*. The passive form is illustrated by the Cruzan case. The active form is illustrated by a physician, Jack Kevorkian, who has assisted a number of people in taking their own lives with his "suicide machine."

THE MEDICAL ESTABLISHMENT

Medicine is *a social institution concerned with combating disease and improving health*. As such, it represents an aspect of *health care*, which is *any activity intended to improve health*. For most of human history, the individual and family were responsible for health care. In preindustrial societies, traditional healers, from herbalists to acupuncturists, provide for the health needs of their society's members. Medicine emerges within technologically complex societies as people fill specialized roles as healers.

The Rise of Scientific Medicine

Scientific medicine dominates health care in the U.S., meaning the logic of science is applied to research and treatment of disease and injury.

In colonial America, medicine was the domain of herbalists, druggists, midwives, and ministers. The ratio of such medical people to the total population is equivalent to the current ratio of medical doctors to the total population.

In colonial times here in America and in Europe, little formal medical training existed. Medical care was plagued by unsanitary conditions and ignorance.

During the early 19th century, medicine came under the control of medical societies. By 1900 there were 400 medical schools in the U.S. Licensing became the order in the second-half of the 19th century. Medical standards were established and directed by the American Medical Association (AMA), which was founded in 1847. By the early 1900s state licensing boards would only certify AMA approved physicians.

The AMA established physicians as scientific professionals with high prestige and earnings. At the same time, it restricted the practice of medicine to an affluent elite, dominated by urban, white males. In 1995, 78 percent of physicians were men, while 97 percent of nurses were women. Approximately 4 percent of physicians in the U.S. are non-white.

Those supporters of alternative approaches other than scientific medicine, like midwives, herbalists, and chiropractors, have been defined as a fringe area of medicine, with much less prestige and earnings. The average earning for a physician in the U.S. in 1993 was $175,000. Further, as the **Seeing Ourselves** box (p. 547) in *National Map 20-1* suggests, the availability of physicians in the U.S. is not evenly distributed across the country.

Holistic Medicine

Holistic medicine is *an approach to health care that emphasizes prevention of illness and takes account of a person's entire physical and social environment.* Holistic practitioners are critical of scientific medical specialists for being focused on symptoms and diseases rather than with people. They believe if drugs and surgery must be used, they must be incorporated into the broader perspective of a person's life. The following are identified and discussed as major concerns of the holistic approach: (1) *Patients are people*, (2) *Responsibility, not dependency* is stressed, with a focus on an *active* approach rather than a *reactive* one, and (4) *A personal treatment* environment is sought.

Paying for Health: A Global Survey

Medicine in Socialist Societies

In societies like the People's Republic of China, the Commonwealth of Independent States, government directly controls medical care. Medical costs are paid for by public funds, and medical care is distributed equally among all.

320

The People's Republic of China is still a relatively poor agrarian society which is just beginning to industrialize. With over 1 billion people, reaching everyone within one system is virtually impossible. While attempting private medical care for a time, in 1989 China returned to a government operated system.

Barefoot doctors, equivalent to paramedics in the U.S., bring modern methods to millions of rural residents in China. Traditional healing arts remain strong in China and medical care in China is quite adequate by world standards.

The former Soviet Union provided health care paid for through taxes. People have not chosen their own physician, but go to a government health facility near their home. Physicians, 70 percent of whom are women, have lower prestige and income than U.S. physicians. Equality in care was achieved in the former Soviet Union, however its rigid bureaucracy created a highly standardized and impersonal system.

Medicine in Capitalist Societies

In capitalist societies, citizens provide for themselves based on their own resources and preferences. Government assistance is provided to varying degrees.

In Sweden there exists a compulsory, comprehensive system of government medical care. The program is paid for through taxes. This type of system is known as *socialized medicine, a health care system in which the government owns and operates most medical facilities and employs most physicians.*

Great Britain has a dual system in which socialized medicine exists, but for those who wish, and can afford it, private care is available.

The Canadian system does not offer a true socialized medicine. The government reimburses citizens for Medicare according to set fees. Physicians operate privately.

In Japan, a combination of private insurance and government programs pay for medical costs. Large Japanese corporations cover their employees well. For those not covered, the government pays 70 percent of the medical costs. Physicians operate privately.

Except for the U.S., capitalist societies have three major benefits in common. First, basic medical care is available to all, regardless of income. Second, the government protects citizens from catastrophic medical costs. And third, the system's structure in each of these societies encourages "well" people to use medical facilities, often preventing more serious illnesses from occurring.

Medicine in the United States

While European governments pay about 80 percent of their citizens' medical costs, the U.S. government pays less than half. For the most part, the U.S. medical system is a private, profit-making industry. It is identified as a *direct-fee system*, or *a medical care system in which patients pay directly for the services of physicians and hospitals.*

The combination of no comprehensive national medical care program, and greater economic inequality than found in Europe, poor people in the U.S. have less access to medical care than their counterparts in Europe. The relative health of people in the U.S.

is worse than is found in European societies. In 1995 the U.S. was the only industrialized society without a government-sponsored medical system for every citizen.

The U.S. has not developed a national health-care program for several reasons. We in the U.S. have traditionally not been open to government intervention in the economy. There is little support for national health-care programs by the public. Also, the AMA has worked hard against dismantling the direct-fee system.

The technological advances in medicine have caused tremendous increases in the cost of medical care. These rising costs are displaced in *Figure 20-3* (p. 549). Currently, medical care absorbs 14 percent of our GNP (about 900 billion dollars).

In 1992, 61 percent of the population of the U.S. received some medical-care benefits from a family member's employer. About 14 percent of people in the U.S. purchased some form of private coverage. So, a total of 75 percent of the U.S. population are covered by *private insurance programs*.

Public insurance programs also exist. Medicare and Medicaid were created in 1965. Medicare currently covers a portion of the medical costs for 13 percent of the population, and Medicaid covers another 11 percent of the population.

HMOs, or **health maintenance organizations** are *organizations that provide comprehensive medical care to subscribers for a fixed fee*. These have become popular over the last decade or so, with 15 percent of the U.S. population being covered by such programs.

In all, a total of 85 percent of the people in the U.S. have some medical care coverage. Most is privately funded. Failures in the current medical-care system in the U.S. involve incomplete coverage in terms of costs for serious illness, exclusion of certain medical needs, and the fact that about 14 percent of our population have no medical coverage. President Bill Clinton is proposing a universal health care coverage program for the U.S. He terms his proposal one that will generate "managed competition." His reform intends to shift medical care away from the tradition private fee-for-service system toward various HMO and government-funded programs. There are many critics of this approach who suggest government interference will limit choice and raise costs.

THEORETICAL ANALYSIS OF HEALTH AND MEDICINE

Structural-Functional Analysis

Given its focus on society as a complex system that is stable and well integrated, structural-functionalism provides a view of illness that sees it as dysfunctional. Every society must therefore establish means of dealing with illness.

The Sick Role

The key concept in structural-functionalist analysis of illness is the *sick role*, or *patterns of behavior that are socially defined as appropriate for people who are ill*. As developed by Talcott Parsons, the sick role has four characteristics, including: (1) a sick person is exempted from routine responsibilities, (2) a person's illness is not deliberate, (3) a sick person must want to be well, and (4) a sick person must seek competent help.

The Physician's Role

The physician is expected to cure illness. According to Parson's, a hierarchy exists in which physicians expect compliance from their patients. Cross-culturally, the physician's role varies as illustrated by Japan physicians who are very likely to conceal from patients information about the patient's illness. The *patient's rights movement* in the U.S. has increased the amount of information shared by doctors with their patients.

Criticism of the structural-functional view of society includes a failure to recognize the inequalities in medical care services in the U.S.. Also, Parson's physician's role concept fits contemporary scientific medicine, but not holistic medicine.

Symbolic-Interaction Analysis

The Social Construction of Illness

The health of any person must be put into the context of the general health of the society. The definition of health and healthy life-styles vary cross-culturally and historically. Further, research by David Mechanic is cited to illustrate how definitions of illness are negotiated within particular social situations. The concept *psychosomatic disorder*, referring to how a person's state of mind affects physical well-being is discussed.

The Social Construction of Treatment

Research by Joan Emerson involving gynecological exams is used to illustrate how physicians "craft" their physical surroundings to make specific impressions on others.

A strength of this perspective is that it reveals the relativity of illness and health. A problem with the symbolic-interaction approach is that it minimizes an objective sense of health and illness.

Social-Conflict Analysis

The Access Issue

Unequal access to medical care is the central concern of the proponents of this perspective. Inequality for social-conflict theorists is rooted in the capitalist class system, which does not equitably distribute its resources, including medical and health care.

The Profit Motive

According to social-conflict theorists, the medical system is comprised of multi-million dollar corporate conglomerates out to make a profit. It is pointed out that three-fourths of all surgery in the U.S. each year is elective, not prompted by medical emergencies. Ivan Illich's research suggests that perhaps 1 million people each year in the United States have an adverse reaction to a medical drug. Moving toward socialism is viewed as necessary in order to improve medical care.

Medicine as Politics

The scientific model of medicine dominates our understanding of health. It is argued that even this approach can be guided by political motivations. The medical establishment, for example, has a history of racism and sexism. The **Global Sociology** box (p. 553) examines the practice of female circumcision which is practiced in many countries in African and in the Middle East.

Objections to this approach include the fact that it minimizes the improvements in medical care brought about by scientific medicine.

LOOKING AHEAD: HEALTH AND MEDICINE IN THE TWENTY-FIRST CENTURY

Members of our society take for granted good health. The advances in medicine which have been occurring over this century are expected to continue. There are many encouraging trends. Yet, health problems will continue, especially for the poor. An important need is to provide for the health care needs of all people. The **Controversy and Debate** box (p. 555) looks at the issue of genetic research and what information it can provide for us. The question is--Do we really want to know?

PART IV: KEY CONCEPTS

Define each of the following concepts in the space provided or on separate paper. Check the accuracy of your answers by referring to the key concepts section at the end of the chapter in the text as well as by referring to italicized definitions located throughout the chapter.

AIDS
anorexia nervosa
direct-fee system
euthanasia
health
health care
HIV
HMO
holistic medicine
kwashiorkor
living will
psychosomatic
scientific medicine
sick role
social epidemiology
WHO

PART V: STUDY QUESTIONS

True-False

1. T F The World Health Organization defines *health* as the absence of disease.
2. T F The top five *causes of death* in the United States have changed very little since 1900.
3. T F *Sex* is a stronger predictor of longevity than is ethnicity or race.
4. T F Research suggests affluent people live longer and suffer less from illness than do other people in the U.S.
5. T F *Venereal diseases* first appeared during the colonialization of Africa and Asia by European nations.
6. T F Approximately 70 percent of physicians in the Commonwealth of Independent States are *women*.
7. T F The United States is unique among the industrialized societies in *lacking* government programs that ensures basic medical care to every citizen.
8. T F Only about 25 percent of the United States population has some *private* medical insurance coverage.
9. T F Japanese physicians, due to the more holistic nature of their approach, tend to be much more "open" and less authoritarian with their patients about medical matters than U.S. physicians.
10. T F Most surgery in the United States is *elective*, or not prompted by a medical emergency.

Multiple-Choice

1. The *health* of any population is shaped by:

   (a) the society's cultural patterns
   (b) the society's technology and social resources
   (c) the society's social inequality
   (d) all of the above

2. In early societies, such as hunting and gathering societies, about one-half of the people died by age 20, and few persons lived past the age of:

   (a) 27 (b) 32 (c) 40 (d) 50 (e) 60

3. The improvement in health in the 19th century was primarily due to:

   (a) the rising standard of living
   (b) medical advances
   (c) changes in cultural values toward medicine
   (d) increases in the number of medical personnel to treat people
   (e) all of the above

4. The study of the distribution of disease or relative health in the population of a society is called:

   (a) scientific medicine   (c) holistic medicine
   (b) social epidemiology   (d) epistemology

5. Which of the following is *accurate*?

   (a) a larger proportion of males smoke as compared to females
   (b) a larger proportion of people with little formal education smoke as compared to highly educated people
   (c) a smaller percentage of people in the U.S. smoke today as compared to 1960
   (d) all above are accurate
   (e) none are accurate

6. The institutionalization of scientific medicine by the *AMA* resulted in:

   (a) expensive medical education
   (b) domination of medicine by white males
   (c) an inadequate supply of physicians in rural areas
   (d) all of the above
   (e) (a) and (b) only

7. *Holistic medicine* is a reaction to scientific medicine. Which of the following is *not* an emphasis advocates of holistic medicine share?

   (a) an emphasis upon the environment in which the person exists
   (b) an emphasis upon the responsibility of society for health promotion and care
   (c) an emphasis upon optimum health for all
   (d) an emphasis upon the home setting for medical treatment

8. Approximately what percentage of our *GNP* is related to health care?

   (a) 2   (b) 8   (c) 14   (d) 23   (e) 30

326

9. A formal organization that provides comprehensive medical care for which subscribers pay a fixed fee is termed:

(a) WHO
(b) AMA
(c) HMO
(d) DFS

10. Which of the following theoretical paradigms in sociology utilizes concepts like "sick role" and "physician's role" to explain health behavior?

(a) social-conflict
(b) symbolic-interaction
(c) structural-functionalist
(d) exchange
(e) materialism

Fill-In

1. Famine stricken children in Africa who have bloated bodies are suffering from a *protein deficiency* known as _____.
2. The leading cause of death today in the U.S. is _____, while in 1900 it was _____ and _____.
3. _____ is the study of the distribution of health and disease.
4. The number of people who prematurely die each year in the U.S. as a direct result of *cigarette smoking* is roughly _____.
5. AIDS, acquired immune deficiency syndrome, is caused by *HIV*, or a _____ _____ _____.
6. _____ *medicine* is an approach to health care that emphasizes prevention of illness and takes account of the whole person within the physical and social environments.
7. About _____ percent of U.S. physicians are *women*.
8. While European governments pay for about _____ percent of their people's medical costs, in the U.S. the government pays for less than _____ percent.
9. Between 1950 and 1994 expenditures for medical care in the U.S. rose _____-fold.
10. Medical experts have long noted the existence of _____ disorders, in which a person's state of mind affects physical well-being.

Definition and Short-Answer

1. It is pointed out in the text that the health of any population is shaped by important characteristics of the society as a whole. What are the three *general characteristics* identified? Provide an example of each.
2. How have the *causes of death* changed in the U.S. over the last century in terms of which one account for most deaths?
3. What is *social epidemiology*? Provide two illustrations of patterns of health found using this approach.

4. What is *AIDS*? How is AIDS transmitted? How widespread is it globally? In the U.S.?

5. What are the two types of *euthanasia*? Discuss the Cruzan and Kevorkian cases to illustrate. Relate these cases to the "ethical issues confronting death" as reviewed in the chapter.

6. What is meant by the *sick role*? What are its components? Provide an illustration, suggesting how it is functional for society.

7. Describe the characteristics of *holistic medicine*. How do they differ from those of scientific medicine?

8. How do health care systems operate in *socialist* societies? Provide specific examples.

9. In what ways does the health-care system of the United States *differ* from health-care systems in other *capitalist* systems? What are your recommendations for improving our health care system? Be specific.

10. What are *social-conflict* analysts' arguments about the health care system in the United States?

11. Discuss how *symbolic-interactionists* help us understand our health care system and our sense of health and illness, making reference to the issues of the "social construction" of illness and treatment.

PART VI: ANSWERS TO STUDY QUESTIONS

True-False

1.	F	(p. 533)	6.	T	(p. 547)
2.	F	(p. 538)	7.	T	(p. 548)
3.	T	(p. 539)	8.	F	(p. 548)
4.	T	(p. 539)	9.	F	(p. 550)
5.	F	(p. 541)	10.	T	(p. 552)

Multiple-Choice

1.	d	(p. 534)	6.	d	(p. 547)
2.	c	(p. 535)	7.	d	(p. 546)
3.	a	(p. 536)	8.	c	(p. 548)
4.	b	(p. 538)	9.	c	(p. 549)
5.	d	(p. 539)	10.	c	(p. 550)

Fill-In

1. kwashiorkor (p. 536)
2. heart disease, influenza, pneumonia (p. 538)
3. social epidemiology (p. 538)
4. 450,000 (p. 540)
5. human immunodeficiency virus (p. 541)

6. holistic (p. 546)
7. 16 (p. 547)
8. 80, 50 (p. 548)
9. 880 billion (p. 548)
10. psychosomatic (p. 551)

PART VII: ANALYSIS AND COMMENT

Global Sociology

"Killer Poverty: A Report From Africa"

Key Points: Questions:

"Female Genital Mutilation: When Medicine Is Politics"

Key Points: Questions:

Controversy and Debate

"The Genetic Crystal Ball: Do We Really Want To Look?"

Key Points: Questions:

Window on the World

"Global Map 20-1 The Availability of Physicians in Global Perspective"

Key Points: Questions:

"Global Map 20-2 HIV Infection of Adults in Global Perspective"

Key Points: Questions:

Seeing Ourselves

"National Map 20-1 The Availability of Physicians Across the U.S."

Key Points: Questions:

Population and Urbanization

21

PART II: LEARNING OBJECTIVES

1. To learn the basic concepts used by demographers to study population.

2. To describe, compare, and contrast the Malthusian theory and the demographic transition theory.

3. To explain how populations differ in industrialized societies and nonindustrialized societies.

4. To suggest ways in which the study of demography will provide guidelines to understanding and dealing with the earth's large population.

5. To compare and contrast the first cities of the world, preindustrial cities in Europe and industrial-capitalist cities in Europe.

6. To trace the transformation of the United States into an urban civilization from colonial settlement through urban expansion and the metropolitan era to urban decentralization.

7. To compare and contrast the characteristics of rural and urban life by explaining the theoretical views of Toennies, Simmel, Park, and Wirth.

8. To describe the key ideas of urban ecology and the related models of city structure.

9. To understand the causes of urbanization in poor countries of the world and the future prospects of cities in these countries.

PART III: CHAPTER REVIEW

This chapter begins with a brief review of Cortes' discovery and destruction of the great Aztec city of Tenochtitlan in the early 16th century. In its place he began to build Mexico City, which is expected to have a population of almost thirty million by the year 2000. It is a city which is part of a poor nation in great crisis. This chapter focuses on the processes of population growth and urbanization.

DEMOGRAPHY: THE STUDY OF POPULATION

Demography is *the study of human population*, investigating the size, age, sex composition and migration patterns of given populations. It is a quantitative discipline, however crucial questions about the consequences of these variables are analyzed and have great qualitative significance. Several basic concepts central to demographic analysis are discussed in the following sections.

Fertility

Fertility is *the incidence of childbearing in a society's population*. A female's childbearing years last from the beginning of menstruation to menopause. But, *fecundity*, or potential childbearing, is greatly reduced by health and financial constraints, cultural norms, and personal choice.

A typical measurement used for fertility is the **crude birth rate**, or *the number of live births in a given year for every thousand people in a population*. In the United States in 1995, there were 4.0 million live births in a population of 263 million, for a crude birth rate of 15.2. The term "crude" relates to the fact that comparing such rates can be misleading because it doesn't focus on women of childbearing age, and doesn't consider varying rates between racial, ethnic, and religious groups. It is however easy to calculate.

Mortality

Mortality is *the incidence of death in a society's population*. The **crude death rate** refers to *the number of deaths in a given years for every thousand people in a population*. There were 2.3 million deaths in the U.S. in 1995, for a crude death rate of 8.8.

The **infant mortality rate**, refers to *the number of deaths among infants under one year of age for each thousand live births in a given year*. The infant mortality rate in the U.S. in 1995 was 7.8. *Figure 21-1* (p. 560) compares fertility, mortality and infant mortality rates for countries around the world. Significant differences exist between nations.

Life expectancy, or *the average life span of a society's population*, is negatively correlated with a society's infant mortality rate. For males born in the U.S. in 1994 life expectancy is about 72 years and for females about 79 years.

Migration

Migration is *the movement of people into and out of a specified territory*. Some is involuntary, such as the historical existence of slave trading, while most is voluntary and based on various "push-pull" factors. Various examples of such factors are discussed.

Movement into a territory is termed *immigration*, and is measured by the number of people entering areas for every 1000 people in the total population. Movement out of an area, termed *emigration*, is measured by using the number of people leaving an area for every 1000 people in the population. The differences between the two figures is termed *net-migration rate*.

333

Population Growth

Migration, fertility, and mortality each affect a society's population size. The *natural growth rate* of a society is determined by subtracting the crude death rate from the crude birth rate. This figure for the U.S. in 1995 was 6.4 per thousand, or 0.64 percent annually. The projected rates for different world regions during the 1990s are presented in *Global Map 21-1* as the focus of the **Window on the World** box (p. 562). Industrialized regions, Europe, North America and Oceania have very low rates, while the poor countries in Asia, Africa and Latin America have relatively high rates. An annual growth rate of 2 percent (as found in Latin America) doubles a population in 35 years. In Africa, the growth rate is 3 percent. The *doubling time* concept is discussed.

Population Composition

The **sex ratio** refers to *the number of males for every hundred females in a given population* In the U.S. in 1995 the sex ratio was 95.2. A more complicated descriptive device is the **age-sex pyramid** which is *a graphic representation of the age and sex of a population. Figure 21-2* (p. 563) presents the age-sex pyramids for the U.S. and Mexico. Very different demographic histories and likely futures are seen in the data. For the U.S. the *baby boom* and *baby bust* birth cohorts are discussed.

HISTORY AND THEORY OF POPULATION GROWTH

Until relatively recently in human history, societies desired high birth rates as high birth rates meant more human resources for productivity. High birth rates were needed to offset high death rates. Also, until the development of the rubber condom 150 years ago, birth control was very unreliable. A critical point in world population growth occurred in the middle of the 18th century as the earth's population began a sharp increase, resulting more from a drop in the mortality rate than from a rise in the birth rate. In the 20th century alone the world's population has increased *fourfold*. Currently there are a little over 5 billion people on earth. Around 1850 the world popu- lation reached 1 billion, in 1930 it reached 2 billion, in 1962 it reached 3 billion, in 1974 it reached 4 billion, and in 1987, 5 billion. By 2025 the world's population is projected to reach 8 billion. *Figure 21-3* (p. 564) shows the increase in world population (actual and projected) 1700-2100.

Malthusian Theory

In the late 18th century Thomas Malthus developed a theory of population growth in which he warned of disaster. He predicted population would increase according to a geometric progression, while food production would only increase in arithmetic progression.

Malthus saw *positive checks*, such as famine, disease, and war; and *preventative checks*, such as artificial birth control and delayed marriage as the only two limits to population growth. The former he felt was immoral, and the latter he was not optimistic about.

For several reasons his projections have not been realized. First, the birth rate in Europe began to drop in the 19th century as children became less of an economic asset. He also under-estimated human ingenuity, specifically in terms of technological applications in solving food production and population related problems.

But his warnings still need to be taken seriously. Technology has caused problems for the environment, and population growth in poor nations remains very high. Even if their population growth rate is reduced, any rate of increase in the long-range can be dangerous.

Demographic Transition Theory

Demographic transition theory has now replaced Malthusian theory and is *a thesis linking demographic changes to a society's level of technological development. Figure 21-4* (p. 565) illustrates three stages of technological change, and the related birth and death dates. Stage 1 is represented by the preindustrial agrarian society with high birth rates and high death rates. Stage 2, represented by industrialization, marks the beginning of the demographic transition, with high birth rates continuing, but death rates dropping significantly. In stage 3, the fully industrialized society, birth rates begin to drop significantly and death rates remain stable and low.

The lower birth rate in the third stage is related to a higher standard of living, resulting in children being a greater economic burden. Smaller families are also more functional as a higher percentage of women work outside the home. Further, a higher level of technology makes birth control widely available and reliable.

This view provides far more optimism than Malthusian theory. It has been incorporated into modernization theory. Dependency theorists have therefore been critical of this view.

Global Population Today: A Brief Survey

Using demographic transition theory important differences between industrialized and nonindustrialized societies can be noted in terms of population patterns.

The Low-Growth North

Shortly after industrialization began the population growth in Europe and America peaked at 3 percent annually. It has been generally declining since, and since 1970 has not been above 1 percent. Europe and the U.S. are near population replacement level of 2.1 births per women, a point known as *zero population growth*, or *the level of reproduction that maintains population at a steady state*. In certain European societies, a fourth stage may have even been reached where there is actually a population decline. Several factors, including the increasing cost of raising children, working women, and delaying marriage, are discussed as reasons for low birth rates in industrialized societies. A very significant factor remains birth control technology and its availability. Even Catholics no longer differ from other people in the U.S. in their contraceptive practices. Abortion, legal in the U.S. since 1973, also is a factor.

The High-Growth South

Few societies are still represented by stage 1. Most poor nations, having a combination of agrarian and industrial economies, fall in stage 2. *Figure 21-3* (p. 565) shows that two-thirds of the world's population is now found in poor societies. The demographic change, historical and projected· (1700-2100) is illustrated. The decreasing death rates in nonindustrialized societies has resulted in the population explosion in these countries.

Birth rates are high for age-old reasons, the economic asset of children to the family and high infant mortality rates. The cultural norm of patriarchy also is a factor in the continuation of high birth rates. The link between social status of women and fertility rates is addressed in the **Critical Thinking** box (p. 568).

Infant mortality rates are still high, and life expectancy compared to industrialized societies is still relatively low, but improvements are being made. Overall, it is *primarily* the declining death rates in poor societies which is responsible for the rapid population growth.

URBANIZATION: THE GROWTH OF CITIES

Urbanization is *the concentration of humanity into cities.* Its history has been characterized by three urban revolutions, which are discussed in the text.

The Evolution of Cities

Preconditions of Cities

The *first urban revolution* occurred about 12,000 years ago with the emergence of permanent settlements. Two factors are discussed as enabling urbanization to occur, a *favorable* ecology and *changing* technology.

The First Cities

The first city is argued to have been Jericho, just north of the Dead Sea, coming into existence about 8000 B.C.E. By 4000 B.C.E. there were several cities within the Fertile Crescent in present day Iraq and along the Nile in Egypt.

Cities emerged independently in at least three other areas of the world--in present day Pakistan (about 2500 B.C.E.) in China (about 2000 B.C.E.), and in Central and South America (about 1500 B.C.E.).

Preindustrial European Cities

Urbanization began in Europe about 1800 B.C.E. on Crete and spread throughout Greece in the form of hundreds of city states. Athens is the most well known. Ancient Athens, as an example of urban life, is discussed. As Greek civilization faded, the city of Rome grew to almost 1 million by the 1st century B.C.E. The militaristic Roman Empire had expanded throughout Europe and Northern Africa.

The fall of the Roman Empire started a period of urban decline. Cities became smaller, surrounded by "defensive" walls. By the 11th century medieval cities began to remove their walls to facilitate trade. Personal and family ties were strong in such cities. These cities in Europe were characterized by "quarters," or areas in the city where particular occupational groups were represented.

Industrial European Cities

The new trading class, affluent, urban, and middle-class or *bourgeoisie* steadily increased in power during the middle ages in Europe. The *second urban revolution* was under way by about 1750. Industrial productivity caused cities to grow rapidly. Besides population changes, cities were transformed in terms of their physical layout. Factories, businesses, and broad boulevards dominated the urban landscape. Urban social life began to change as well as crowding, impersonality, inequality, and crime became more and more characteristic of cities during the 18th and 19th centuries.

The Growth of U.S. Cities

Native Americans established few permanent settlements. The Spanish made their first settlement in St. Augustine in Florida in the year 1565. The English founded Jamestown in Virginia in 1607. Today, more than three-quarters of the U.S. population lives in urban areas.

Colonial Settlement: 1624-1800

The changing face of settlements in the northeastern U.S. during the 17th century is discussed. *Figure 21-5* (p. 570) contrasts the different urban development patterns of the early 17th and late 17th century, showing how the traditional European shape of winding and narrow roads were replaced by grid-like patterns.

The first U.S. census in 1790 counted 4 million U.S. citizens. *Table 21-1* (p. 573) shows the change in the number and percentage of people living in urban areas between 1790 and 1990.

Urban Expansion: 1800-1860

Important transportation developments are discussed which influenced the development of cities in the East to the Midwest. By 1860 about one-third of the people in the U.S. lived in cities.

The Great Metropolis: 1860-1950

Table 21-4 (p. 577) illustrates the rapid growth of cities in the late 19th century. It further shows population changes in cities during the 20th century. By 1900, New York City had about 4 million inhabitants. Chicago had about 2 million inhabitants. The growth between 1860-1900. This marked the beginning of the era of the *metropolis, a large city that socially and economically dominates an urban area.* By the end of World War I most of the U.S. population lived in cities.

·Urban Decentralization: 1950-present

Since 1950, people have been moving away from the central cities in the U.S.. *Table 21-2* (p. 573) illustrates how many northeastern and Midwest cities have been experiencing either stable or declining populations. Urbanization continues however with the growth of suburbs.

Suburbs and Central Cities

Suburbs, the urban areas beyond the political boundaries of a city, have been expanding in recent decades. Suburbs first appeared in the late 19th century, as some of the well-to-do moved from the hectic cities. Racial and ethnic intolerance also increased the movement to the suburbs. The post-World War II economic boom, more affordable cars, and an increased birth rate all were factors in the rapid growth of suburbia. By 1970, more people lived in the suburbs than in the central cities.

Shopping and industry also began to move out of the cities to the suburbs during this period. The loss of tax revenue caused many cities to decay, some reaching the brink of bankruptcy. The government responded with *urban renewal programs,* or government programs intended to revitalize cities. Many inner-cities have been rebuilt, yet critics argue this has benefited business, not the poor residents.

Postindustrial Sunbelt Cities

In 1940 the "Snowbelt" contained 60 percent of the population of the United States. In 1992 the "Sunbelt" contained 56.2 percent of our population. This regional migration is linked to the post-industrial economy. This demographic shift is portrayed in *Table 21-2* (p. 573). Six of the ten largest cities (by population) are now found in the sunbelt. These Sunbelt cities, developed after decentralization began, tend to be larger in areas than Snowbelt cities. The **Sociology of Everyday Life** box (p. 574) presents and discusses figures that show how the largest Sunbelt and Snowbelt cities fared between 1980 and 1992 in terms of population.

Megalopolis: Regional Cities

Decentralization has created regional cities. The Census Bureau officially recognized 253 regional cities in the U.S. in 1993. These are called *metropolitan statistical areas* (MSAs). MSAs must include a city with a population of at least 50,000, plus densely populated surrounding counties. A *megalopolis* is *a vast urban region containing a number of cities and*

338

their surrounding suburbs. The largest MSAs are called *consolidated metropolitan statistical areas* (CMSAs). In 1993 there were 18 of these in the U.S. When several of the CMSAs geographically meet, like on the east coast from Boston to northern Virginia, a *megalopolis*, or vast urban region containing a number of cities and their surrounding suburbs, is created.

URBANISM AS A WAY OF LIFE

Ferdinand Toennies: Gemeinschaft and Gesellschaft

This German sociologist of the late 19th century differentiated between two types of social organization. The first *gemeinschaft* refers to *a type of social organization by which people are bound closely together by kinship and tradition.* It describes social settings dominated by primary groups and small villages. Its meaning is similar to Durkheim's mechanical solidarity. In contrast, *gesellschaft* is *a type of social organization by which people have weak social ties and considerable self-interest.* This represents city dwellers, and is similar to Durkheim's concept of organic solidarity.

Emile Durkheim: Mechanical and Organic Solidarity

Durkheim agreed with much of what Toennies had to say about urban life. Again, Durkheim saw *mechanical solidarity* being replaced by *organic solidarity*, paralleling Toennies concepts of *gemeinschaft* and *gesellschaft*. Durkheim was far more optimistic about the changes than Toennies.

Georg Simmel: The Blase Urbanite

This German sociologist used a micro-level analysis of how urban life shaped the behavior and attitudes of people. He argued city dwellers needed to be selective in what they responded to because of the social intensity of such a life. They develop then a *blase' attitude* out of necessity.

The Chicago School: Robert Park and Louis Wirth

The first major sociology program in the U.S. to focus on urban development was at the University of Chicago. Robert Ezra Park is perhaps the most famous urban researcher to have worked at Chicago. His is introduced in the **Profile** box (p. 577). He saw the city as a highly ordered mosaic of distinctive regions. Cities were viewed as complex social organisms by Park.

As another of the Chicago urban researchers, Louis Wirth identified three factors that define urbanism: large population, dense settlement, and social diversity. He saw cities as impersonal, superficial, and transitory.

Mixed support for Park's and Wirth's views on city life have been found in recent decades. While a greater sense of community exists in rural areas, the difference compared to cities can be exaggerated. Also, early sociologists were incorrect in their projection that urban life would neutralize the effects of class, race, and sex.

Urban Ecology

Urban ecology is *the study of the link between the physical and social dimensions of cities.* One issue focused on is why cities are located where they are. Another issue concerns the physical design of cities. Several models explaining urban form are identified and discussed, including the *concentric zone* model, the *sector* model, the *multicentered* model, the *social area analysis* model, and *wedge-shaped sectors* model.

Criticism of this view include the argument that urban ecologists paint an overly simplified picture of urban life, and that they have focused only on one historical period of cities.

The Historical Importance of Cities

Thomas Jefferson in 1800 and Rudyard Kipling in 1900 each indicated a distaste for urban life. The ancient Greeks, on the other hand, saw cities as the only path to find the "good life." We are ambivalent about cities. They seem to comprise the best and the worst social life has to offer. It should be remembered, the Latin root *civis* means "city dweller." Early Greeks saw the connection between civilization and cities as *polis*, meaning city, is the root of politics, the core of Greek life.

URBANIZATION IN POOR SOCIETIES

Previously described were the first and second urban revolutions. A third urban revolution began about 1950. In 1950, about 25 percent of the population in poor countries was urbanized, by the year 2005 this figure is expected to reach 50 percent (it currently is at about 40 percent). In the **Window on the World** box (p. 585) *Global Map 21-2* puts urbanization in global perspective. Seventy-five percent of the people living in industrialized societies now live in urban areas. Fewer than one in ten people living in many African and Asian countries live in cities. *Table 23-6* (p. 580) compares the world's ten largest cities in 1980 and the projected sizes of certain cities for the year 2000. In the year 2000 only four of the largest cities by population are expected to be in industrialized societies.

As the poor countries of the world continue through the second stage of the demographic transition, and migration to urban areas in these countries continues, their cities are expected to experience further conflict and hardships. The Mexico City situation outlined at the beginning of the chapter is further discussed as an example of this pattern.

LOOKING AHEAD: POPULATION AND URBANIZATION IN THE TWENTY-FIRST CENTURY

Modernization and underdevelopment theories provide different answers to what is needed in order to stabilize and nurture the urban growth patterns in poor countries. Each year 90 million new people live on our planet, most in the least economically developed countries. The recent global population growth is described as "a great wave," and the future of the entire world is tied to changes occurring in the poor nations of the globe. The **Controversy and Debate** box (p. 582) provides a brief discussion on this issue.

KEY CONCEPTS

Define each of the following concepts in the space provided or on separate paper. Check the accuracy of your answers by referring to the key concepts section at the end of the chapter in the text as well as by referring to italicized definitions located throughout the chapter.

age-sex pyramid
concentric zone model
crude birth rate
crude death rate
demographic transition theory
demography
emigration
fecundity
fertility
gemeinschaft
gesellschaft
immigration
infant mortality rate
integrated analysis
life expectancy
Malthusian theory
megalopolis
metropolis
migration
mortality
multi-nuclei model
natural growth rate
sector model
sex ratio
social area analysis
suburbs
urbanization
urban ecology
urban renewal
zero population growth

PART V: STUDY QUESTIONS

True-False

1. T F Demographers using what is known as the *crude birth rate*, only take into account women of childbearing age in the calculation for this figure.

2. T F In general, population is moving from the coasts *toward* the heartland of the United States.

3. T F A significantly larger percentage of the U.S. population over the next two decades will be comprised of *childbearing aged women* than at any other period in our nation's history.

4. T F *Africa* has the highest annual population growth rate of all the continents.

5. T F According to *demographic transition theory*, population growth patterns are linked to a society's level of technological development.

6. T F Protestants are more likely than Catholics in the U.S. to use *contraceptive practices*.

7. T F *Urbanization* in Europe began in about 1800 B.C.E.

8. T F Today, over three-quarters of the people in the U.S. live in *urban areas*.

9. T F Most of the ten largest cities in the U.S. (in terms of population) are in the *Sunbelt*.

10. T F Compared to Louis Wirth, Robert Park had a relatively *negative* view of urban life.

Multiple-Choice

1. Cortes reached the *Aztec capital* of _____ in 1519.

    (a) Cuzco
    (b) Tikal
    (c) Montezuma
    (d) Tenochtitlan

2. The *sex ratio* in the U.S., or the number of males for every one-hundred females is:

    (a) 85   (b) 90   (c) 95   (d) 100   (e) 105

3. During the 20th century the world's population has increased _____ times.

    (a) 2   (b) 4   (c) 10   (d) 20   (e) 30

4. The *first city* to have ever existed is argued to be:

   (a) Athens   (d) Cairo
   (b) Tikal   (e) Jericho
   (c) Rome

5. According to the text, the *second urban revolution* was triggered by:

   (a) the fall of Rome
   (b) the Industrial Revolution
   (c) the fall of Greece
   (d) the post-World War II baby boom
   (e) the discovery of the New World

6. The period of *1950 to the present* is described in the text as:

   (a) urban decentralization   (c) the metropolitan era
   (b) urban expansion   (d) the second urban revolution

7. Ferdinand Toennies' concept that refers to the *type of social organization* with weak social organization as a result of cultural pluralism and impersonal social relationships is:

   (a) megalopolis   (d) sector model
   (b) gesellschaft   (e) multi-nuclei model
   (c) gemeinschaft

8. One issue studied by *urban ecologists* is the physical design of cities. Which of the following is not a model used to explain urban form:

   (a) concentric zone   (d) social area analysis
   (b) multicentered   (e) all are used as models
   (c) sector model

9. What percentage of the population in poor nations is expected to be living in *urban areas* in the year 2005:

   (a) 10   (b) 25   (c) 37   (d) 50   (e) 67

10. Which of the following is expected to be the *largest urban area* (in terms of population) in the year 2000:

    (a) Tokyo-Yokohama   (d) Shanghai
    (b) New York   (e) Buenos Aires
    (c) Mexico City

Fill-In

1. _____ is the *incidence of childbearing* in a society's population.

2. People's movement *into* a territory--commonly termed _____, while people's movement *out of* a territory is commonly termed _____.

3. The richest countries of the world, including the U.S., Canada, and the nations of Europe, have *growth rates* below _____ percent. The nations of Latin America and Asia typically have growth rates approaching ____ percent, which double a population in thirty-five years. The continent of _____ has an overall growth rate of _____ percent, which cuts the doubling time to less than twenty-four years.

4. A handy rule of thumb is that dividing society's *growth rate* into the number seventy yields the _____ _____ in years.

5. Thomas Malthus saw two limits to population growth: _____ checks, such as famine, and _____ checks, such as birth control.

6. _____ _____ *theory* is the thesis that population patterns are linked to a society's level of technological development.

7. Two factors are identified which set the stage for the *first urban revolution*. The first factor was a favorable _____, and the second factor was changing _____.

8. The era of the *great metropolis* is characterized in the text as existing from _____ to _____.

9. A _____ is a very large city that socially and economically dominates an urban area.

10. The Bureau of the Census recognizes 253 *regional cities* in the U.S. which they call _____ _____ _____, or MSA's.

11. _____ refers to a *type of social organization* with strong solidarity based on kinship and tradition.

12. The *model of urban development* established by Ernest Burgess is called the _____ _____ model.

13. The "third urban revolution" began in about _____, and is taking place in _____ societies.

Definition and Short-Answer

1. What are the three basic factors which determine the *size* and *growth rate* of a population? Define each of the three concepts.

2. Differentiate between *Malthusian theory* and *demographic transition theory* as perspectives on population growth.

3. What are the *three stages* in the demographic transition theory? Describe each.

4. Identify and describe the five *periods* of growth of U.S. cities presented in the text.

5. Differentiate between the concepts of *metropolis* and *megalopolis*.

6. Differentiate between the *perspectives* of Louis Wirth and Robert Park concerning urbanization in the U.S.

344

7. What factors are causing *urban growth* in poor nations?
8. How are urbanization patterns changing worldwide?
9. Differentiate between the work of Ferdinand Toennies and Emile Durkheim in terms of their views on *urbanization*.
10. What are the major points being made by the author concerning the *historical importance* of cities?
11. What do the terms "low-growth-north" and "high-growth south" mean? What are the factors related to the differences in demographics for these two parts of the world?
12. Select any two *tables* in this chapter and summarize, analysis, and interpret the data contained in them.
13. Select any two *figures* in this chapter and summarize, analyze, and interpret the data contained within them.

PART VI: ANSWERS TO STUDY QUESTIONS

True-False

1.	F	(p. 560)	6.	F	(p. 567)
2.	F	(pp. 563-64)	7.	T	(p. 569)
3.	F	(p. 563)	8.	T	(p. 571)
4.	T	(p. 563)	9.	T	(p. 573)
5.	T	(p. 565)	10.	F	(p. 576)

Multiple-Choice

1.	d	(p. 559)	6.	a	(p. 572)
2.	c	(p. 563)	7.	b	(p. 574)
3.	b	(p. 564)	8.	e	(pp. 577-78)
4.	e	(p. 569)	9.	d	(p. 580)
5.	b	(p. 570)	10.	a	(p. 580)

Fill-In

1. fertility (pp. 559-60)
2. immigration, emigration (p. 561)
3. 1, 2, Africa, 2.8 (p. 562)
4. doubling time (p. 563)
5. positive, preventative (p. 565)
6. demographic transition (p. 565)
7. ecology, technology (p. 569)
8. 1860, 1950 (p. 571)
9. metropolis (p. 572)

10.   metropolitan statistical area (p. 573)
11.   gemeinschaft (p. 574)
12.   concentric zone (p. 577)
13.   1950, poor (p. 580)

PART VII: ANALYSIS AND COMMENT

Critical Thinking

"Empowering Women: The Key to Controlling Population Growth"

Key Points: Questions:

Sociology of Everyday Life

"Heading for the Sunbelt"

Key Points: Questions:

Profile

"Robert Ezra Park (1864-1944)

Key Points: Questions:

Controversy and Debate

"Apocalypse Soon? Will People Overwhelm the Earth?"

Key Points: Questions:

Window on the World

"Global Map 21-1 Population Growth in Global Perspective"

Key Points: Questions:

"Global Map 21-2 Urbanization in Global Perspective"

Key Points: Questions:

Seeing Ourselves

"National Map 21-1 Population Change Across the United States"

Key Points: Questions:

The Natural Environment 22

PART I: CHAPTER OUTLINE

I.   Ecology: The Study of the Natural Environment
        A. The Role of Sociology
        B. The Global Dimension
        C. The Historical Dimension
        D. Population Increase
        E. Cultural Patterns: Growth and Limits
            1. The Logic of Growth
            2. The Limits of Growth
II.   Environmental Issues
        A. Solid Waste: The "Disposable Society"
        B. Preserving Clean Water
            1. Water Supply
            2. Water Pollution
        C. Clearing the Air
        D. Acid Rain
        E. The Rain Forests
            1. Global Warming
            2. Declining Biodiversity
III.   Society and the Environment: Theoretical Analysis
        A. Structural-Functional Analysis
        B. Cultural Ecology
        C. Social-Conflict Analysis
        D. Environmental Racism
IV.   Looking Ahead: Toward a Sustainable Society and World
V.   Summary
VI.   Key Concepts
VII. Critical-Thinking Questions
VIII. Suggested Readings

PART II: LEARNING OBJECTIVES

1. To understand the global dimension of the natural environment.
2. To be able to discuss the impact of technology and population growth on the ecology of the globe.
3. To be able to discuss the dimensions of the "logic of growth" and the "limits to growth" as issues and realities confronting our world.
4. To be able to identify and discuss the major environmental issues confronting our world today.
5. To be able to discuss the two contrasting theories concerning the relationship between society and the environment--Structural-functional analysis and social-conflict analysis.
6. To begin to develop a sense about the ingredients for a sustainable society and world in the century to come.
7. To be able to identify the key strategies being suggested to create a sustainable ecosystem.
8. To begin to think about the fundamental changes necessary in our ways of thinking about ourselves and our world to better support a sustainable ecosystem.

PART III: CHAPTER SUMMARY

The beginning paragraphs of this chapter address the issue of the global depletion of "natural" surroundings. Nauru, a tiny island in the Soouth Pacific, is discussed as an example of environmental desruction. The inhabitants of this island are among the richest in the world, and yet their island is no longer habitable.

ECOLOGY: THE STUDY OF THE NATURAL ENVIRONMENT

Ecology is *the study of the interaction of living organisms and the natural environment*. It is an interdisciplinary study, involving social and natural sciences. One key concept being focused on is the **natural environment** which refers to *the earth's surface and atmosphere, including various living organisms as well as the air, water, soil, and other resources necessary to sustain life*. Like all living species, humans are dependent on the natural environment. However, humans are unique in a capacity for culture which allows us to remake the world according to our own interests and desires.

The Role of Sociology

Environmental concerns fall within the scope of sociology. There are three main reasons why sociology can help us better undertand and deal with the environmental crises of our time. First, sociologists can explore what "the environment" means to people of varying social backgroounds. Second, sociologists can monitor the public pulse on many environmental issues. And third, sociologists can demonstrate how human social patterns have caused mounting stress on the natural environment.

The Global Dimension

Our planet consists of one *ecosystem,* or *the system composed of the interaction of all living organisms and their natural environment.* The Greek meaning of "eco" is house. All living things in the natural environment are *interrelated.* The use of chlorofluorocarbons is used as an example. Further illustration is provided in the **Global Sociology** box (p. 589) which takes a look at the connection between hamburger chains in the U.S. and the ecological consequences in Latin America.

The Historical Dimension

Culture, specifically *technology* poses a threat to the natural environment. The more complex the technology of a culture, the greater the impact on the natural environment. Simple technologies, such as found in hunting and gathering societies, intermediate technologies as found in pastoral and horticultural societies, and complex technologies found in industrial societies are briefly discussed. In the **Window on the World** box (p. 590) *Global Map 22-1* illustrates where in the world energy use is highest. High use is linked to industrialization. High energy use is only part of the problem though, as the products produced through technology creates solid waste.

Humans threaten the natural environment. Ecologists describe this as *environmental deficit,* meaning *a situation in which our relationship to the environment, while yielding short-term benefits, will have profound nd negative long-term consequences.* Three important ideas are implied by this concept. These are: (1) the state of the environment is a *social issue,* (2) the damage done to the environment is often *unintentional,* and (3) in some but not all instances the damage done is *reversible.*

As we reach the postindustrial era people in technologically advanced societies seem to be coming to the realization that concern is needed for environmental quality.

Population Increase

Besides powerful technology, another threat to the environment is a population explosion. As the Industrial Revolution progressed, rising living standards in Europe sent death rates down dramatically. In 1850 the world's population reached one billion people. Five thousand years ago humanity numbered about 50 million, in 1930 2 billion people inhabited the globe, in 1962 there were 3 billion, and today we number about 5.75 billion. The net gain of people each day worldwide is 250,000.

By the end of the next century some experts predict 10 billion people will be living on earth. The highest growth rates are found in the poorest countries. Rapid population growth and poverty go hand in hand. Industrialization in poor societies, given current population levels and projections would greatly stress the world's natural resources.

Cultural Patterns: Growth and Limits

The point is being made that the planet suffers not just from economic *under*development in some parts of the world but also from economic *over*development in others.

The Logic of Growth

The core values in our society of *material comfort*, *progress*, and *science* underlie the *logic of growth* view. This is an optimistic view, one seeing productive technology improving over time. But, as many of the earth's resources are *finite*, this view helps create many environmental problems. This issue is discussed.

The Limits to Growth

Environmentalists argue that the logic of growth view has contributed to the deterioration of the natural environment. They argue that humanity must implement policies to control the growth of population, material production, and use of resources in order to avoid environmental collapse. Projections are discussed and are illustrated in *Figure 22-1* (p. 593).

ENVIRONMENTAL ISSUES

Surveys suggest that people in the poorest countries are the most unhappy with their surroundings. People in the U.S. rate their local environments higher than people in poor countries, but lower than people in other industrial societies. Two-thirds of the U.S. population is concerned that the natural environment has "gotten worse." We *perceive* the natural environment to be in danger. *Figure 22-2* (p. 594) show data from a global survey on the rating of local environments. European societies rate their local environments as being of higher quality than we do in the U.S.

Solid Waste: The "Disposable Society"

For our nation as a whole, over one billion pounds of solid waste are generated every day. We have been labeled the *"disposable society."* We not only consume many products per capita, but also throw away a great deal. Much of that discarded waste is the packaging materials that the products come in. Examples are discussed. Only about 20 percent of what we throw away is burned or recycled. The dumping in landfills poses several problems, including the space limits for waste material, the water pollution created, and the fact that much of what is discarded is not biodegradable. *Recyclying* is a critical issue and is placed in global perspective by our author. Compared to Japan, for example, we recycle very little. The Fifty percent of what households throw away in the U.S. includes paper products. *Figure 22-3* (p. 595) shows data concerning the composition of household trash in the U.S. The **Global Sociology** box (pp. 596-97) provides a look at one recycling effort in Egypt which has been quite successful. The story told concerns the Zebaleen, a religious minority--Coptic Christians--in a predominately Muslim society, who actually live in the Cairo dump.

351

Preserving Clean Water

While the earth naturally recycles water and refreshes the land through a process known as the *hydrological cycle*, two key concerns exist--supply and pollution.

Water Supply

Concern of the supply of water is actually an issue which dates back to ancient times in civilizations in Egypt, China, and Rome. Current and projected problems in Asia and North Africa are discussed. Increasing population and complex technology are major factors. Industry industry draws 25 percent of all global water usage. Households account for 10 percent of usage.

Water Pollution

Most people in the U.S. take water quality for granted. But water contamination is a steadily growing problem in our country. Only recently have water supplies had the protection of the law. A major step was taken in 1972 with the federal government's Clean Water Act. Yet still, 500 million pounds of toxic waste is absorbed into rivers and streams across our country each year. Things in certain respects are improving though. Before federal legislation took effect Cleveland's Cayahoga River was so polluted it actually caught on fire. So, both water *supply* and water *quality* are critical issues in our society.

Clearing the Air

People in this country seem to be more aware of air pollution than they are about contaminated water. Industrialization has impacted negatively on air quality. Factories and automobiles are major sources of this problem. Laws which are helping reduce the problem are discussed. In the **Seeing Ourselves** box (p. 600) *National Map 22-1* shows the level of air pollution for all the states in the U.S.

Acid Rain

Acid rain refers to *precipitation that is made acidic by air pollution so that it destroys plant and animal life. Figure 22-4* (p. 601) illustrates how acid rain is formed. One phenomenon which is demonstrated is how one form of pollution causes another. The global scope of the problem is clear.

The Rain Forests

Rain Forests are *regions of dense forestation, most of which circle the globe close to the equator.* The **Window on the World** box (p. 598) presents *Global Map 22-2* which show he location of rain forests around the world. Today, approximately 7 percent of the earth's land surface is covered by rain forest. The largest is in South America, primarily in Brazil. The world's rain forests are being deforested at the rate of 1 percent each year.

Global Warming

Rain forests play an important role in removing carbon dioxide from the atmosphere. The burning of the rain forests released even more carbons into the atmosphere. Today the atmospheric concentration of carbon dioxide is 10-20 percent higher than it was 150 years ago. What is being created is a *greenhouse effect*, or *a rise in the earth's average temperature due to increasing concentration of carbon dioxide in the atmosphere*. Projections indicate that the average global temperature of 60 degree fahrenheit today could rise 5 to 10 degrees during the next century.

Declining Biodiversity

The *biodiversity*, or the array of plant and animal life, is decreasing around the globe. Rain forest hold approximately one-half of all the living species in the world. Why should we be concerned about the world's declining biodiversity? First, biodiversity provides a varied source of food. Second, it provides a vital genetic resource. Third, the beauty and complexity of our natural environment is diminished. It is also important to remember that extinction is irreversible.

SOCIETY AND THE ENVIRONMENT: THEORETICAL ANALYSIS

Structural-Functional Analysis

The structural-functionalists offer three important insights about the natural environment. These include: (1) the fundamental importance of *values* and *beliefs* to the operation of a social system, (2) the interconnectedness of various dimensions of social life, and (3) strategies for responding to environmental problems.

Critics of this view stress that it overlooks the issues of inequality and power. Further, many environmentalists are skeptical about the optimism held by people holding this view concerning our capacity to improve the natural world.

Cultural Ecology

Cultural ecology, which is closely allied with structural-functional theory, is *a theoretical paradigm that explores the relationship of human culture and the physical environment*. Marvin Harris' analysis of India's sacred cow provides an informative illustration of this approach and its application to the relationship between humans and the natural environment. Limitations of this perspective involve oversimplifying the connections between cultural and physical forces.

Social-Conflict Analysis

This view directs us to see problems in the natural environment being the result of social arrangements favored by elites. Capitalism is seen as a major contributor to environmental crisis. They further stress the significance of inequality between nations as a major factor in the exploitation of the natural world.

Critics of this view argue that capitalism is no more hostile to the natural world than other systems. Many strides toward environmental protection are being made in capitalist societies, even more so than in socialist countries. Also, poor countries are also putting stress on the natural environment, particularly given their population growth rates.

Environmental Racism

Environmental racism refers to *the pattern by which environmental hazards are greatest in proximity to poor people and especially minorities.* Historically, factories have been built in and near poor neighborhoods. Examples in the United States are discussed.

Criticisms of this view include the fact that elites have not been able to stop legislation that proects the environment and workers, capitalist countries have better records of environmental protection than socialist societies, and environmental problems are worsening in poorer countries as they develop economically.

LOOKING AHEAD: TOWARD A SUSTAINABLE SOCIETY AND WORLD

An environmental deficit exists anywhere humans live. A *sustainable ecosystem,* referring to *a way of life that meets the needs of the present generation without threatening the environmental legacy of future generations,* is given focus in this section. Three basic strategies for achieving such an existence are identified. These include: (1) conservation, (2) reducing waste, and (3) bringing world population growth under control.

Environmental strategies are not enough though. Four changes in terms of how we perceive ourselves and our world are discussed. These include: (1) seeing the present as being tied to the future, (2) seeing that humans are linked in countless ways to all other species of life, (3) the needs for global cooperation, and (4) a critical reevaluation of the logic of growth view.

PART IV: KEY CONCEPTS

acid rain
biodiversity
cultural ecology
disposable society
ecology
ecosystem
environmental deficit
environmental racism

greenhouse effect
natural environment
rain forest
recycling
sustainable ecosystem

PART V: STUDY QUESTIONS

True-False

1. T F The cultural values of material comfort, progress, and science form the foundation for the *logic of growth thesis*.
2. T F The *limits to growth* model puts great faith in human ingenuiety and science to resolve problems of scarcity and environmental depletion.
3. T F People in the U.S. rate their local environment *more favorably* than people in poor societies do, but compared to those people living in other industrial societies the U.S. population is more negative.
4. T F The Japanese *recycle* over three times more solid waste per capita than people in the U.S.
5. T F Households around the world account for more *water use* than does industry.
6. T F California and Pennsylvania are two of the *least polluted* U.S. states.
7. T F *Biodiversity* tends to be relatively low in rain forest environments.
8. T F The *greenhouse effect* is the result of too little carbon dioxide in the atmosphere.
9. T F One criticism of *structural-functional theory* is that it fails to take account of the interconnectedness of various dimensions of social life.
10. T F According to *social-conflict theorists*, rich nations are overdeveloped and consume too much of the world's natural resources.

Multiple-Choice

1. The Greek meaning of the word *eco* is:

    (a) weather   (d) satisfaction
    (b) house   (e) work
    (c) material

2. Riddle: A pond has a single water lily growing on it. The lily doubles in size each day. In thirty days, it covers the entire pond. On which day did it cover half the pond?

    (a) 5   (b) 8   (c) 15   (d) 21   (e) 29

3. How many pounds of solid waste are generated in the U.S. each and every day?

   (a) 15 million   (d) 1 billion
   (b) 100 million   (e) 8 billion
   (c) 250 million

4. In which of the following countries do the people rate their local environment more poorly than people in the U.S. rate their own?

   (a) Poland   (d) Russia
   (b) Canada   (e) both (a) and (d)
   (c) Ireland

5. What percentage of the solid waste in the U.S. is either recycled or burned?

   (a) 2   (b) 8   (c) 20   (d) 35   (e) 50

6. Which type of solid waste represents about one-half of all household trash in the U.S.?

   (a) metal products   (d) yard waste
   (b) paper   (e) plastic
   (c) glass

7. The federal government's *Clean Water Act* of _____ was a first step toward cleaning this country's water.

   (a) 1867   (d) 1983
   (b) 1972   (e) 1990
   (c) 1958

8. *Rain forests* cover approximately _____ percent of the earth's land surface.

   (a) .01   (b) 2   (c) 7   (d) 11

9. The world's *largest* rain forest is found in:

   (a) South America   (d) Indonesia
   (b) North America   (e) Asia
   (c) Africa

10. The *structural-functional* paradigm offers three important insights about the natural environment. These include:

   (a) the importance of values and beliefs to the operation of a social system
   (b) the interconnectedness of various dimensions of social life
   (c) some strategies for responding to environmental problems
   (d) all of the above
   (e) none of the above

11. Strategies recommended for creating a *sustainable ecosystem* include:

   (a) conservation
   (b) reducing waste
   (c) bring population growth under control
   (d) all of the above
   (e) none of the above

12. A collection of environmental strategies alone will not succeed with some *fundamental changes* in the ways in which we think about ourselves and our world. Important points to consider include:

   (a) the present is tied to the future
   (b) humans are linked in countless ways to all other species of life
   (c) achieving a sustainable ecosystem is a task that requires global cooperation
   (d) a critical reevaluation of the "logic of growth" thesis is required for a sustainable society
   (e) all of the above

Fill-In

1. An _____ is defined as the system composed of the interaction of all living organisms and their natural environment.
2. The typical adult in the U.S. consumes up to _____ times more energy each year than the average member of the world's poorest societies.
3. Our planet gains an additional _____ people each day.
4. Core values that underlie cultural patterns in the U.S. include progress, material comfort, and science. Such values form the foundation for the _____ ___ _____ *thesis*.
5. The _____ ____ _____ *thesis* states that humanity must implement policies to control the growth of population, material production, and the use of resources in order to avoid environmental collapse.
6. The results of a general survey of twenty-two nations reveal a serious concern about the environment. However, the people of _____ scored the *quality* of their natural environment higher than all other nations surveyed.

7. The earth *naturally recycles* water and refreshes the land through what scientists call the _____ _____.

8. It is estimated that fifty percent of *household trash* is _____.

9. Experts estimate the atmospheric concentration of *carbon dioxide* is now _____ to _____ percent higher than it was 150 years ago.

10. *Structural-functional analysis* is criticized for overlooking the issues of _____ and _____ and how these affect our relationship with the natural environment.

11. Strategies for creating a *sustainable ecosystem* include _____, _____ _____, and bringing _____ _____ under control.

12. Environmental strategies alone won't succeed without some *fundamental changes* in the way we think about ourselves and our world. We must see that the present is tied to the _____, humans are linked in countless ways to all other _____ of life, achieving a sustainable ecosystem is a task that requires _____ _____, and a critical reevaluation of the logic of _____ thesis is necessary for a sustainable society.

Short-Answer

1. Differentiate between the concepts *ecology* and *natural environment*.

2. What three important ideas are implied by the concept *environmental deficit*?

3. Briefly describe the pattern of world *populaiton growth* prior to and after the Industrial Revolution.

4. Critically differentiate between the *logic of growth* and the *limit to growth* views concerning the relationship between human technology and the natural environment.

5. What is meant by the term *disposable society*? Provide evidence discussed in the text which suggests that this label applies to the U.S. today.

6. Review the global research presented in the text concerning either *water pollution* or *air pollution*.

7. Discuss the connection between the depletion of the *rain forests* and *global warming* and *declining biodiversity*.

8. Differentiate between the *structura-functional* and *social-conflict* views on the relationship between human society and the natural world. What are the three important insights offered by structural-functionalists? What are the key issues highlighted by the social-conflict theorists? Identify one criticism of each approach.

9. What is *cultural ecology*? How does India's sacred cow illustrate this perspective? What are the criticism of this perspective?

10. What are the three strategies identified for creating a *sustainable ecosyseem*? What are strategies would you suggest?

11. What is *environmental racism*? What is the evidence that it exists? What are three criticisms of this perspective?

12. What are the *fundamental changes* in the ways we think about ourselves and the world which are being suggested in the text? What other changes in our thinking would you suggest be made?

PART VI: ANSWERS TO STUDY QUESTIONS

True-False

1.	T	(p. 592)	6.	F	(p. 600)
2.	F	(p. 593)	7.	F	(pp. 601-02)
3.	T	(p. 594)	8.	F	(p. 601)
4.	T	(p. 595)	9.	F	(p. 603)
5.	F	(p. 598)	10.	T	(p. 605)

Multiple-Choice

1.	b	(p. 588)	7.	b	(p. 599)
2.	e	(p. 591)	8.	c	(p. 601)
3.	d	(p. 594)	9.	a	(p. 601)
4.	e	(p. 594)	10.	d	(p. 603)
5.	c	(p. 595)	11.	d	(p. 607)
6.	b	(p. 595)	12.	e	(pp. 607)

Fill-In

1. ecosystem (p. 592)
2. 100 (p. 594)
3. 250,000 (p. 594)
4. logic of growth (p. 596)
5. limits to growth (p. 597)
6. Norway (p. 599)
7. hydrological cycle (p. 600)
8. paper (p. 601)
9. 10-20 (p. 605)
10. inequality/power (p. 607)
11. conservation/reducing waste/population growth (p. 610)
12. future/species/global cooperation/growth (p. 610)

PART VII. ANALYSIS AND COMMENT

Global Sociology

"The Hamburger Connection: The Global Consequences of What We Do at Home"

    Key Points: Questions:

Social Policy

"The Second Time Around: Recycling in the U.S."

    Key Points: Questions:

Controversy and Debate

"Is the Environmental Movement Radical? Should It Be?"

    Key Points: Questions:

Window on the World

"Global Map 22-1 Energy Consumption in Global Perspective"

    Key Points: Questions:

"Global Map 22-2 The Earth's Tropical Rain Forests"

    Key Points: Questions:

Seeing Ourselves

"National Map 22-1 Air Pollution Across the U.S."

    Key Points: Questions:

Collective Behavior and Social Movements

23

PART I: CHAPTER OUTLINE

I.   Studying Collective Behavior
II.   Localized Collectivities: Crowds
        A. Mobs and Riots
        B. Crows, Mobs, and Social Change
        C. Explaining Crowds
                1. Contagion Theory
                2. Convergence Theory
                3. Emergent-Norm Theory
III.   Dispersed Collectivities: Mass Behavior
        A. Rumor and Gossip
        B. Public Opinion
        C. Panic and Mass Hysteria
        D. Fashions and Fads
IV.   Social Movements
        A. Types of Social Movements
        B. Explaining Social Movements
                1. Deprivation Theory
                2. Mass-Society Theory
                3. Structural-Strain Theory
                4. Resource-Mobilization Theory
                5. New Social Movements Theory
        C. Gender and Movements
        D. Stages in Social Movements
        E. Social Movements and Social Change
V.   Looking Ahead: Social Movements in the Twenty-First Century
VI.   Summary
VII.   Key Concepts
VIII.   Critical-Thinking Questions
IX.   Suggested Readings

PART II: LEARNING OBJECTIVES

1. To identify the problems associated with studying collective behavior from a sociological perspective.
2. To explain the general characteristics of collectivities that distinguish them from social groups.
3. To distinguish among the concepts of crowds, mobs, riots, and panics.
4. To describe, compare and contrast contagion theory, convergence theory, and emergent- Norm theory in terms of how each orients researchers in the study of collective behavior.
5. To describe the relationships of crowds to politics and social change.
6. To describe, compare, and contrast the various dispersed collectivities: rumor, public opinion, mass hysteria, fashion, and fads.
7. To identify and describe the four types of social movements.
8. To compare and contrast the four theories of social movements: deprivation theory, mass- society theory, structural-strain theory, and resource mobilization theory.
9. To describe the four stages of a social movement.
10. To explain the relationship between social movements and social change.

PART III: CHAPTER REVIEW

This chapter begins with the story of the "Million Man March" in 1995 held in Washington, D.C. African-American males from around the country participated in this national display of pride, brotherhood, and determination to bring about change.

The focus of this chapter is *social movements*, or *organized activity that encourage or discourages social change*. Social movements are one of the most important types of *collective behavior*, referring to *activity involving a large number of people, often spontaneous, and typically in violation of established norms*.

STUDYING COLLECTIVE BEHAVIOR

Studying collective behavior is difficult for several reasons, including (1) this concept is very **wide ranging,** (2) it is a very **complex** concept, and (3) it is often **transitory** in nature. It is pointed out that this is perhaps true for all issues studied by sociologists. However, a particularly significant problem here is limited theoretical analysis of this domain of social inquiry.

A *collectivity* is *a large number of people whose minimal interaction occurs in the absence of well-defined and conventional norms*. Two types of collectivities are (1) *localized* collectivities, referring to people in physical proximity to one another, and (2) *dispersed* collectivities, or *mass behavior*, meaning people influencing one another, often from great distances.

These collectivities are distinguished from social groups on the basis of three characteristics, including (1) **limited social interaction**, (2) **no clear social boundaries**, and (3) **weak and unconventional norms**.

363

LOCALIZED COLLECTIVITIES: CROWDS

A **crowd** is *a temporary gathering of people who share a common focus of attention and whose members influence one another*. Herbert Blumer identifies four types of crowds, based in part on their level of emotional intensity. These include: the *casual* crowd, or a loose collection of people who have little interaction; the *conventional* crowd, resulting from deliberate planning of an event and conforming to norms appropriate to the situation; the *expressive* crowd, which forms around an event that has emotional appeal; and an *acting* crowd which is a crowd energetically doing something. Crowds can change from one type to another. A fifth type, or *protest* crowd, not identified by Blumer, is a crowd which has some political goal.

Mobs and Riots

When an acting crowd becomes violent it is classified as a **mob**, *a highly emotional crowd that pursues some violent or destructive goal*. Lynching is a notorious example in the history of the United States. The freeing of the slaves, which provided African Americans with political rights and economic opportunities were perceived by whites as a threat. Lynching was used as a form of social control to exert white supremacy over African Americans. Lynchings were at their peak between 1880 and 1930. Most of the 5,000 lynchings which were officially reported to the police during this time occurred in the deep South.

A violent crowd with no specific purpose is termed a **riot**, or *a social eruption that is highly emotional, violent, and undirected*. Throughout U.S. history riots have resulted from a collective expression against social injustice. Examples from U.S. history are reviewed. It is also pointed out that rioting behavior can result from positive feelings as evidenced by the riots involving college students on Spring Break.

Crowds, Mobs, and Social Change

Over history, crowds have been able to effect social change, and have also provoked controversy. Crowds enable people to challenge or support their society. Ordinary people gain power through collective activity.

Explaining Crowd Behavior

Contagion Theory

The unconventional behavior of crowds has been a topic of sociological concern for many years. One of the first social scientists to try and explain such behavior was Gustave Le Bon, who developed *contagion theory*. This theory maintains that crowds can exert a hypnotic effect on its members. Anonymity of a crowd creates a condition in which people lose their identity and personal responsibility to a collective mind.

Critics claim that many crowds do not take on a life of their own separate from the thoughts and actions of their members. The tragic deaths at a Who concert in Cincinnati in 1979 is used as an example to illustrate.

Convergence Theory

Convergence theory leads researchers to see motives which drive collective action as emerging prior to the formation of a crowd. The idea is that people of like-mind come together for a particular purpose and form a crowd. As opposed to contagion theory, which focuses our attention on irrational forces, this perspective provides a view of rational processes creating a crowd.

Emergent-Norm Theory

Ralph Turner and Lewis Killian developed *norm-emergent theory*, and argue like convergence theorists, that crowds are not merely irrational collectivities. However, they further suggest that patterns of behavior emerge within the crowds themselves. The New Bedford, Massachusetts tavern rape in 1983 is used to illustrate this process.

This view fits into the symbolic-interaction approach to the study of social life. Crowd behavior is seen, in part, as a response to its members motives, but that norms emerge and guide behavior within the development of the crowd itself. Critics of this view argue that not all members follow emergent norms.

DISPERSED COLLECTIVITIES: MASS BEHAVIOR

Mass behavior refers to *collective behavior among people dispersed over a wide geographical area.*

Rumor and Gossip

Rumor, or *unsubstantiated information people spread informally, often by word of mouth*, is one example. Rumor has three essential characteristics, including *thriving in a climate of ambiguity, being unstable,* and *being difficult to stop.* The **Sociology of Everyday Life** box (p. 619) discusses the case of the rumored death of Beatle Paul McCartney in 1967.

Closely related to rumor is *gossip*, or *rumor about the personal affairs of others*. Gossip is referred to as being more localized than rumor. It can be an effective means of social control.

Public Opinion

Public opinion is a form of highly dispersed collective behavior. No one "public opinion" exists on key social issues, but rather is represented by a diversity of opinion. However, sharing particular traits in common with others can create certain patterns in attitudes.

365

A public grows larger and smaller over time as interest in a particular issue changes. The women's movement is used as an illustration. Certain categories of people are argued to have more social influence than others when it comes to shaping public opinion.

Propaganda is defined as *information presented with the intention of shaping public opinion*. It can be accurate or false, positive or negative. Various forms exist from politics to advertising. The **Seeing Ourselves** box (p. 620) *National Map 23-1* shows data concerning support for public broadcasting across the United States.

Panic and Mass Hysteria

A *panic* is *a form of localized collective behavior by which people react to a perceived threat or other stimulus with irrational, frantic, and often self-destructive behavior*. Generally some threat provokes a panic, as in the case of a fire in a crowded theater.

Mass hysteria is *a form of dispersed collective behavior by which people respond to a real or imagined event with irrational, frantic, and often self-destructive behavior*. The 1938 CBS radio broadcast of a dramatization of the novel War of the Worlds, is used as an example to illustrate how mass hysteria can emerge.

Fashions and Fads

Fashion is *a social pattern favored for a time by a large number of people*. Fashions are transitory and occur for two reasons, the future-orientation of people in industrial societies and the high social mobility representing such societies.

U.S. sociologist Thorstein Veblen originated the term *conspicuous consumption*, referring to the practice of spending money with the intention of displaying one's wealth to others.

A *fad* is *an unconventional social pattern that people embrace briefly but enthusiastically*. They are sometimes referred to as *crazes*. While fads are truly "passing fancies," fashions tend to reflect fundamental human values and social patterns that evolve over time.

SOCIAL MOVEMENTS

Three characteristics differentiate social movements from other types of collective behavior: a higher degree of internal organization; typically longer duration, often spanning many years; and the deliberate attempt to reorganize society itself.

While being rare in preindustrial societies, social movements are common in industrialized societies. They develop around a wide range of social issues.

Types of Social Movements

Social movements are classified along two basic dimensions, *breadth*, concerning the proportion of the population in society involved and *depth*, concerning the question of how superficial or extensive the change being sought is for the society.

Four types of social movements are identified based on these dimensions. *Figure 23-1* (p. 624) presents a model of the different types identified along these two dimensions. These

366

types include: *alternative social movements*, which pursue limited change for certain individuals (planned parenthood being an example); *redemptive social movements*, which focus on a limited number of individuals, but seek to change them radically (fundamentalist church organizations are an example); *reformative social movements*, which seek limited social change for the entire society (proponents of holistic health care are an example); and *revolutionary social movements*, which seek basic transformations of the entire society (the John Birch Society is an example).

Explaining Social Movements

Deprivation Theory

Deprivation theory holds that social movements arise as people react to feeling deprived of things they consider necessary or believe they deserve. This approach is implicit in Karl Marx's expectation that industrial workers would eventually organize in opposition to capitalism.

Relative deprivation is *a perceived disadvantage arising from some specific comparison.* In the middle of the 19th century, Alexis de Tocqueville studied the question as to why a revolution occurred in France and not in Germany in the late 1790s. What puzzled him was that social conditions in Germany were far worse than they were in France. His answer to this apparent paradox was that German peasants had known nothing but feudal servitude and thus had no basis for feeling deprived. Improving social conditions in France had raised the expectations of its people during the latter part of the 18th century.

Figure 23-2 (p. 625) illustrates the model developed by Jamie Davies predicting that social movements are more likely to occur in a society when an extended period of improvement in the standard of living is followed by a shorter period of decline.

Weaknesses with this perspective include its inability to help us explain why social movements emerge among some categories of people and not others, and the apparent circular reasoning involved in this approach. This latter point refers to the fact that deprivation is identified as a condition only if a social movement emerges.

Mass-Society Theory

This approach, first developed by William Kornhauser, suggests people who feel isolated and insignificant within a broad, complex society are attracted to social movements. Using this perspective, involvement in social movements is viewed as being more *personal* than *political.*

Research provides inconsistent support for this approach. The Nazi movement in Germany; for example, primarily recruited people who were not socially isolated. Further, political goals of urban rioters in the U.S. have been shown to be part of the participants' purpose.

367

Structural-Strain Theory

This perspective was developed by Neil Smelser in the early 1960s. In this theory, six social conditions are identified as fostering social movements. These include: (1) **structural-conductiveness**, (2) **structural strain**, (3) **growth and spread of an explanation**, (4) **precipitating factors**, (5) **mobilization for action**, and (6) **lack of social control**. Each of these conditions is explained in the text.

This approach is identified as being distinctly social, rather than psychological. This theory however contains the same circularity of argument as found in the relative deprivation theory. Further, it fails to incorporate the important variable of resources, such as the mass media, into a formula for explaining social movements and their relative success or failure.

Resource-Mobilization Theory

Resource-mobilization theory argues that social movements are unlikely to emerge, and if they do, are unlikely to succeed without necessary resources.

This theory's dual focus on discontent and available resources for the success of a social movement provides critical insight for researchers. However, critics argue that powerless segments of the population can promote successful social movements if they organize effectively and have strongly committed leaders. It is also pointed out that power struggles within the status quo of society itself must be taken into account.

New Social Movements Theory

A major question focused on by researchers using this approach concerns how and why many recent social movements are different from those of the past. Theorists using this view are concerned with issues such as global ecology, women's and gay's rights, and risks of nuclear war. Two features of this approach is a national (and sometimes international) scope and concern for the quality of life. This view also highlights the power of the state and the mass media. *Table 23-1* (p. 629) identifies and summarizes the six theories of social movements.

Gender and Movements

There have traditionally been many gender barriers for women who want to, or do, participate in social movements. Examples are discussed. Nonetheless, women have played key roles in different social movements, as examples, the abolitionist and feminist movements.

Stages in Social Movements

While recognizing each social movement is unique, four stages are identified which most move through. These stages include: *emergence, coalescence, bureaucratization*, and *decline*.

These are reviewed in the text. *Figure 23-3* (p. 630) illustrates the stages.

A social movement declines for several reasons, including the accomplishment of its goals, poor political leadership, inability to counteract forces from the status quo, repression by leaders over their followers, and finally, some social movements may eventually become an accepted part of the system.

Social Movements and Social Change

Social movements either encourage or resist social change. Social change is both a cause and a consequence of social movements. Many past social movements, though taken-for-granted by most people today, did much to affect our social lives.

LOOKING AHEAD: SOCIAL MOVEMENTS IN THE TWENTY-FIRST CENTURY

The U.S. has been relatively calm in terms of social movements since the 1960s. However, social movements are a significant part of our history, and many of our most profound social problems remain unsolved. It is being suggested that the scope of social movements in the U.S. is likely to increase in the future given new technologies and the emerging global connections of many issues/problems facing people today. The **Controversy and Debate** box (p. 632) asks the question--Are you willing to take a stand? National surveys reveal that most people express considerable pessimism and apathy about the state of society. Included are survey data concerning the political involvement of students who entered college in 1995.

PART IV: KEY CONCEPTS

Define each of the following concepts in the space provided or on separate paper. Check the accuracy of your answers by referring to the key concepts section at the end of the chapter in the text as well as by referring to italicized definitions located throughout the chapter.

acting crowd
alternative social movement
casual crowd
collective behavior
conspicuous consumption
contagion theory
conventional crowd
convergence theory
crowd
deprivation theory
dispersed collectivities
emergent-norm theory

expressive crowd
fad
fashion
gossip
mass hysteria
mass-society theory
mob
panic
propaganda
redemptive social movement
reformative social movement
relative deprivation
resource-mobilization theory
revolutionary social movement
riot
rumor
social movements
structural-strain theory

PART V: STUDY QUESTIONS

True-False

1.	T	F	People gathered at a beach or observing an automobile accident are used in the text as examples to illustrate *conventional crowds*.
2.	T	F	Using *contagion theory*, it is argued that people lose their individual identities and surrender personal will and responsibility to a collective mind.
3.	T	F	*Mass behavior* refers to collective behavior among people dispersed over a wide geographic area.
4.	T	F	According to the text, *social movements* are rare in preindustrial societies.
5.	T	F	According to the text, reformative social movements have greater depth, but less scope than redemptive social movements.
6.	T	F	The post-Civil War Ku Klux Clan and Jim Crow laws are presented in the text to illustrate deprivation theory.
7.	T	F	Using mass-society theory, social movements are viewed as more personal than political.
8.	T	F	*Mass-society theory* argues that social movements attract socially isolated people who feel personally insignificant.
9.	T	F	According to *structural-strain theory*, people form social movements because of a shared concern about the inability of society to operate as they believe it should.

10. T   F   According to our author, *social change* characteristic of large and complex societies is a consequence, but not a cause of social movements.

Multiple-Choice

1. Which of the following is *not* identified as a difficulty in researching collective behavior using the sociological perspective?

    (a)   the concept of collective behavior is broad
    (b)   collective behavior is complex
    (c)   collective behavior is often transitory
    (d)   all are identified as difficulties

2. Herbert Blumer identified several *types* of crowds based on their level of emotional intensity. Which of the following is not a type of crowd identified by Blumer?

    (a)   casual   (d)   acting
    (b)   conventional   (e)   emergent
    (c)   expressive

3. A *theory of crowds* which claims that the motives which drive collective action do not originate within a crowd, but rather precede its formation is called _____ theory.

    (a)   contagion   (c)   convergence
    (b)   reactive   (d)   subversive

4. One of the first theories of *crowds*, developed by French sociologist Gustave Le Bon, is called _____ *theory*, which focuses on how anonymity in a crowd causes people to lose their identities and surrender personal will and responsibility to a collective mind.

    (a)   mob   (c)   retreative
    (b)   convergence   (d)   contagion

5. A *theory* which argues that crowds are not merely irrational collectivities is

    (a)   consensual theory   (c)   structural theory
    (b)   emergent-norm theory   (d)   reactive theory

6. The radio broadcast by H.G. Wells "War of the Worlds" is used to illustrate:

(a) gossip
(b) rumor

(c) mass hysteria
(d) panic

7. What *type* of social movement seeks limited social change for the entire society?

(a) revolutionary
(b) redemptive
(c) deprivation

(d) alternative
(e) reformative

8. The pro-democracy movement in Eastern Europe is used to illustrate which *theory* of social movements?

(a) mass society
(b) structural-strain

(c) resource-mobilization
(d) "new social movements"

9. The following points--people join social movements as a result of experiencing relative deprivation; social movement is a means of seeking change that brings participants greater benefits; social movements are especially likely when rising expectations are frustrated, best fit which *theory* of social movements?

(a) deprivation theory
(b) resource-mobilization

(c) structural-strain
(d) mass-society

10. Emergence is identified as stage 1 of a social movement. Which of the following is *not* identified as a stage in the evolution of a social movement?

(a) bureaucratization
(b) coalescence

(c) decline
(d) realignment

Fill-In

1. Riots, crowds, fashions, fads, panics, mass hysteria, public opinion, and social movements are all examples of _____ _____.
2. *Collective behavior* is difficult for sociologists to study for the following three reasons: collective behavior is _____ _____, collective behavior is _____, and much collective behavior is _____.
3. A _____ is a large number of people who interact little, if at all, in the absence of well-defined and conventional norms.
4. Three key *differences* between *social groups* and *collectivities* are that the latter are based on _____ social interaction, have no clear _____ _____, and engender _____ and _____ norms.

5. Five *types of crowds* are identified in the text, including: _____, _____, _____, _____, and _____.

6. _____ *theory* holds that motivations for collective action are not born in the crowd but are brought to the crowd by individual participants.

7. *Rumor* has three essential characteristics, including: thriving on a climate of _____, being _____, and difficult to _____.

8. _____ refers to information presented with the intention of shaping public opinion.

9. While _____ is a form of collective behavior by which people react to a perceived threat or other stimulus with irrational, frantic, and often self-destructive behavior, _____ _____ is a form of *dispersed* collective behavior by which people respond to a real or imagined event with irrational, frantic, and often self destructive behavior.

10. Thorstein Veblen defined _____ _____ as the practice of spending money with the intention of displaying one's wealth to others.

11. A _____ is an unconventional social pattern that people embrace briefly but enthusiastically and are truly passing fancies, whereas _____ is a social pattern favored for a time by a large number of people and tends to reflect fundamental human values and social patterns that evolve over time.

12. _____ _____ is a perceived disadvantage based on some comparison.

13. Using *mass-society theory*, social movements are viewed as more _____ than _____.

14. According to Neil Smelser's *structural-strain theory* there are six factors that foster social movements, including: structural _____, structural _____, growth and spread of an _____, precipitating _____, mobilization for _____, and lack of social _____.

15. One clear strength of _____ _____ _____ *theory* is its recognition that social movements are increasing in scale in response to the growing power of the state and the development of a global political system.

16. The third *stage* of a social movement after emergence and coalescence is _____.

Definition and Short-Answer

1. What are three basic characteristics of *dispersed collectivities*?

2. Differentiate between the four *types of crowds* identified by Herbert Blumer on the basis of level of emotional intensity.

3. Differentiate between *contagion theory*, *convergence theory*, and *emergent-norm theory* in terms of how each explains crowd behavior.

4. Differentiate between the concepts of *rumor* and *gossip*.

5. Using structural-strain theory, Smelser identifies *six social conditions* that help foster social movements. What are these social conditions?

6.   What are the *five theories* of social movements? Compare and contrast each of these in terms of how they help us explain social movements.

7.   What are the *four stages* of social movements? Define and provide an illustration for each.

8.   What are the *four types* of social movements identified in the text? Select two of these and provide an illustration for each.

9.   Differentiate between the concepts *mass hysteria* and *panic*. Provide examples of each.

10.   Why are social movements expected to increase in *scope* over the next decades? Do you agree? Why?

PART VI: ANSWERS TO STUDY QUESTIONS

True-False

1.	F	(p. 614)	6.	T	(p. 624)
2.	T	(p. 617)	7.	T	(p. 625)
3.	T	(p. 618)	8.	T	(p. 625)
4.	T	(p. 623)	9.	T	(p. 626)
5.	F	(p. 624)	10.	F	(p. 633)

Multiple-Choice

1.	d	(p. 613)	6.	c	(p. 621)
2.	e	(p. 614)	7.	e	(p. 624)
3.	c	(p. 617)	8.	b	(p. 626)
4.	d	(p. 617)	9.	c	(p. 631)
5.	b	(p. 617)	10.	d	(pp. 629-30)

Fill-In

1.   collective behavior (p. 613)
2.   wide ranging, complex, transitory (p. 613)
3.   collectivity (p. 614)
4.   limited, social boundaries, weak, unconventional (p. 614)
5.   casual, conventional, expressive, acting, protest (pp. 614-15)
6.   convergence (p. 617)
7.   ambiguity, unstable, stop (p. 618)
8.   propaganda (p. 620)
9.   panic, mass hysteria (p. 621)
10.   conspicuous consumption (p. 622)
11.   fad, fashion (pp. 622-23)
12.   relative deprivation (p. 624)

13. personal/political (p. 625)
14. conductiveness, strain, explanation, precipitating, action, control (pp. 526-27)
15. new social movements (p. 628)
16. bureaucratization (p. 630)

PART VII: ANALYSIS AND COMMENT

Sociology of Everyday Life

"The Rumor Mill: Paul Is Dead"

    Key Points: Questions:

Controversy and Debate

"Are You Willing to Take a Stand?"

    Key Points: Questions:

Seeing Ourselves

"National Map 23-1: Support for Public Broadcasting Across the United States"

    Key Points: Questions:

Social Change: Traditional, Modern, and Postmodern Societies

PART I: CHAPTER OUTLINE

I. What Is Social Change?
II. Causes of Social Change
    A. Culture and Change
    B. Conflict and Change
    C. Ideas and Change
    D. The Natural Environment and Change
    E. Demographic Change
III. Modernity
    A. Key Dimensions of Modernization
    B. Ferdinand Toennies: The Loss of Community
    B. Emile Durkheim: The Division of Labor
    C. Max Weber: Rationalization
    D. Karl Marx: Capitalism
IV. Theoretical Analysis of Modernity
    A. Structural-Functional Theory: Modernity as Mass Society
        1. The Mass Scale of Social Life
        2. The Ever-Expanding State
    B. Social-Conflict Theory: Modernity as Class Society
        1. Capitalism
        2. Persist Inequality
    C. Modernity and the Individual
        1. Mass Society: Problems of Identity
        2. Class Society: Problems of Powerlessness
    D. Modernity and Progress
    E. Modernity: Global Variation

PART II: LEARNING OBJECTIVES

1.   To know the four general characteristics of social change.
2.   To know the different sources of social change.
3.   To understand the four general characteristics of modernization.
4.   To compare and contrast the explanations of modernization offered by Toennies, Durkheim, Weber, and Marx.
5.   To explain the difference between modern and traditional societies on the basis of: scale of life, social structure, cultural patterns, and social change.
6.   To identify the key ideas in two major interpretations of modern society: mass society and class society.
7.   To know the problems faced by individuals in "class society" and "mass society."
8.   To explain the relationship between modernity and progress.
9.   To be able to discuss the ideas of postmodernist thinkers and critically consider their relevance to our society.
10.   To explain the key ideas of modernization theory.
11.   To explain the key ideas of dependency theory.

PART III: CHAPTER REVIEW

The radical transformation of the Kaiapo culture living in Brazil's Amazon region is discussed. Many profound questions concerning social change are raised.

WHAT IS SOCIAL CHANGE?

Social change, the transformation of culture and social institutions over time is the focus of this chapter. Four general characteristics represent the process of social change:

(1)   Social change happens everywhere, although the rate of change varies from place to place;

(2)   Social change is sometimes intentional but often unplanned;

(3)   Social change often generates controversy; and,

(4)   Some changes matter more than others.

377

Examples for each of these characteristics are discussed to illustrate. For example, William Ogburn's theory of *cultural lag*, which recognizes that material culture usually changes faster than nonmaterial culture, is discussed in reference to (1) above.

CAUSES OF SOCIAL CHANGE

It is being argued that the causes of social change are found both inside and outside of a given society.

Culture and Change

Cultural change results from three basic processes: *invention*, *discovery*, and *diffusion*. Examples for each are presented.

Conflict and Change

Tension and conflict within a society can be a source of social change. The work of Karl Marx is briefly reviewed as an illustration of theory which links social structure and social change.

Ideas and Change

Max Weber's thesis concerning the influence of the Protestant work ethic on industrialization in Europe and America reflects the influence of ideas on social change. His argument was that the disciplined rationality of Calvinists was fundamental in this process of change.

The Natural Environment and Change

The controlling of the natural environment and its resources by colonists in America demonstrates the power human groups have in manipulating nature. However, examples from India and Crete are pointed out to demonstrate the devastating power of nature of humans and our social lives.

Demographic Change

Demographic factors are discussed to show their affect on how societies change. Examples include: the amount of territory a nation controls, the population composition by age of the nation, the extent of urbanization, and the amount of geographic mobility of the nation's population.

Focusing on our society, we are a very urban people by residence. Our country is very large in terms of territory. Also, the U.S. is an aging society. In 1900 only about 4 percent of our population was over the age of 65 while today over 13 percent are 65 or over. By the year 2030 it is projected that 20 percent of the U.S. population will be 65 or older. The U.S.

also has a very geographically mobile population. This latter point is illustrated in the **Seeing Ourselves** box (p. 641) in *National Map 24-1*.

MODERNITY

Modernity refers to *social patterns linked to industrialization*. **Modernization** is therefore *the process of social change initiated by industrialization*.

Key Dimensions of Modernization

Peter Berger has identified four general characteristics of modernization:

(1)   The decline of small, traditional communities;
(2)   The expansion of personal choice;
(3)   Increasing diversity in beliefs, and
(4)   Future orientation and growing awareness of time.

Examples for each of these characteristics are discussed to illustrate. Peter Berger is cited as arguing that modern societies increase autonomy and personal freedom, which Berger refers to as the process of *individualization*. However, such societies also offer less personal and enduring social ties.

Ferdinand Toennies: The Loss of Community

Ferdinand Toennies is introduced to us in the **Profile** box (p. 643). His classic book Gemeinschaft and Gesellschaft focuses on the process of modernization and his reaction to the impersonalization of the world. He did not see modern society as "worse" than preindustrial society, but he was critical of growing individualism.

His concepts of *gemeinschaft* and *gesellschaft* are discussed in some detail using changing conditions in the U.S. as illustrations.

One feature of gesellschaft is geographical mobility of a society's population. While synthesizing various dimensions of social change, Toennies's work did not clarify cause and effect relationships between the variables he studied. He also has been criticized for being a romanticist.

Emile Durkheim: The Division of Labor

Central to Durkheim's analysis of modernity is his view of the increasing division of labor in society. Durkheim did not see modernization as the loss of community, but rather as a change in the basis of community from *mechanical solidarity*, or shared sentiments and likeness, to *organic solidarity*, or community based on specialization and mutual dependency. These two types of solidarity are similar in meaning to Toennies' concepts of gemeinschaft and gesellschaft. Durkheim was more optimistic than Toennies about the effects of modernity, yet he feared anomie could result given increasing internal diversity of society.

379

Max Weber: Rationalization

Max Weber argued that ideas and beliefs are what caused social change. For him, modernity meant increased rationality and a corresponding decline in tradition. In this process bureaucracy increased as well. Compared to Toennies and Durkheim, Weber was pessimistic and critical about the effects of modernity. He was concerned that rationalization would erode the human spirit. A question asked by his critics concerns whether it is bureaucracy which causes alienation or just social inequality.

Karl Marx: Capitalism

While other theorists of the late 19th and early 20th centuries were concentrating their thoughts and research on moral consensus and social stability, Marx focused on social conflict. He saw the Industrial Revolution as primarily a *capitalist revolution*. He agreed with Toennies' analysis of the changing nature of community. He was concerned with Durkheim's sense of the increase in the division of labor. His position also supported Weber's view about increasing rationality and declining tradition. However, for Marx, these processes were all changes which supported the growth of capitalism, and of this he was very critical. Such changes, for Marx, would eventually lead to social revolution.

THEORETICAL ANALYSIS OF MODERNITY

As explained in the text, modernity is a complex process involving many factors. *Table 24-1* (p. 647) summarizes the characteristics of traditional and modern societies along the dimensions of scale of life, social structure, cultural patterns, and social change. Sixteen different variables, including seven institutional domains and nine relating to social structures and social processes are focused upon comparing the two types of societies.

Structural-Functional Theory: Modernity as Mass Society

One approach to the study of social change is viewing modernization as a process which creates mass societies. A *mass society* is *a society in which industry and expanding bureaucracy have eroded traditional social ties.*

The Mass Scale of Modern Life

This approach draws on the work of Toennies, Durkheim, and Weber. Two points are stressed using this perspective. First, the expanding scale of social life creates impersonality and cultural diversity to an extent which is overwhelming for individuals, drawing meaning out of their lives. Second, the expanding role of the government dominates the regulation of people's lives through a complicated and impersonal bureaucratic structure.

The Ever-Expanding State

In preindustrial America and Europe, limited community size, social isolation, and a strong traditional religion created homogeneous cultural values (Durkheim's mechanical solidarity and Toennies' gemeinschaft).

Industrialization created geographical mobility, urbanization, and large organizations which provided greater opportunities for a variety of social groups. All of this created what Durkheim referred to as organic solidarity, and what Toennies called gesellschaft.

Preindustrial Europe was essentially governed by local nobility. As time passed, governments became more centralized; consequently power has come to reside in large bureaucracies. This has resulted in the depersonalization of human life.

Modernization is viewed both positively and negatively using the mass society approach. It is accepted by many social and economic conservatives who support conventional morality and oppose the expanding power of the government.

Social-Conflict Theory: Modernity as Class Society

This approach is largely derived from Karl Marx's analysis of society. A *class society* is *a capitalist society with pronounced social stratification*. The social inequality present is understood as producing feelings of powerlessness among the people.

Capitalism

For Karl Marx, it was the growth of capitalism, not the industrial revolution which caused the increasing scale of social life during the 19th century in Europe and North America. He saw the profit motive, which emphasized self-interest and greed, as forces which broke down social ties which bound small-scale communities.

Marx also saw advances in science as a reason for such change. He believed science and the technological solutions it offered gave legitimacy to the status quo.

Persistent Inequality

While many theorists argue that modernization began to break down rigid categorical distinctions, proponents of the theory of class society see a greater concentration of power and wealth occurring.

A criticism of this approach, however, is that it tends to underestimate the ways in which egalitarianism has increased in modern societies. The mass-society theory and the class-society theory are summarized in *Table 24-2* (p. 650).

Modernity and the Individual

While mass-society theory and the theory of class society have been discussed to this point as perspectives focusing on macro-level issues concerning patterns of change, they also offer micro-level insights into how modernity affects individuals.

Mass Society: Problems of Identity

According to this view, establishing an identity becomes more difficult with the social diversity, atomization, and rapid social change which modernization brings about.

David Riesman developed the term *social character* to mean *personality patterns common to members of a particular society*. He views preindustrial societies as promoting *tradition-directedness*, or *rigid conformity to time-honored ways of living*. This would be associated with Toennies' gemeinschaft and Durkheim's mechanical solidarity. In culturally diverse and rapidly changing industrial societies, another type of social character emerges. This type, called *other-directedness*, refers to *a receptiveness to the latest trends and fashions, often expressed in the practice of imitating others*. In the U.S., for example, people tend to conform to peers and easily become influenced by fads.

Class Society: Problems of Powerlessness

According to this view, individual freedom is undermined by the persistence of social inequality. Herbert Marcuse, using this perspective, challenges Weber's contention that modern society is rational. For Marcuse, because society is failing to meet the basic needs of many people it is actually irrational.

Modernity and Progress

Generally, people view modernity as *progress* (from the Latin "a moving forward), but this conception ignores the complexity of social change. The Kaiapo of Brazil, highlighted earlier in this chapter, illustrate this point. In global context, *Figure 24-1* (p. 652) show the U.S. population has considerable confidence in science to improve our lives.

An interesting perspective is offered in the **Sociology of Everyday Life** box (p. 653), in which the concepts of *honor* and *dignity* are discussed in relation to the idea of human rights.

The issue of individual choice and freedom versus social responsibility and social obligation is addressed. Social change does not proceed in a predictable, linear fashion, and cannot merely be understood as *"progress."*

Modernity: Global Variation

Around the world, traditional and modern social patterns coexist. The mixing of the old and the new, for example, in Japan and among he Kaiapo, is more the rule than the exception.

POSTMODERNITY

Postmodernity refers to *social patterns characteristic of postindustrial societies*. What this precisely means is really still a matter of debate. Many variants of postmodern thinking exist, however, the five following themes have emerged:

      (1)   In important respects, modernity has failed.
      (2)   The bright promise of "progress" is fading.
      (3)   Science no longer holds the answers.
      (4)   Cultural debates are intensifying.
      (5)   Social institutions are changing.

The underlying contention seems to be that modernity in the U.S. and elsewhere has failed to meet human needs. Yet, modernity has raised the standard of living for many people all around the world. Further, postmodernist thinkers have not suggested any alternatives to "progress." Yet, there are many disturbing social trends in the U.S., some of which are addressed in the **Critical Thinking** box (p. 655) in which it is being asked: Is the U.S. a nation in decline? Increased per capita government spending, increasing numbers of welfare recipients, lower achievement test scores in schools, high divorce rates, and more violent crime are all seen as evidence for the failings of how we are experiencing modernization.

LOOKING AHEAD: MODERNIZATION AND OUR GLOBAL FUTURE

Modernization theory and *dependency theory* which are both discussed in great detail in Chapter 11, are reviewed. Modernization theorists see modernity as increasing the standard of living among the people of a society. However, many problems are involved as well, including an increasing materialistic approach to life, which this approach tends to underemphasize.

Dependency theory, on the other hand, views social change as something which is not under the control of individual societies. Placing our understanding of social change within a global perspective is argued to be of vital importance. The **Controversy and Debate** box (pp. 656-57) addresses the issue of whether personal freedom and social responsibility can coexist in modern society. Emitai Etzioni's "communitarian movement, which rests on the premise that "strong rights presume strong responsibilities," is discussed.

PART IV: KEY CONCEPTS

Define each of the following concepts in the space provided or on separate paper. Check the accuracy of your answers by referring to the key concepts section at the end of the chapter in the text as well as by referring to italicized definitions located throughout the chapter.

class society
diffusion
discovery
gemeinschaft
gesellschaft
individualization
invention
mass society
mechanical solidarity
modernity
modernization
organic solidarity
other-directedness
postmodernity
progress
social change
social character
tradition-directedness

PART V: STUDY QUESTIONS

True-False

1.   T   F   Max Weber argued that technology and conflict are *more* important than ideas in transforming society.
2.   T   F   By the year 2050, it is estimated that about 13 percent of the U.S. population will be over age *sixty-five*.
3.   T   F   According to Peter Berger, a characteristic of modernization is the expression of *individual choice*.
4.   T   F   The concepts of *gemeinschaft* and *gesellschaft* were developed by Ferdinand Toennies.
5.   T   F   According to our author, Emile Durkheim's view of modernity is both more *complex* and more *positive* than that of Ferdinand Toennies.
6.   T   F   Compared to Emile Durkheim, Max Weber was *more critical* of modern society, believing that the rationalization of bureaucracies would cause people to become alienated.

7. T F A *mass society* is one in which industrialization and expanding bureaucracy have weakened social ties.
8. T F *Class-conflict theory* maintains that persistent social inequality undermines modern society's promise of individual freedom.
9. T F According to David Reisman, a type of *social character* he labels other-directedness represents rapidly changing modern societies.
10. T F According to the text, the concept of *honor* is diminishing in significance for most members of modern society, while the concept of *dignity* is becoming more important.

Multiple-Choice

1. The Kaiapo:

    (a) is a small society in Brazil
    (b) is a ritual among the Mbuti of the Ituri forest
    (c) is a sacred tradition involving animal sacrifice which has been made illegal by the Canadian government
    (d) are a people of Asia who represent the gesellschaft concept developed by Toennies
    (e) is a ritualistic war pattern of the Maring, a New Guinea culture of horticulturists

2. William Ogburn's theory of _____ states that material culture changes *faster* than nonmaterial culture.

    (a) modernity   (d) cultural lag
    (b) modernization   (e) anomie
    (c) rationalization

3. The rapid development of medical devices to prolong the life of seriously ill people has outpaced our ability to define death clearly. This situation is an illustration of:

    (a) modernity   (d) anomie
    (b) cultural lag   (e) gemeinschaft
    (c) mechanical solidarity

4. Which of the following is *not* a general source of social change?

    (a) ideas   (d) the natural environment
    (b) population   (e) social structure
    (c) genetic heritage

5. As the power of tradition declines, a society's members come to see their lives as an unending series of options. Peter Berger refers to this process as:

    (a) modernization
    (b) gesellschaft
    (c) rationalization
    (d) alienation
    (e) individualization

6. Which of the following is *most accurate*?

    (a) Durkheim's concept of organic solidarity refers to social bonds of mutual dependency based on specialization
    (b) Toennies saw societies as changing from social organization based on gesellschaft to social organization based on gemeinschaft
    (c) Peter Berger argued that modern society offers less autonomy than is found in preindustrial societies
    (d) Durkheim's concept of mechanical solidarity is very similar in meaning to Toennies's concept of gesellschaft

7. Emile Durkheim's concepts of *mechanical* and *organic solidarity* are similar to the notions of:

    (a) mass-society and class-society
    (b) tradition-directedness and other directedness
    (c) anomie and progress
    (d) gemeinschaft and gesellschaft
    (e) none of the above

8. _____ *theory* focuses on the expanding scale of social life and the rise of the state in the study of modernization.

    (a) mass society
    (b) social class
    (c) dependency
    (d) modernization
    (e) rationalization

9. Which social scientist described *modernization* in terms of its affects on social character?

    (a) David Reisman
    (b) Peter Berger
    (c) David Klein
    (d) William Ogburn
    (e) Herbert Marcuse

10. _____ suggested that we be *critical of Max Weber's view* that modern society is rational because technological advances rarely empower people; instead, we should focus on the issue of how technology tends to reduce people's control over their own lives.

   (a)   Emile Durkheim   (d)   Herbert Spencer
   (b)   David Reisman   (e)   Herbert Marcuse
   (c)   Ferdinand Toennies

Fill-In

1. _____ refers to the transformation of culture and social institutions over time.
2. *Social change* results from three basic processes: _____, _____, and _____.
3. _____ refers to patterns of social life linked to *industrialization*.
4. Emile Durkheim's concept of *organic solidarity* is closely related to Toennies' concept of _____.
5. For Emile Durkheim, *modernization* is marked by an increasing _____ _____.
6. *Mass society theory* draws upon the ideas of _____, _____, and _____.
7. _____ is a society in which capitalism has generated pronounced social stratification.
8. _____ refers to *personality patterns* common to members of a society.
9. David Reisman argues that preindustrial societies promote _____, or rigid conformity to time-honored ways of living.
10. *Modernization* enhances concern for people as _____, which is expressed in the concept of _____.
11. Five themes have emerged as part of *postmodern thinking*. These include that in important respects, _____ has failed; The bright promise of "_____" is fading; _____ no longer holds the answers; Cultural debates are _____; And, social institutions are _____.
12. In the Critical Thinking box concerning the question of whether the U.S. is a nation in decline, from William Bennet's point of view, the primary _____ of any society are not set by _____ but by _____ living in communities and, especially, by _____ raising their children.

Definition and Short-Answer

1. What are the four general *characteristics* of *social change*?
2. Five general domains which are involved in *causing social change* are identified and discussed in the text. List these and provide an example for each.

3. Peter Berger identifies four general *characteristics* of *modern societies*. What are these characteristics?
4. Differentiate between Toennies', Durkheim's, Weber's and Marx's perspectives of *modernization*.
5. What factors of modernization do theorists operating from the *mass-society theory* focus upon?
6. What factors of modernization do theorists operating from the theory of *class society* focus upon?
7. What are the two *types* of *social character* identified by David Reisman?
8. What are the arguments being made by *postmodernists* concerning social change in modern society? What do critics of this view have to say?
9. Referring to *Table 24-1*, select a nonindustrialized society and compare it to the U.S. on four of the elements of society identified in the table. Provide a specific illustration representing a relative comparison for each element.

PART VI. ANSWERS TO STUDY GUIDE QUESTIONS

True-False

1.	F	(p. 639)	6.	T	(p. 645)
2.	F	(p. 640)	7.	T	(p. 646)
3.	T	(p. 641)	8.	T	(p. 649)
4.	T	(p. 642)	9.	T	(p. 651)
5.	T	(p. 644)	10.	T	(p. 653)

Multiple-Choice

1.	a	(p. 637)	6.	a	(pp. 641-644)
2.	d	(p. 638)	7.	d	(p. 644)
3.	b	(p. 638)	8.	a	(p. 646)
4.	c	(p. 639)	9.	a	(p. 650)
5.	e	(p. 641)	10.	e	(p. 651)

Fill-In

1. social change (p. 638)
2. invention, discovery, diffusion (p. 639)
3. modernity (p. 640)
4. gesellschaft (p. 643)
5. division of labor (p. 644)
6. Toennies, Durkheim/Weber (p. 646)
7. class society (p. 649)
8. social character (p. 650)
9. tradition-directedness (p. 650)

10. individuals, dignity (p. 653)
11. modernity, progress, science, intensifying, changing (pp. 653-54)
12. values/government/people/families (p. 655)

PART VII: ANALYSIS AND COMMENT

Profile

"Ferdinand Toennies (1855-1936)

    Key Points: Questions:

Critical Thinking

"The U.S.: A Nation In Decline?"

    Key Points: Questions:

Sociology of Everyday Life

"What's Happened to Honor"

    Key Points: Questions:

Controversy and Debate

"Personal Freedom and Social Responsibility: Can We Have It Both Ways?"

Key Points: Questions:

Seeing Ourselves

"National Map 24-1 Moving On: Migration Across the U.S.

Key Points: Questions: